DOING RESEARCH ON WOMEN'S COMMUNICATION:
PERSPECTIVES ON THEORY AND METHOD

COMMUNICATION AND INFORMATION SCIENCE

Edited by
BRENDA DERVIN
The Ohio State University

Recent Titles

Doing Research on Women's Communication: Perspectives on Theory and Method

Edited by

Kathryn Carter
Department of Communication Arts
Wayne State College

and

Carole Spitzack
Department of Communication
Tulane University

 ABLEX PUBLISHING CORPORATION
NORWOOD, NEW JERSEY

Library of Congress Cataloging-in-Publication Data

Doing research on women's communication : perspectives on theory and
   method / edited by Kathryn Carter and Carole Spitzack.
      p. cm.—(Communication and information science)
   Bibliography: p.
   Includes index.
   ISBN 0-89391-483-5 (cloth); 0-89391-616-1 (ppk)
    1. Women—Communication—Research—Methodology. 2. Feminism—
Research—Methodology. I. Carter, Kathryn, 1954–
II. Spitzack, Carole, III. Series.
P94.5.W65D65   1989
302.2′088042—dc20

89–14900
CIP

Ablex Publishing Corporation
355 Chestnut Street
Norwood, New Jersey 07648

CONTENTS

Preface

This book is the result of several years of discussing the meaning, personally and politically, of doing research in general and feminist research in particular. As teachers and scholars, we gradually became aware that a lack of connection exists between two general types of research in gender and communication. In the area of applied research, scholars have uncovered gender differences in diverse communication contexts, but few have critically questioned the relationship between approaches to research and the sociopolitical contexts in which differences become comprehensible. In metatheoretical analyses, conversely, feminist scholars integrate the findings in applied research, placing them in a sociopolitical context, but have not clearly specified alternatives for conducting applied research. Both types of research, taken separately, contribute to our knowledge of gender and communication. From here, the insights generated by these two approaches need to be interrelated so that the political insight afforded by metatheoretical analyses is implemented in the conduct of applied research.

Our book provides a bridge between metatheory and research practices. Each chapter offers guidelines for coordinating applied research for women and alterations in research procedures. The authors present women's experiences as valid and complex, posing the question: How can women's communication be examined so it can be revealed as richly competent? Such investigations generate greater coherence between the strategies and styles found in women's communication and the methods used to study them.

This volume provides expanded critical possibilities for gender and feminist communication researchers. First, by valuing women's communication on its own terms, the richness and complexity of female expression is given visibility. Second, novel investigative strategies can be designed, offering a more comprehensive understanding of women's interactions in diverse communication contexts. In combination, these activities allow female *and* male scholars to rethink the place of gender within our disciplinary tradition.

Many people contributed their skills and support in the writing of this book. We would like to thank the people who made valuable critical suggestions and comments on earlier drafts: Thomas Benson, Celeste Condit,

Mary Anne Fitzpatrick, Cheris Kramarae, Richard Lanigan, Ana Lopez, and Kathleen Turner.

Brenda Dervin, as editor of the Communication and Information Science Series for Ablex, not only offered her editorial expertise, but provided personal support and enthusiasm for this project.

We both wish to thank our departments for enabling the successful completion of this book. Kathryn Carter received a faculty research award from Wayne State College that provided necessary release time and funding. Kathryn also expresses grateful appreciation to Jo Taylor, head of the humanities division at Wayne State College, for moral and departmental support. Carole Spitzack wishes to thank John Patton, chair of the communication department at Tulane University, for providing expanded computer resources, traveling funding, and encouragement. Carole expresses appreciation to Jim Hikins for numerous lively discussions concerning feminist research.

We express our gratitude to the authors who contributed to this volume. Each author not only provided personal and professional support, but extended our knowledge and understanding of feminist research. In this context, we thank: Mary Ellen Brown, Catherine Dobris, Karen Foss, Sonja Foss, Deanna Hall, Katherine Hawkins, Kristin Langellier, Sheila McNamee, Jenny Nelson, Michael Presnell, Constance Courtney Staley, and Pamela Shockley-Zalabak.

Finally, we thank the many women who provided the context for this work. From the women who do feminsit research to the women who offer their experiences for study, we express our profound gratitude.

Introduction

Like many feminist scholars, our interest in the relationship between gender and research practices developed gradually. In the process of becoming acclimated within the speech communication tradition, we learned much about prevailing theoretical paradigms, research methods, and the particular perspectives that inform various areas within the field. As women, we began to realize that our disciplinary boundaries did not adequately account for our experiences. Approaches and findings that did not account for gender seemed, in important ways, to ignore or simplify the complexity of women's communicative behavior. The studies about women were few and far between and the methods used by researchers did not allow for rich analyses of women's communication. The invisibility of women became the impetus for our current research, which seeks to incorporate a feminist perspective within the communication research tradition.

As our interest in feminist scholarship developed, we encountered numerous prohibitions which promote a tacit exclusion of women's communication from mainstream communication studies. As other women in the field can probably attest to, the choice to conduct feminist research is often met with resistance at a number of levels. Perhaps the most pervasive argument against feminist research is the claim that communication studies operate from a position of gender neutrality; hence women *are* included in disciplinary practices. Feminists, then, are viewed as persons who "stir up trouble" over nonissues. The charge of irrelevancy masks a complex process of patriarchal silencing. Mainstream resistance is rarely expressed as an open condemnation of women's issues. Rather, we are told that it is in our best professional interest to avoid such issues. Among the reasons given are: the very term "feminist," with its negative social implications, negatively influences hiring practices; feminist concerns comprise a "fringe" area which leads to difficulty in publishing; an inability to publish creates problems at the time of tenure or promotion.

If one decides, in spite of professional difficulties, to pursue research from a feminist perspective, another set of problems becomes apparent. Because of professional discouragement, there is a dearth of information about women's perceptions of their own experiences within the tradition of communication research. One's familiarity with the literature, which is central in the establishment of academic respectability, is often difficult to demonstrate. We are not suggesting that feminist scholarship does not exist; rather, that it rarely appears in mainstream communication publications. Feminist scholarship appears in publications that are devoted to women's concerns, falsely implying that these concerns have no place in mainstream communication studies.

The dilemma for feminist researchers is further complicated by traditional investigative strategies. Because research strategies are informed by human experiences, and because women and men are socialized to have separate experiences, we can expect differing scholarly choices depending on the gender orientation of particular researchers. That is, it is likely that women and men will have different perceptions of relevant questions, data collection techniques, subject selection, data interpretation, and the relationship between researcher and researched. The problem is not the existence of differing perspectives, but that only one—typically male—is offered in texts which present research procedures. Thus, when feminist scholars seek guidelines for conducting research on women, they are often met with procedures that cannot account adequately for the rich complexity of women's lives.

When faced with methodological inadequacies, feminist researchers must rethink methodological choices. This rethinking may not always involve the development of new methodologies, but may entail an examination of prevailing research dichotomies—qualitative/quantitative methods, soft/hard approaches, impressionistic/scientific grounding—through a new lens. Thus, feminist scholars, in formulating a basis for critique or revision, draw from existing approaches. At the same time, however, existing approaches are often redesigned to allow for sensitive and accurate interpretations of women's experiences.

A woman-centered rereading of traditional approaches takes many forms. Many feminist scholars test existing research guidelines by checking the fit between procedural dictates and women's experiences. For example, a researcher may utilize the precepts of content analysis to analyze women's turn-taking behavior and find that the standard definition of a turn does not account for women's conversational moves. Other feminist researchers work from within the boundaries of traditional methodology to develop research procedures that suit the particularities of women's communication behavior. Finally, some feminist scholars attempt to develop explicitly feminist methodologies, which include critiques of the politics of androcentrism.

While the barriers for feminist researchers may be discouraging, they can also produce immeasurable insight. Because of our simultaneous status as "insiders" within the communication field, and "outsiders" as women in a patriarchal culture, women are able to see the perspectival nature of claims made about human experience. When perspectives formerly thought to be gender-neutral are found to have a basis in male experiences, possibilities for disciplinary expansion are uncovered. The questions asked in research and the methods of analysis, for example, can be expanded to include experiences and strategies previously considered marginal or nonrepresentative.

A primary purpose of this volume is to describe the relationships between gender, theory, methodology, and methods. There is much disciplinary confusion regarding distinctions between method, methodology, theory, applied theory, and philosophy. In various ways, each chapter in the anthology confronts these distinctions. The central point in the book concerns the importance of making explicit the implicit assumptions which inform the research process. These assumptions are not easily categorized as theory *or* method *or* philosophy. Rather, philosophy informs theory, theory informs methodology, and methodology trains and clarifies researcher vision. Thus, a relationship of interdependence characterizes the multileveled process of research.

Women's communication is often perceived to be deficient, we believe, because the interdependent nature of assumptive bases remains invisible and thus safe from critical examination. Some of our authors undertake critical examination by addressing the intricate relationship between theory and methodology, some focus on the "breakdown" of traditional methodologies when faced with the dynamics of women's experiences, and others address the politics of the research process. The data collection process has political import because research procedures make possible particular ways of seeing data. The authors suggest that there are novel and useful readings of research assumptions, and alternative ways of seeing the process of research. Such alternatives not only lend insight into the communication community in general, but, from our perspective, become essential in understanding women's communication. All of our contributors discuss the need for studying women's communication within a feminist perspective.

An issue of crucial importance in feminist communication scholarship is the task of questioning taken-for-granted assumptions. The authors herein provide novel uses of, and applications for, varied perspectives in the context of women's communication. Consistent with the feminist tradition, we believe that women scholars find ways of rethinking the place of women's communication *within* our disciplinary tradition.

The first section, *Problematics of Feminism and Social Science*, begins the process of rethinking by examining the implicit masculine assumptions within the communication tradition. In various manners, authors point to disciplinary biases that have prohibited an inclusion of gender in our approaches to research, challenge these biases by making them visible, and propose alternative guidelines for the conduct of feminist research.

Carole Spitzack and Kathryn Carter show that our supposedly gender-neutral views of research practices are in fact gender-laden. The socialization of women and men imbues women with characteristics associated with softness, subjectivism, irrationality; men, conversely, are characterized as hard, objective, and rational. These oppositional qualities suggest implicitly that women are ill-equipped for the rigors of serious scholarship. The gendered gatekeeping process informs judgments made regarding research by and for women. Feminist scholarship, then, is often deemed marginal or insignificant because, first, it is seen to represent a fringe group of women, and second, it is not worthy of serious concern since it is judged to be lacking in rigor. Added to these difficulties is the issue of scientific impartiality. Specifically, because feminists argue that political dimensions infuse social knowledge, and because feminist studies advocate respect for women, our work is seen to contain bias.

Katherine Hawkins further illustrates the association between masculinity and objectivity within the tradition of science. Drawing from the work of Keller and Fee, Hawkins not only provides a critique of masculine science, but proposes an alternative feminist approach to research. Her alternative is characterized by dynamic rather than static objectivity, a research goal of understanding instead of control, and a sensitive and personalized treatment of subjects rather than one which is controlled and impersonal. Finally, she uses the study of sexual harassment to illustrate the tenets of a feminist perspective within an applied research context. Hawkins demonstrates that a feminist approach to science provides for rigorous and rich analyses of human experience.

Karen Foss and Sonja Foss show that feminist perspectives have not been fully incorporated into mainstream communication journals. A feminist perspective creates a dilemma for scholars because the outlets available for publication exist largely within traditional frameworks, thus forcing feminist scholars to conduct research within conventional boundaries. Thus, the ability of the feminist perspective to challenge the discipline is often minimized when studies must rely on traditional frameworks for legitimacy. But, as Foss and Foss argue, the feminist perspective constitutes a major challenge to communication research because it allows women to speak in their own voices and does so by using methodologies that differ from those used in traditional paradigms. Their analysis of articles relating to gender and women published in four mainstream communication journals during the past decade reveals the ways in which attempts to incorporate a feminist perspective have been complicated. Researchers using a feminist perspective make accommodations to gain access to mainstream scholarship. Although these accommodations facilitate publication, a primary purpose of a feminist perspective is to challenge the discipline. Only by challenging traditional frameworks can a feminist perspective be fully realized in the discipline.

The next section, *Theoretics of Feminism and Communication Studies*, shows how the genderization of science biases research in general and women's communication strategies in particular. Each author provides approaches to science that account adequately for gender and women's communication.

Sheila McNamee addresses human interaction within a family therapy context to highlight alternative approaches to social scientific research. In particular, she shows that the Milan model of family therapy is consistent with feminist models. Both models give attention to the personal experience of social actors, allow for a plurality of perspectives, and reveal that intervention, whether in a clinical or research context, must be acknowledged. She argues that the Milan model, like feminist models, can serve to inform social scientific research. In combining Milan and feminist approaches, McNamee challenges masculine views of science by offering a model that criticizes the androcentric tradition of positivistic science.

Michael Presnell argues that masculine biases prohibit an inclusion of female discourse in the study of narrative. Presnell employs the distinction between oral and literate discourses to ground an understanding of female-male differences in narrative. He suggests that the distinction can be used to avoid bias in favor of male narrative forms and to promote new ways of understanding female narratives. Gilligan's studies of moral development are analyzed to show how the oral-literate distinction can be used to study the form and content of women's speaking. He further connects the oral-literate distinction to methodological choices by arguing that gender-inclusive research assumptions provide greater coordination among research questions, data collection, and interpretation. Presnell's analysis of the impact of gender on narrative allows for a more comprehensive narrative paradigm which promotes a truly inclusive understanding of human discourse.

Catherine Dobris suggests that dominant rhetorical paradigms are designed to investigate male communication strategies and styles. Because of masculine bias, Dobris argues for a rhetorical theory that accounts for gender. She examines existing research in the area of gender differences in information processing, communication behaviors, and stereotypes of women and men in interaction contexts. Her rhetorical theory emphasizes gender differences so that women's communication dynamics are incorporated into rhetorical paradigms. A rhetorical theory accounting for gender, Dobris shows, includes a feminist perspective and expands research choices. A feminist perspective facilitates analyses of previously ignored rhetoric by women, provides unique contributions to feminist scholarship, and includes women's concerns, thereby encouraging a genuinely pluralistic rhetorical tradition.

Mary Ellen Brown examines the role of ideology in the research process. Her scrutiny of soap opera as a devalued cultural form shows that patriarchal discourse influences methodological choices and the selection of research topics. By examining her own experience as a woman researcher in male-dominated scholarship, she realizes that her conceptions of research are influenced by patriarchal values. Brown's recognition leads to the development of a woman-centered research methodology, which minimizes the distance between researcher and researched, defines interviews as conversational rather than bidirectional, and views subjects as active instead of passive agents. Moreover, in her selection of soap operas as a valid area of investigation, Brown challenges traditional notions of topical relevancy within scholarly research. Brown's analysis of soaps as a type of feminine discourse reveals that studies of women's culture can function as resistance to dominant ideology.

In the context of feminist critiques, researchers generate new readings of the research process in applied studies. Investigations of women's communication indicate that women and men use different interactional strategies for different purposes, which necessitates alternative methodological choices on the parts of researchers. In particular, feminist scholars question the separation of knower and known and the distinction between subjective and objective ways of knowing. By recognizing that women are coproducers of their communicative climates, feminist scholars enter into nonhierarchal and reciprocal relationships with the women whose lives they seek to understand. The final section, *Methods for Studying Women's Communication*, shows how feminist views alter the conduct of applied communication research.

Kristin Langellier and Deanna Hall argue that, although interviewing is a standard research instrument, the process of interviewing is rarely described by researchers. By demystifying the interviewing process, Langellier and Hall promote data collection techniques that allow for effective coordination between feminist theories and the methods used to study women's communication. Their approach combines phenomenology and feminism so that interviews can be used to tap into the processual complexities of women's experiences. As an empirical illustration, they analyze the interview process in Hall's (1985) study of mother-daughter storytelling. Langellier and Hall's study, by giving attention to the politics of *researcher* communication, invites us to conduct research *for* women rather than on women. Research for women empowers female subjects and female scholars.

Jenny Nelson, like Langellier and Hall, suggests that a combination of feminism and phenomenology can be used to conduct interviews. Rather than focusing on the interaction between researcher and researched, Nelson calls attention to the process of data interpretation. She explores the feminist claim that personal choices have political import by examining her own choices in the role of interpreter. The phenomenological procedures of description, reduction, and interpretation are delineated in relation to Nelson's experience as a female researcher. By using examples from her study of televisual experience, Nelson demonstrates the ways in which interview transcripts can be interpreted. This examination calls for a rejection of superior-subordinate power roles in the research setting, replacing them with the practices of coresearchers. Nelson's study is consistent with the feminist tradition because she argues that, as researchers, we are not only responsible for examining the experience of subjects, but for the impact of our own experiences on the interpretive process.

Constance Courtney Staley and Pamela Shockley-Zalabak examine another communication context wherein women's skills are evaluated through the lens of patriarchy. Their survey of the research on female-male organizational performance demonstrates that, although few significant differences are found in actual behaviors, there is a prejudicial evaluation of professional women. Furthermore, mixed findings within gender and communication research in general are traceable to a lack of coordination between methods and the phenomenon under study. Staley and Shockley-Zalabak propose multileveled triangulation as a method for more effective integration. Triangulation provides a holistic, contextual, objective approach to the study of gender and communication. The benefits of triangulation are demonstrated in their research design to study female-male communication behavior during decision-making activities. Staley and Shockley-Zalabak's proposal is valuable because it shows that the study of women's interaction is not limited to a single methodology, but can draw insights from multiple approaches to research.

A major issue in each chapter concerns the research process. Authors discuss the relationship between research, data, researcher, and culture. We hope that, in addition to generating new information about women's communication, the knowledge gained from a critical analysis of research practices makes a place for feminist perspectives within the communication discipline.

Each author in this volume, consistent with feminist theorists, recognizes the danger of promoting a unitary definition of women's communication. Our collective and individual examinations of the research process militate against a single, and thus exclusionary, definition. In addition, authors delineate the social construction of gender, revealing that women's communication is characterized by diverse strategies. Such revelations highlight the mechanisms within the research process, which are made visible through feminist critical sensibilities. In a very rich manner, then, each chapter promotes a pluralistic view of research practices within the communication tradition.

I

Problematics of Feminism and Social Science

Research on Women's Communication: The Politics of Theory and Method

CAROLE SPITZACK
Department of Communication
Tulane University

KATHRYN CARTER
Department of Communication Arts
Wayne State College

The communication discipline is known for its openness to critical debate. Practitioners in our field invite theoreticians, methodologists, and empirical researchers to assist in the development of communication paradigms. Our acceptance of a wide variety of perspectives may be partially explained by our attempts to achieve disciplinary unity. The field "has struggled to achieve recognition as a legitimate discipline" (Bochner & Eisenberg, 1985, p. 299) and to accomplish a definition within the cultural domain of scholarly research (Cohen, 1985; Pearce, 1985; Williams, 1973). While some scholars have argued for an integrative perspective of communication (e.g., Delia, 1979), others question whether the discipline can become legitimized by having a coherent, unified perspective (e.g., Bochner & Eisenberg, 1985). Such openness to debate coupled with diversity of interests has generated multiple definitions and perspectives concerning the parameters of the field. It is only by tolerating differences and considering the diversity of the field, argue Bochner and Eisenberg (1985, p. 315–321), that the communication discipline can achieve cohesiveness and respectability.

In addition to valuing diverse theoretical perspectives within the scope of the communication discipline, a wide variety of human communication behaviors must also be valued. Our self-proclaimed liberal status, according to Roderick Hart (1985), demands attention to, and respect for, many forms and levels of human interaction, ranging from the everyday communication of social actors to intellectually sophisticated proposals by persons engaged in theory construction. Those who are underrepresented or silenced within society should, with our assistance, be given a voice because we "accept all comers into the world of human discourse" (Hart, p. 164). Only through a plurality of voices can a community of communication scholars understand each other and the society we examine through research efforts. Indeed, our commitment to equality not only militates against elitism and singular vision, but can offer enriched accounts of human interaction.

As with most academic disciplines, however, the openness to multiple perspectives encouraged within communication studies is tempered by a tacit valuing process wherein some questions are considered more laudable or interesting than others, the lives of some individuals are likely to receive our attention to the exclusion of others, and some approaches to research are praised while others are ignored, distorted, or disparaged.

A particular blind spot in our discipline concerns the impact of gender on the research process, from selecting research questions to theorizing about human communication (Rakow, 1986; Spitzack & Carter, 1987; Thorne, Kramarae, & Henley, 1983). In this chapter we argue that there is sufficient evidence in the area of feminist and gender studies to demand an explicit inclusion of gender within communication theory and research. We accomplish our argument in four sections. First, we review disciplinary research practices to clarify the particular ways in which the boundaries surrounding the study of communication in general are challenged or perpetuated through critical activity. In the second section we argue that the communication discipline has not only excluded an explicit consideration of gender, but assumes a masculine view of the world which, by implication, disparages female experience.[1] Our third section elaborates the gatekeeping mechanisms within communication studies that prevent gender and gender theory considerations from reaching "mainstream" scholarship. Finally, we highlight the particular commitments encompassed in a feminist approach to research.

BORROWING FROM THE TRADITION OF SCIENCE: HUMAN OR PHYSICAL?

Communication is a unique area of academic study. In few disciplines are scholars required to take as their data base the very language and cultural

---

[1] We have argued elsewhere that a masculine view of the world disparages female experience (Spitzack & Carter, 1987). We are not suggesting that male views, in and of themselves, are detrimental to women. Rather, within sociocultural hierarchies, women are placed historically at lower levels. Hierarchies entail a tacit valuing process whereby those who are perceived to exist at lower levels are afforded less power, less visibility, and less credibility.

systems used by researchers to describe or explain various interactional phenomena. Communication scholars examine the dynamics of everyday human interaction and present their findings by using language and relational conventions that are drawn from the general human communities they are attempting to understand or explain. By definition, then, communication researchers are enmeshed in the social and cultural systems about which they speak and write. Moreover, only through a recognition of emersion—an ability to see and interpret the everyday communication of social members—are researchers able to produce sensible and realistic explanations of communication behavior.

The unique character of our discipline has created dilemmas for scholars who wish to position the study of communication within the domain of science. The call for a traditional scientific approach to communication research often takes as valid the pursuit of a unified communication theory, akin to a Kuhnian (1962) vision of normal science. Because the practice of normal science was viewed as a means to legitimize the discipline, and because our field has been plagued with fragmentation and a lack of coherency, a unified theory was seen by some scholars as promising affinity with disciplines whose histories afford respectability and power.

The call for a unified theory is complicated by the inherently processual and complex nature of human communication. Kenneth Williams (1973, p. 246), in delineating a vision of science within communication, argues that a paradigm for our field "cannot be 'grand' or formal theory based on the hypothetico-deductive model because hypotheses must be grounded in processual phenomena rather than in logical postulates." Although the study of communication has gained attention by contributing greatly to enriched understandings of human behavior, the unique character of data within our field contributes to ambiguity in conceptual and theoretical precision. As Jeremy Tunstall (1983, p. 92) observes, "All disciplines, fields, and departments have their agonies of definition, theory, method, relevance, finance, and integrity—the problem with communication studies is simply that it has more of these." Kenneth Sereno and C. David Mortensen (1970, p. 2) echo Tunstall's concerns: "Although astonishingly popular as an object of research, the field of communication has not established any sharply-defined boundaries or domains" (p. 2). In 1972, Frank Dance and Charles Larson found 125 definitions of communication. Many of these definitions were conceptually distinct and even antagonistic (in Trenholm, 1986, p. 8). Herman Cohen (1985, p. 283) defines speech communication as a "field without a history," which leads to a crisis in identity because "we are often not certain who we are."

Efforts to provide theoretical unity to the study of communication, thereby legitimizing our status as a discipline, have often been grounded in the assumption that natural science models, where objectivity or researcher distance is given priority, should function as the exemplar for communication research. Communication researchers, then, began to use the research methods of experimentation and quantification. Science, as understood and revered culturally, promised an identity for communication scholars. That is, if we could "act like" scientists, perhaps our discipline would command equivalent levels of legitimacy and respect.

The discipline, by borrowing the scientific method, also adopted certain ontological and metaphysical assumptions. Within the tradition of the physical sciences, an underlying conceptual framework containing theoretical and methodological precepts grounds intellectual activities. Although the framework is susceptible to change through scientific discovery, an intact paradigm helps to guide research efforts during particular historical periods.

Scientists share a discourse—a way of talking about what they do—that provides a consensual means by which to evaluate or assess the validity of scientific discoveries. Becoming a member of the scientific community entails a mastery of conceptual information which, in later stages of development as a scientist, can be applied competently and comprehensibly to the phenomena under investigation. To define oneself as a "scientist" rests on a demonstrated familiarity with the conceptual underpinnings that inform the language of the scientific community. The language of science itself, however, is not seen to have an interpretive or subjective impact on the object of study; rather, a mastery of scientific discourse gives adequate preparation for the ability to see natural and interdependent organization within the environment. If someone is presented as a "chemist" and cannot identify the periodic chart of the elements, for example, it is unlikely that she or he will be accorded the status of a scientist because a "real" chemist would be able to identify the elements.

The scientific unity promised to the communication discipline through the adoption of the research methods of the natural sciences was called into question with the publication of Thomas Kuhn's (1962) work, *The Structure of Scientific Revolutions.*[2] Kuhn argues that the process of scientific discovery is not linear, objective, and progressive; rather, the history of science is comprised of "paradigm shifts" which occur when competing paradigms within the scientific community battle for supremacy and one paradigm emerges as the temporary victor. The implication of Kuhn's work for scientists, according to Evelyn Fox Keller (1985, p. 5), "is that not only different collections of facts, different focal points of scien-

---

[2] Keller (1985, p. 5) notes that, although Kuhn was not the only historian of science to question progressive views of science, Kuhn's work "provided a welcome alternative to the view maintained by scientists themselves, and until then unchallenged by most historians: the view that science is autonomous and absolutely progressive—approximating ever more closely a full and accurate description of reality 'as it is'."

tific attention, but also different organizations of knowledge, different interpretations of the world, are both possible and consistent with what we
call science." Science, then, is "not simply defined by the exigencies of
logical proof and experimentation," but is the name given to a set of practices which fall under the general rubric of science (Keller, p. 4). Scholars
engaged in social studies of science reveal that science can no longer be
seen as a systematic and impartial uncovering of reality, but as a communal activity in which shared cultural definitions and meanings inform the
process of discovery.

The Kuhnian proposition that science is affected by social and political
forces generated fresh debates within the communication discipline. The
natural science paradigm that promised us clarity was now seen to share
our definitional partiality, our emersion in cultural and social practices.

Thus, during the late 1960s and early 1970s, communication scholars
reexamined the implications of scientific paradigms for theory and research within our discipline. Central in this critical process, defined by
Barnett Pearce (1985, p. 270) as the "great metatheory debate," was a rethinking of the relationship between language or discourse and the activities of researchers. Additionally, communication scholars questioned
the feasibility of using a physical science model to analyze human behavior. Scholars representing the humanistic tradition, for example, drew distinctions between persons and objects and maintained the presence of
fundamental differences between the two (Stewart, 1973). The unique
character of human beings, humanists argued, necessitated modifications
in model building to account for this uniqueness (Barnlund, 1973; Stewart,
1973).

Other scholars provided alternative, though related, ways of conceptualizing the differences between physical and human sciences. Williams
(1973, p. 239) argued that while physical sciences aim to produce "accurate measurement and prediction which presuppose explanations based
on principles of causality and determinism," a human science "aims at
sensitively accurate understandings of social and cultural experience
which require explanations based on principles of teleology and volunta-
rism." In essence, communication scholars began to argue that human
agents, unlike physical matter, are volitional, reflective, choice-making beings; thus a model borrowed from the tenets of a physical science has
limited applicability within our discipline.

As is evidenced in *Speech Communication in the 20th Century* (1985)
and a special issue of the *Journal of Communication* (1983) titled "Ferment in the Field," the present decade has produced more studies about
human communication, but methodological and theoretical clarity has not
been achieved. Because communication scholars take as data everyday
human speech and utilize language in sharing their discoveries, analyses

of the relations between language, thought, and human knowledge have been undertaken to promote a critical understanding of the dynamics of theory building within the discipline. The dynamic nature of communication study, in conjunction with its demand for sociocultural sensitivity, require a continuous reconsideration of investigative frameworks.

Many scholars, in the spirit of Kuhn's work, have critiqued the reductive elements of the normal science tradition. Investigators engage in critical analyses of the methodological and theoretical commitments made when the field, without question, adopts quantitative approaches to communication scholarship (e.g., Miller, 1983; Pearce, Cronen, & Harris, 1982). The feasibility of alternative perspectives and research methods is often explored, in association with attendant critiques of the tacit disparagement imposed on researchers who do not use quantitative methods. Stanley Deetz (1973a), for example, compares "normative" and "interpretive" paradigms and suggests that the field has largely misunderstood interpretive approaches by judging them according to the legitimacy criteria found within the normative paradigm. Deetz argues (p. 141) that although "interpretive studies are often confused with studies based on introspection, subjective impressions, and 'soft data' which are of questionable scientific status," interpretive investigations "are as valid, objective, and rigorous as quantitative research if judged with appropriate criteria and if separated from simple impressionistic insights."

Methodological and theoretical gatekeeping is criticized not only because the silencing of alternative perspectives often involves distortion, but because research is framed in language that has little to do with everyday spoken interaction. Moreover, the normative paradigm is limited by a focus on literal or directly observable phenomena because much of the meaning derived from human interaction takes place at the level of implicature. For instance, playful insults exchanged between family members may at times be experienced as an instantiation of love and cohesiveness; at other times the same insults may acknowledge hostility and distance. To miss the implicit interpretation of what appears to be the same behavior is to distort the meaning of insults for family members. Because the normative paradigm has as its goal literal description, Deetz (1973a, p. 142) notes, the description "inherently distorts process and emergence." Thus, the abilities of normative paradigm users to provide accurate descriptions of everyday communication are diminished by their own commitments to objectivity: "The theoretical findings described in the normative paradigm terms, while objective and unambiguous in themselves, show fewer implications than the same behavioral datum described in everyday language" (p. 142). Proponents of the interpretive paradigm, by contrast, "explicate the implications which are present but hidden in the observation of the behavior rather than to literally describe and give an independent explanation" (p. 143). In the hypothetical family, then, interpretive strategies may well provide a more *accurate* description of speech acts as understood by family members.

An additional problem for proponents of a normative paradigm occurs when the language of science is used to describe interactional phenomena. Explanatory power becomes questionable in the research context because the concepts or names given to communicative phenomena unite a host of otherwise (seemingly) random and unpredictable behaviors. Conceptual grounding permits a coalesence of behaviors and enables a researcher to identify patterns, rules, and conventions which inform everyday behavior. Although the patterns of communicative action are named by researchers, the lay person may not be fully aware of, and would be largely unable to identify, the patterns found by researchers. Yet, as Leonard Hawes (1973, p. 16–17) observes, "Once the researcher specifies the rules . . . communication is explained as being generated from the rules and thereby understood even though the communicators may be only tacitly aware of them."

Hawes suggests that research can involve an act of imposition. Specifically, researchers impose on experience a conceptual apparatus which is used to identify and quantify subsequent behavior patterns. As empirical evidence accumulates, the conceptual framework is validated or legitimized. Empirical validation renders difficult the task of challenging an explanatory device because the behavior is viewed as *an instantiation of* a preordained framework, which becomes reified. That is, the framework comes to be viewed as a set of explanatory principles, existing apart from the whims or biases of individual researchers: the operative explanatory principles are defined as objective. Due to the perceived unreliable nature of individual observation, Donald Darnell (1971, p. 9) suggests that objectivity is achieved through "intersubjective confirmation" or "perceptions or judgments which can be confirmed by comparison with the perceptions or judgments of other individuals (also unreliable)." Thus explanatory principles are validated consensually and accepted within a community of scholars, because the principles are thought to transcend the subjective impressions of an individual actor or scholar. The original and repeated imposition of a priori postulates is forgotten because, through increasing community acceptance, individual responsibility for an explanatatory scheme is diffused.

Once these impositions are revealed we see that knowledge generates from those who are in a position to "see" consistency in human behavior. Concomitantly, the experiences of those studied are named through the power of imposition whether the imposition is collective or individual. Many of us can probably recall times when students have offered accounts of their experiences, only to have a professor offer a seemingly "better" or more "accurate" way of seeing. We are not suggesting that concepts are inherently dangerous or inaccurate. We do argue, however, that as scholars and teachers we must be aware of the power given to us by way of conceptual mastery.

In sum, the scientific method is designed to eliminate researchers' personal values and biases. But, scientists do not exist in a vacuum. Researchers are shaped by their culture as are their research questions and research methods. Ruth Bleier (1984, p. 194), borrowing from Foucault, points out that knowledge, as discourse, works to "reflect, express, and generate relations of power." These power relationships determine which questions can be asked or not asked, which research is considered worthy of discussion, and which answers or perspectives are "true." Bleier further argues (p. 194) that while science, as a body of knowledge, seems to work to uncover truth, "it rests upon and conceals the struggle between those who have the power to discourse and those who do not. Both by the practices of exclusion and their definitions of what *is*, what is to be discussed, and what is false or true, discourses *produce* rather than reveal truth."

The power appropriated by scientists allows them to define truth and to claim that the scientific method is the primary means for finding this truth. Thus, alternative perspectives and methods which produce differing truths are often "ignored–or attacked as 'unscientific' " (DuBois, 1983, p. 106).

The scientific method, with its "guarantee" of prestige and objectivity, is highly valued in our discipline. Thus, many of our research texts advocate sensitivity to the research context and the particularities of the subject population, arguing that research questions should determine investigative strategies. Most authors, however, go on to embrace the tenets of objectivist science (Anderson, 1987; Bowers & Courtright, 1984; Sereno & Mortensen, 1970; Tucker, Weaver, & Berryman-Fink, 1981).

RECOGNIZING GENDER IN OUR RESEARCH TRADITION

The communication discipline in the past decade has critiqued the field's overreliance on quantitative empirical communication research. The "Ferment in the Field" issue of the *Journal of Communication*, mentioned previously, offered many alternatives to the scientific method. But, out of the 35 essays, Treichler and Wartella (1986, p. 3) observe, "not one is a work of feminist scholarship." The journal "frames the 'ferment in the field' of communication as a competitive male struggle for dominance" (Treichler & Wartella, p. 3). Such disregard of feminist alternatives to research indicates the extent to which scholars have not noted the attendant correlations between gender and research conventions.[3]

Communication scholars, then, have criticized our field's preference for quantitative methods, but have not discussed the relationship between a desire for objectivity, control, manipulation, and domination, and a masculine value system. Furthermore, the debate over whether research is "subjective" or "objective" dichotomizes modes of knowing. Such dualisms, feminists maintain, are themselves part of the masculine script. The critique of the scientific method, then, does not begin with feminists (Harding, 1986, p. 91). What does originate with feminists is the suggestion that the scientific method and the division between subjective *versus* objective research may be a cultural construction created by a masculine world view.

Keller (1985, p. 7) observes that the objective/subjective dichotomy tacitly supports a division between male and female identities in which "objectivity, reason, and mind [are viewed] as male, and subjectivity, feeling, and nature [are viewed] as female." The oppositional gender characteristics are linked to the dispositions, roles, and spheres that have been deemed masculine or feminine within sociocultural practices (Pearson, 1985; Spitzack & Carter, 1987; Stewart, Cooper, & Friedley, 1986). Keller (p. 7) writes: "In this division of emotional and intellectual labor, women have been the guarantors and protectors of the personal, the emotional, the particular, whereas science—the province par excellence of the impersonal, the rational, and the general—has been the preserve of men."

Feminist scholars have observed that patriarchy divides the world into a system of dichotomies that are imposed on the world and people in the world. These dichotomies are often incorporated into research practices. For example, Bleier (1984, p. 165) observes that "science has been viewed as the objective investigation of nature for the purpose of both knowledge and its control and domination by 'man'." Here, the dichotomies play out as: "men are to women as culture is to nature, as mind is to body, as subject is to object, as domination is to subordination" (Bleier, p. 164). Science is defined in terms of masculine identity. That is, science is rigorous, rational, impersonal, dispassionate, objective. Cultural notions of science as rational, objective, impersonal are infused with cultural stereotypes of masculine gender identity (Harding, 1986, p. 63). Female gender identity is defined in opposition to masculine and scientific stereotypes.

---

[3] Clearly, many gender and feminist communication scholars have examined these connections (Foss & Foss, 1983; Thorne, Kramarae, & Henley, 1983; Rakow, 1986), but thus far our general knowledge of research practices has not been noticeably altered by feminist insights. Rather, gender and feminist researchers must adapt their work to traditional frameworks if they hope to gain legitimacy (see Chapter 3).

Here, the female is viewed as emotional, personal, subjective, and untamed (Bleier, 1984, p. 196). Thus, "scientific" and "masculine" are compatible while "scientific" and "feminine" are not. Bleier (p. 196) observes, "science is the male intellect: the active, knowing subject; its relationship to nature—the passive object of knowledge, the untamed—is one of manipulation, control, and domination; it is the relationship of man to woman, of culture to nature."

In research terms, the power and control advocated by proponents of objectivity is consistent with persons for whom the individual and collective mastery of nature is central. The goal of orderly compartmentalization within nature, which always entails a domination of nature, requires the devaluing and defacement of nature (Griffin, 1981; Trask, 1986). According to Harding (1986, p. 76), nature is viewed by modern scientists as both passive and threatening to humans. Nature, then, must be tamed and subdued. This conceptualization of nature legitimates a scientific method whose purpose is to control, manipulate, and dominate nature (Harding, 1986, p. 76). Bacon, for example, suggests that the value of science lies in "leading to you Nature with all her children to bind her to your service and make her your slave" (in Keller, 1982, p. 598). The methods of science "have the power to conquer and subdue her, to shake her to her very foundations" (in Keller, 1982, p. 598). Furthermore, Hans Jonas (1963, p. 124), in describing Bacon's view of nature, says, "to be the master of nature is the right of man as the sole possessor of mind."

The domination of nature by (manly) mental powers is related to objectivist attempts to control the research environment. In objectivist approaches researchers are encouraged to "rise above" or transcend the everyday lifeworlds of researcher and researched. "To be objective, to objectify," argues Paul Campbell (1975, p. 398), "is to treat something as an object, as external, as impersonal." If something is treated as an object, it can be manipulated and controlled externally; its uniqueness must be diminished or destroyed in the research setting so that researchers can make generalized claims about human behavior. Schachtel observes: "The scientist . . . looks at the object with one or more hypotheses and with the purpose of his research in mind, and thus 'uses' the object to corroborate or disprove a hypothesis, but does not encounter the object as such, in its own fullness" (in Wyatt, 1986, p. 26).

The gendered implications of objectification are largely unnoticed for two interrelated reasons. First, within culture, a hierarchical valuing process defines intellectual activity as a "higher good" than the interaction of everyday actors. Second, due to inequity within the hierarchy, those who are studied become reduced to the status of mere "data," and by this reduction they lose their status as human beings. Moreover, a built-in inequity between culture and nature posits culture as superior because it strives for rationality; nature, conversely, is messy and often contradictory because it defies concepts of order and consistency. The latter must be controlled by the former in order to ensure the preservation of culture.

Women are equated historically with nature. In turn, nature is linked to the body. Within cultural practices, the naturalness of the body is opposed to the sophistication of reason (Janeway, 1980, pp. 5–7). David Levin (1985, p. 56) writes, "In the Western discourse of cultural symbols, the body has always been associated with the feminine, and especially the matriarchal principle, while the mind (reason, law, intelligence, brainpower) has been traditionally tied to the masculine and the patriarchal." The body represents all that threatens to bring about a demise of reason because nature is viewed as an active and often destructive force. That women are often portrayed as persons who attempt to manipulate men or drive them to acts which reveal male insecurities (e.g., rape) is testament to the potentially destructive capabilities of women's bodies (Spitzack, in press).

The solution to the destructive capabilities of female bodies is active denial and denigration of the natural—the bodily. Rather than viewing the body as a rich encasement for all human action, cultural constructions equate the body with softness, weakness, helplessness, and vulnerability. Nancy Henley (1977) points out, for example, that from earliest socialization, females are draped in soft hues and textures, underscoring their bodies as weak and passive. Males, conversely, are adorned in straightforwardly functional attire, clothing that readies them for action. The bodies of boys must not impede the development of male strength or reasoning prowess, nor can these bodies be "reduced" to the status of *only bodies.* Popular dictates such as "big boys don't cry" epitomize the erasure of body sensation, of softness, within male socialization.

A direct parallel between female and male body experience and research practices is evident in the contrast between "soft" and "hard" approaches to investigation. Soft research approaches are often viewed as unreliable because the findings are viewed as impressionistic, subjective, intuitive observations. Hard approaches, by contrast, are thought to be reliable because knowledge claims are achieved by way of objective evidence and validation. Within the soft/hard opposition, a hierarchy of value lends greater legitimacy to hard approaches because the body of the researcher is presumably erased or "forgotten" in the establishment of consensual validity—sensuality is eradicated. Soft approaches are devalued because within the confines of research, scholars take into account their own personal experiences, biases, and assumptions in relation to the data and the context of research. Claims of objectivity, then, can only be accomplished within the value hierarchy by neutralizing the body.

To examine the language of scholars in the communication discipline is to come face to face with masculine socialization. Our disciplinary roots exhibit a severing of mind and body in which the former is viewed as superior to the latter. Aristotle, for example, believed that "no bodily activity has any connexion with the activity of reason" (in Lange, 1983, p. 6). Texts within the field, in defining communicative competence and describing research practices, emphasize control at the expense of personal connections. For example, Phillips and Wood (1983, p. 74) advise communicators to transcend everyday human involvements by focusing attention "on ideas, not you and the other person. By confining your comments to the issue, you demonstrate your fairmindedness." Self-control, observe Spitzberg and Cupach (1984, p. 11), is "necessary to fulfill the general need of all humans to control their environment." And in the context of scholarly research, Tucker, Weaver, and Berryman-Fink (1981, p. 7) argue, "Competent researchers seek knowledge through careful and controlled inquiry. Those who allow biases and prejudices to confound their investigations come up with nothing more than distorted, slanted, or incorrect findings."

The division between culture and nature, with its attendant polarity in research conventions, is articulated implicitly in descriptions of objective and subjective approaches found in the procedural guidelines in communication research texts. James Anderson (1987), for example, contrasts a "quantitative/deductive/objective/materialist paradigm" with a "qualitative/inductive/subjective/interpretive paradigm" (p. 46). After noting that the former paradigm is "the more dominant of the two,"[4] Anderson adopts the label of "rationalistic" to define quantitative approaches: "The paradigm views human behavior atomistically, as divisible into many independent parts each of which performs in reliably systematic rather than random or capricious ways. Human behavior is organized in response to an ordered, external reality. Human behavior is, in short, fundamentally rational" (p. 46). The qualitative paradigm, called "naturalistic," is defined by a concern with the "situated individual, organization, institution, society, or culture" (p. 46). The individual is understood holistically and behavior is viewed as a process, rather than as a series of disconnected or discrete responses to a preordered universe. Anderson describes the rationalist as an "opportunistic risk-taker," and the naturalist as a "competent inductive thinker" (p. 47). Difference within the domain of sexual difference is mirrored in research practices or conventions. Approaches reflect an oppositional disjunction between deduction and induction, transcendence and immanence.

The sex-role imagery in research texts clarifies the explicit connections

---

[4] Anderson (1987, p. 47) contrasts the dominance of the quantitative paradigm with the relative invisibility of the qualitative paradigm. "The communication paradigm of qualitative research is very much in development. Its history in our discipline is short although its intellectual traditions reach back to the scientific revolution."

between theorizing and gender identity. In *Communication Research Methods,* John Bowers and John Courtright (1984) use a parable to describe the process of scientific discovery. The parable is worthy of considerable discussion here because it brings to the fore innumerable connections between gender and research practices. In the parable, four participants are engaged in a debate concerning the temperature at which water boils. Two participants are male (Gordon and Bernard) and two are female (Charlotte and Joan). As the story unfolds, we learn that Gordon has recently discovered the boiling point of water by developing an accurate measuring instrument. Charlotte "expressed great admiration for Gordon's accomplishments with his new instrument and indicated that she would like to see it work" (p. 3). Bernard later claims to disprove Gordon's result and sends a self-congratulatory telegram to boast his own superior findings. Because Charlotte "became concerned with the deteriorating relationship" between Gordon and Bernard due to their competition for professional recognition, she "confined herself for a month, during which time she pondered the difference between Gordon's studies and Bernard's" (p. 4). During her confinement, she develops her own theory on the temperature of boiling water and Gordon is gracious enough to publish her theory "among his friends" (p. 4). Bernard rejects Gordon's acceptance of Charlotte's theory because "Gordon's quick acceptance of her theory might be explained by personal rather than scientific considerations" (pp. 4–5). Joan, meanwhile, is asked to join the research team. She accepts immediately because she is interested in a romantic relationship with Bernard and, upon receiving his invitation, she "noted the possible personal implications to be inferred" by his invitation (p. 5).

Charlotte's theory is disproved eventually by one proposed by Bernard and Gordon. When the new findings were presented, "Joan and Charlotte applauded, and the coauthors received congratulations with becoming modesty" (p. 5). Later, however, it is Joan who arrives at the definitive explanation for the temperature of boiling water. Although her findings are brilliant, she engages in considerable self-effacement: "You all know that I lay no claim to genius" (p. 6). Moreover, she attributes much of her success to Bernard and Gordon in stating, "I can do nothing but express my admiration for their ingenuity and my envy for their industry. Their scientific contribution certainly will prove to be significant" (p. 6). Indeed, in the parable told by Bowers and Courtright, part of the irony in Joan's discovery stems from her personal interest in Bernard and from her unfailing awe for the scientific genius of Bernard and Gordon. She is, due to her inability to separate personal and professional interests, and her image of herself as inferior, the least likely to succeed in producing the correct result.

The parable is rich in gender implications. Charlotte and Joan function primarily as support for the endeavors of Bernard and Gordon. The males have the power to determine the research issue (the boiling point of water). Charlotte and Joan gain admiration from Bernard and Gordon, in part anyway, because they embrace the issue as an important one. Yet, the women are not accorded equivalent levels of respect in their pursuits. Charlotte's theory is shared only with friends and later debunked. Joan attributes her success essentially to Bernard and Gordon. A primary function of the women is to maintain relationship harmony between two competitive male researchers and to promote the possibility of male-female relationship development.

In order to see the gender implications in the parable told by Bowers and Courtright, we suggest that readers reverse all gender referents. For example, if we assume that Bernard engaged in the study solely for purposes of forming a romantic relationship with Joan, or if we assume that Gordon proved the definitive result and attributed his success entirely to Charlotte and Joan during a self-effacing presentation, traditional gender stereotypes are apparent. Alternatively, if Charlotte and Joan compared the potency of their respective "instruments," and Bernard longed to see Joan's impressive instrument, we may be driven to laughter because the reversal is absurd. If gender holds no place in the development of theory and research, the roles of women and men in the parable should be interchangeable. Clearly, they are not.

The activities of objective scientists are by no means value-free, as is evident in the contrast between soft and hard approaches and the female-male stereotypes found in communication research. Pearce, Cronen, and Harris (1982, pp. 2–3) observe, for example, that "research methods depend on the implicit or explicit theories of the researcher; and these theories derive from the array of often-unstated assumptions about the nature of reality, of knowledge, of humankind. . . ." Bleier (1984, p. 4) argues that a scientist's world view impacts on methodology. That is, questions researchers find interesting to ask incorporate the opinions and values of the researchers. Thus, the question limits the answers supplied (Bleier, p. 4). Similarly, Paul Campbell (1975) argues that "the values are there to start with and removed in the act of scientific study; it is rarely, if ever, the case that one begins with an unvalued reality" (p. 399).

Campbell presents a compelling argument against the assumption of value-free research by asserting that responsible research entails a recognition of *personae* in scientific discourse. The scientific personae is characterized by concerns with control, mastery, and knowledge acquisition, often at the expense of those whom are studied. Campbell calls for awareness regarding the presumed objectivity of science, arguing that the neutrality principle leads to a devaluing of scientific data for which scientists, as *persons*, must be held accountable: "To consider some object/event as unimportant, or dispensable, or destructible via experiment is to regard that something else as worth less than something else, and to so consider it is to devalue it and to bear the responsibility for the act of devaluing" (p. 399).

Campbell takes to task two additional dictates of objectivist science: prediction and control. Competent scientists are partly defined by their abilities to predict the outcome of an experiment, as epitomized by research hypotheses. As Schachtel says, when one has as a goal prediction, "only those aspects of the object are deemed relevant which make it suitable for manipulation or control...." (in Wyatt, 1986, p. 26). If we can accurately predict the results of, say, conflict strategies in marital dyads, we demonstrate competence in the scientific community and gain the respect of colleagues. If an unexpected outcome of our study is the production of tremendous tension between husbands and wives, we are not held accountable for the resulting discord because we did not *predict* tension.

Closely linked to prediction is scientific control. The objectivist, according to Campbell, controls both her or himself and the phenomena studied. The imposition of controls removes both researcher and researched from the temporal dimension of experience (p. 400). The seer and the observed must be "frozen" in time, stripped of dynamic and multifaceted experience, so that ordered, causal, discrete connections can be uncovered. Control functions to reduce the complexity of experience to simple cause-effect relationships. Rhonda Unger (1983, p. 11) observes that, through experimental controls, "the behaviors examined have largely been restricted to those that are amenable to simple observation and/or categorization (and, therefore, devoid of much meaning to the subject); alternative meanings have been eliminated." In the case of our hypothetical marital dyad study, control might be achieved initially by conducting the study in a laboratory setting, followed by a predetermination of what will count as a conflict strategy. The dyads are first removed from their everyday context of interaction, and second, judged according to criteria based on other studies in which the behavior of marital dyads has been predetermined and based on generalization in laboratory settings. The problem with control, then, is double-edged: not only do controls function to disallow individual uniqueness, but they impose constraints which *distort* the data and thus the reliability of findings becomes suspect.

Scholars who argue for a contextually and relationally sensitive treatment of human beings, brought about in part by acknowledging the responsibilities of the researcher vis-á-vis the researched, are often perceived as doing "subjective" or nonscientific research. If the *personae* of a researcher assumed by investigative strategies is taken into account, according to objectivists, the researcher in question is not doing science, but is engaged in a "soft" intuitive enterprise which produces unreliable findings. In fact, the notion of *personae* within "soft" approaches might well be acknowledged by objectivists and used to discount the findings of so-called subjective researchers.

Context sensitivity and a recognition of process are lauded in publications by communication scholars and in the advice and research instructions given to students and colleagues.[5] However, if researchers take these situational tenets to heart and design strategies that tap into the complex and processual nature of communication, they run the risk of being labeled "subjective" or "soft." Overlooked in the labeling process is the position of elitism from which the criticism proceeds. To condemn a research approach because it is "soft" assumes a particular and limited vision of scholarship, one which, in *advance*, has predetermined a single set of criteria for evaluation.

Researchers who argue for objectivist research practices do not openly prohibit alternative approaches. Additionally, traditional scholars who embrace a scientific paradigm would not admit gender bias because an admission of perspective goes against the grain of objectivity. Scholarship, from the objectivist vantage point, should be based on equality within the domain of inquiry. Scholarly equality is insured by an active process of questioning, in which success or failure is presumably removed from the personal qualities of individual researchers. As Barnett Pearce (1985) points out, scholars of science invite critical scrutiny. In the spirit of theoretical and disciplinary progress, scientists make themselves vulnerable by exposing findings and methods to both hostile and supportive colleagues. The scholarly enterprise invites debate and controversy because only through such activities does theory building occur (Bormann, 1980; Tucker, Weaver, & Berryman-Fink, 1981).

Rarely addressed, however, are the ideological components of the research process. Theorists or metatheorists may engage in speculation about ideology,[6] but researchers who conduct applied "scientific" studies must, if anything, ultimately dehistoricize their work. In few statistical or mathematical analyses of communication behavior do we find discussions of ideological factors which underlie research procedures or significant findings. Unger (1983, p. 11) finds that within experimental and laboratory studies, "those actions involving ideology and values have been defined out by fiat as operationally meaningless." To present the world view implicit in research designs acknowledges perspective and can lead to

---

[5] Pearce (1985) presents a typical example of the disjunction between the assumptions or models offered by researchers and the subsequent implementation of models. Pearce notes that in the influential work, *The Process of Communication*, David Berlo (1960) developed "an excellent description of communication as processual in its first chapters, then developed at length a very linear model" (p. 274).

[6] There are numerous examples of theoretical reflection on ideology in the communication discipline. See Campbell (1975); Deetz (1973a, 1973b); Pearce (1985).

charges of bias. Communication theorists are often quite amenable to discussing paradigmatic assumptions because theories are viewed inevitably as products of human activity. In other words, theories themselves are not seen to appear "naturally," hence they are open to question and debate. Yet, when theoretical assumptions filter into the domain of research methodologies and methods, where data collection itself is often not seen in political terms, the constructed nature of theoretical precepts is diffused or lost.

Sarah Trenholm (1986) argues that *ideological masking* is one reason for the lack of critical scrutiny concerning the confusion about our disciplinary boundaries. As Trenholm (1986, p. 7) writes, ideologies "tend to uphold the status quo," but for this very reason, "ideological assumptions appear so natural that we never think to question them." The lack of critical scrutiny encompassed within ideological discourse leads to "uncritical support of particular, and often contradictory, constructions of reality" (p. 8).[7] Ideological masking takes place at all levels of the research process.

The ideology masked in contemporary communication research reflects the history of patriarchy in American culture. Although communication researchers do not define themselves as androcentric—to do so would reveal ideology—the language used to communicate theoretical assumptions and research activities clearly reflects masculine experience. Quite matter-of-factly, researchers may describe "penetrating" explanations, "thrusts" of arguments, and "seminal" works.

Thus, feminist scholars point out the sexual imagery and metaphors in the writings of scholars and researchers. Traditional scholars, however, argue that these sexual images are unrelated to scientific concepts and methods. Alternatively, when nature is viewed as a machine, scientists have another interpretation (Harding, 1986, p. 113). Harding observes:

> Here, we are told, the metaphor provides the interpretations of Newton's mathematical laws: it directs inquiries to fruitful ways to apply his theory and suggests the appropriate methods of inquiry and the metaphysics the new theory supports. But if we are to believe that mechanistic metaphors were a fundamental component of the explanations the new science provided, why should we believe that the gender metaphors were not?

It is hard to believe that women scholars would design a research method that utilizes terminology grounded in viewing nature as a female who needs to be controlled, dominated, subdued, raped, or penetrated.

When selecting research methods, both women and men draw from

---

[7] Trenholm (1986) uses the term "ideological discourse" as developed by semiotician Umberto Eco.

explanatory schemes that are most sensible and realistic, given their respective experiential backgrounds. For example, if a researcher holds a mechanistic view of the world, the methodological precepts of behaviorism are appealing; thus a quantitative or experimental research method is feasible because it affords the promise of control and employs hypothetico-deductive reasoning. A primary concern for this type of researcher is the generation of objective findings which can be generalized to the larger population. If, however, a researcher has been socialized to note the subtle and often implicit (or hidden) mechanics of the communication process, it is likely that she or he would select a descriptive or interpretive method, based in turn on a phenomenological or critical methodology. Both approaches attempt to provide accurate, comprehensive, realistic accounts of human behavior. To suggest that qualitative approaches are subjective is to interpret phenomenological or descriptive approaches with gross inaccuracy. The goal of providing a more comprehensive understanding of human communication is shared by both qualitative and quantitative researchers.

In sum, the task for scholars is to unmask and deconstruct the conceptual dichotomies that bipolarize culture and nature, male and female, mind and body, subject and object, quantitative and qualitative. This deconstructive process reveals the ways in which research is both culture-bound *and* gender-bound.

THE PROBLEM OF INTEGRATION: GATEKEEPING AND GENDER RESEARCH

Once it is realized that communication science contains a gender component, women are given opportunities to make visible their experiences, forms of interaction, and modes of scholarly analysis. The difficulty of translating gender insights into the field of communication, as articulated by Karen Foss and Sonja Foss (Chapter 3), is the traditional disciplinary marginalizing of feminist and gender research which severely limits opportunities for female visibility. Viewed as a specialty area, gender studies have been perceived as having limited applicability to the study of communication in general (Spitzack & Carter, 1987). The cultural devaluing of women further complicates the inclusion of feminist and gender studies within the communication discipline because, by having the right to claim impartiality, patriarchal culture hides behind the guise of gender neutrality.

Research for women, then, is seen within patriarchy as biased because it advocates acknowledging perspective, partiality, and institutional mechanisms which impede the voices of women in research and sociocultural

practices. This acknowledgment is often used against women within patriarchy as evidence to confirm the so-called subjective character of wom-
en's experiences and their research. A conceptual network of dichotomies
is once again brought into play. That is, males are aligned with that which
is objective, impersonal, neutral, and distant; females are placed on the
side of the subjective, the personal, and are seen to be too involved. Thus,
research by and for women can be almost automatically discounted simply because women are not perceived as having the appropriate "scientific" mind.

In this section we delineate some of the major barriers for researchers
who conduct gender and feminist studies. As will become clear, criticisms
of feminist research are based on stereotypes about women. And so the
same persons who purport to be objective are found to embrace gender
arguments when criticizing *female* scholarship, but they exempt themselves from gender stereotypes as applied to, or found in, their own work.
We highlight some of the predominant strategies by which feminist research is discounted within the domain of traditional inquiry.

Perhaps the main argument directed against feminist research, or research on women in general, is the charge of irrelevancy. That is, traditional scholars often claim that a "gender problem" does not exist because
all persons within society should be treated equally. Thus because the gender problem is not really a problem at all, women who conduct feminist
research are thought to generate controversy over nonissues. The ability
to determine the significance of issues signifies the power of privilege.
One of the benefits of privilege is the socially sanctioned right to define
one's own view as the only (reasonable) view.

Similarly, Spender (1982) points out that the notion of objectivity constitutes a double barrier for women. First, by creating the category of objectivity, one does not have to be directly sexist, rather one simply presents his ideas as truth (p. 4). Any objections to this "truth" or any
alternative suggestions can be rejected as non-Truth. Thus, one does not
have to state directly that women are deficient, one only has to present
one's findings as objective and universal for others to be able to see wom-
en's differences as deviant. Second, Spender (p. 34) argues that when
women suggest we are not inferior or deficient but have different experiences or a different view,

> then men can use another weapon they have constructed: they can declare
> that we are being subjective ... men's descriptions and explanations which
> arise from their experience of the world are legitimated by themselves as
> objective. But where women's expressions do not conform, where they arise
> from women's experience of the world, men are able to label the differences
> as subjective.

Spender's observations are directly related to the impact of the gate-keeping process within the domain of research practices. That is, male scholars can label women's research as irrelevant or political, but when the tables are turned, that is, when women suggest that the research concentration on men is irrational, subjective, or political, a hue and cry arises. The question that comes to mind is: If women's research for women is so trivial and irrelevant, and, worst of all, political, then why the outrage? If it's so trivial, it ought to be ignored. The outrage may come from the assumption that there is only one reality. Addelson (1983, p. 165) shows that if we believe there is only one reality, then we also assume there is only one truth, and that the scientific method is the means to understand and know this truth.

Feminist researchers from diverse areas have called attention to the accusation of subjective bias in research by and for women. In her critical analysis of rape in American culture, Susan Brownmiller (1977) points out that, in collecting data, she was asked repeatedly by librarians, public officials, assistants, "have you ever been raped?" Similarly, in a study of women's experiences of childbirth, Ann Oakley (1981) found much attention centered on whether or not she had given birth. And in Spitzack's (in press) analysis of women's experiences of dieting, the author was often asked by subjects and colleagues if she had suffered from a weight problem or eating disorder.

The preceding examples suggest that when women conduct research on issues of concern to women, researchers are assumed to hold a vested experiential interest in the issues that are investigated. Feminist researchers would not deny this charge because, from a feminist perspective, personal actions and choices are indeed tied to personal history. As Unger (1983, p. 24) states, "Since even those females involved in scholarship have had a different subjective reality from their male counterparts, it is not surprising that they focus on different aspects of experience and/or evaluate it differently." The problem is that those who criticize feminist scholarship on subjective grounds fail to account for their own degree of experiential bias. The accusation of subjective bias, directed at research for women, acknowledges a different personal history on the parts of critics.

The charge of subjective bias is tied to an assumption that feminist researchers are motivated in part by their own rejection within patriarchal culture. Those who stereotype feminists often feel confident that feminists have had negative experiences with men. The anger expressed in feminist scholarship is interpreted as an overly emotional response to men, in line with the assumption that women take things too personally. Yet, we might indeed wonder who is taking things personally when feminist research is received consistently with defensiveness. Only persons who assume they are at the center of culture—the primary reference point—feel the need to defend themselves when others challenge the centrality of their position. Even when the female stereotype portrays women as inherently nurturing and motivated by the need to have relationships, there may be a rejection of findings indicating that women are more competent in relational communication than men. That is, women are expected to excel in promoting relationship harmony, but not if their abilities involve an explicit or implicit critique of male relationship behaviors. Moreover, as Andrea Dworkin (1987) argues, male authors who speak about women by using degrading and violent imagery are seldom asked if their work is motivated by a personal rejection from women.

Male scholars within the communication discipline who advocate alternative approaches to research are not, to our knowledge, asked if they have been personally hurt by the assumptions contained in traditional approaches, hence their motivation for critique. Indeed, such an admission by male scholars, within traditional conceptions of scholarship, would border on the humorous: "I am studying marriage because I have been divorced three times and find that quantitative approaches do not capture my experience."

The issue of emotion is related to the research concepts of subjective bias and personal involvement. Specifically, women who criticize the dominance of male scholarship and male versions of reality violate two dimensions of female stereotypes. Women are socialized to be passive and compliant; when they question their place within society, they violate the traditional feminine role. In addition, women are socialized not to express anger so that the expression of *any* anger is viewed negatively. In a review of Kappeler's *Pornography of Representation,* for example, Lawrence Rosenfield (1987, p. 258–259) notes anger in Kappeler's work and summarizes her contribution with the following observation: "It is unlikely that Kappeler's book will achieve currency as a major source of ammunition in the war between the sexes. As rhetoric it illustrates how self destructive to the process of public debate are those arguments which are both overtly hostile and overly moralistic." From our perspective, the metaphors of "war," "ammunition," and "currency" equally reflect a particular view of the world—one which contains hostility and its own brand of destructiveness. Moreover, we argue that traditional rhetoric is hardly free of moralistic tendencies. Plato's dictate, "a good man speaking well," is packed with moral (and gender) implications. Alternatively, as indicated above, the history of rhetoric is replete with views that oppose reason to the body, following religious contrasts between heaven and hell, body and soul.

Feminist research is often discounted within patriarchy on technical grounds. Dale Spender (1985) observes that traditionalists discredit feminist studies by finding fault with their research procedures. A rejection of work that challenges the dominant position of men rarely evolves through explicit censoring. Spender (1981, p. 191), in describing an observation made by Kuhn, argues that "those who have established reputations (and who are likely to be editors, reviewers or advisors) often have a vested interest in preserving the authority of their work and can suppress fundamental novelties which challenge, or reflect unfavourably on their work." Thus, Spender (p. 191) continues, "gatekeepers are in a position to perpetuate their own schemata by exercising sponsorship and patronage towards those who classify the world in ways similar to their own." Because censorship is antithetical to academic freedom, research that challenges the status quo is rejected not because it is a challenge per se, but because traditional scholars claim the author used ineffective data collection techniques, drew inaccurate conclusions, performed a simplistic analysis of the data, used an inappropriate sample population, or failed to provide adequate controls for the testing of variables.

Reports of research findings can also perpetuate sex-role stereotypes. Numerous feminist scholars have pointed out that many empirical studies begin by assuming sex differences (Thorne et al., 1983; Unger, 1983). Mary Anne Fitzpatrick (1983) describes a study in which self-perceptions of same- and opposite-sex friends were determined by using a scale of behaviors ranging from control to nurturance. Although only two dimensions showed difference, the discussion section of the paper focused almost completely on the two differences found. Similarly, Unger (1983) delineates a controversial study in which the authors argued that they had discovered innate sex differences in mathematical abilities. The study received much attention by both popular and scholarly audiences. Objections to the study and qualifications made by the authors themselves, however, "received less attention from the journal and far less from the popular press, which had picked up on the original study without paying attention to cautionary statements by the authors themselves that numerous interpretations were consistent with the data" (p. 20).

Feminist scholarship, then, offers alternative perspectives, values, and truths. Because feminist researchers openly acknowledge the political dimensions of their work, arguing that women's experiences are legitimate and worthy of study, feminist insights are seen to be tainted within mainstream academia. At best, gender is simply viewed as another variable to study; at worst feminist research is attacked as unscientific or subjective. The partiality and politics assumed in "mainstream" scholarship, conversely, are protected from critique under the cloak of "objectivity." Harding (1986) argues that feminist scholarship seeks to develop theories which reveal women's lives as valid and gender as an important explanatory concept in social activities. "There is nothing 'subjective' about such a project," Harding (p. 138) observes, "unless one thinks only visions distorted by gendered desires could imagine women to be fully social and gender relations to be real explanatory variables."

DOING FEMINIST RESEARCH

Feminist scholars argue that subjective and objective ways of knowing cannot be polarized because they are not independent of each other (e.g., Du Bois, 1983; MacKinnon, 1982; Stanley & Wise, 1981). Even researchers who use experimental research designs derive their theories and concepts from life experiences. Moreover, female and male researchers are dependent on affirmation of their findings from other persons who also have life experiences which inform their judgments. For any research to have meaning, scientists must develop their concepts from real world situations which are in turn reflected in research choices. In addition, the all-too-easy linkage between subjective-qualitative and objective-quantitative research must be rejected.

Hilary Graham (1983, p. 136) argues that the "wholesale adoption of qualitative research by and for women may reinforce the very divisions that feminists are seeking to destroy." Existing cultural divisions, placing women on the side of emotion and men on the side of reason, may be tacitly and dangerously underscored through an uncritical matching of research approach to gender. Graham (p. 136), in examining traditional feminist critiques which attempt to give women a place within the scientific community, explains:

> [T]he logic of critique suggests that qualitative methods are better suited to the structure of women's lives, while quantitative methods are reserved for the study of (and by) men. Such a sexual division may yield useful data, but only at the same time, by reinforcing the tendency to analyse women's and men's lives separately. In so doing, it underlines the notion that women are locked into a 'woman's world', marginal to mainstream culture and integrated into society only through the mediation of men.

Similarly, Sandra Coyner (1983) argues that while feminists denounce objectivity, control, and neutrality, we are not restricted to opposite methods: subjectivism or intuition. Coyner (p. 63) points out, "in our [feminist] reactions to the limitations of previous scholarship we don't need to emphasize the opposite, but create a new spectrum of methods which is more inclusive."

Given the inevitability of the personal in the research process for women *and* men, feminist scholars argue for a redefinition of subjectivity and objectivity so that the two are not set in opposition to one another. Reinharz (1979, p. 255) proposes a research method of "experiential analysis," suggesting that "objectivity should thus be redefined from the elimination of the influence of the investigator's personal features to a clear understanding of their influence." Rather than a systematic removal of researcher bias, then, experiential analysis demands a critical scrutiny of the underlying perspective in research, including the biases of individual or collective researchers. The activity of critical scrutiny does not revert to impressionistic or unsystematic procedures. Rather, Reinharz (p. 355) states:

> The introspective subjective position is expanded so that the researcher is reflecting on experiences embodied in action and interaction during the course of ongoing, patterned social events.... The experiential researcher stands at the intersection of subjectivity and objectivity, between the observer and the thing observed.

Du Bois (1983) argues that subjectivity and objectivity are not opposed to each other. Rather, "objectivity and subjectivity are modes of knowing, analyses, interpretation, understanding. They are not independent of each other and should not be" (p. 111).

We suggest that researchers must reexamine the relationship between the knower and the known, the researcher and the subject. Traditional science views the relationship between knower and known as separate. To insure objectivity, the knower is expected to distance her/himself from the subject. The methods of traditional science demand an impersonal relationship between researchers and subjects. For example, traditional scientists may well look askance at a researcher who conducts systematic interviews with friends and loved ones. The impersonal relationship between researcher and researched places the former in a position of superiority with respect to the latter. The "superior" researcher is able to control emotions and maintain distance from the everyday flow of life. According to Hawes (1975), traditional research is elitist because researchers assume they can provide "better" accounts of subjects' behavior and meanings than can the subject her-or himself (in Deetz, 1976). Thus there is an implicit power factor in the relationship between researcher and subject—the researcher is powerful (due to an ability to control and manipulate the setting), while the subject is powerless. The subject retains the status of a "good" subject only by complying to the researcher's demands. A one-way process of intrusion allows a researcher to demand disclosure from a subject, potentially disrupting the subject's lifeworld, then walk away from the research setting with personal identity intact. As Reinharz (1979, p. 95) explains, researchers "intrude into their subjects' privacy, disrupt their perceptions, utilize false pretense, manipulate the relationship and give little or nothing in return. When the needs of researchers are satisfied, they break off contact with the subject."

Feminist scholars have likened the intrusion of impersonal researchers into the lives of human beings to the act of rape (e.g., Lather, 1982, p. 6; Reinharz, 1979, p. 95). Although it may be argued that researchers gain the consent of subjects for participation in a project, the consent becomes suspect with the realization that, in traditional research, subjects are misled as to the purpose of the study. And a survey by Gordon (1983, p. 221) indicates that 68 percent of communication researchers believe that it is "acceptable to mislead or misinform a subject, as long as the subject is debriefed afterward." Forty-six percent of those surveyed believed that "subjects do not mind being deceived during participation in experimental research" (Gordon, p. 221). Thus, the majority of communication researchers who responded to the survey believe that deception is a justifiable approach to communication research.

We argue, however, that most people feel violated if they are led to participate in an activity under false pretenses. They might indeed use adjectives such as manipulative, deceptive, and thoughtless to describe the person who solicited their participation. Gordon (1986), at a conference on gender and communication, argued against the employment of dissimulation in research practices, stating that the most ethical way to do research is through collaboration (in Wyatt, 1986, p. 27). Similarly, Wyatt (1986) argues that we must involve our subjects as collaborators. "We have to include them [subjects] in the research process as partners in the discovery and understanding of human communication.... using deception, we deceive ourselves.... studying people as objects-in-use, we demean ourselves" (27). We support Wyatt's and Gordon's views and argue that researchers cannot be given the luxury of exempting themselves from ethical conduct simply because the context of research appears to require deception.

Feminist research reveals that the researcher and the researched cannot be separated; they are both enmeshed in the sociocultural world. Rather than deceiving the "subjects" in research, which assumes that the researcher knows what is best for those whom are studied, feminists argue that subjects can speak for themselves and can lend insight to scholarly endeavors. We endorse Westkott's (1979) and Renata Duelli Klein's (1983) concepts of intersubjectivity in research arrangements. Westkott argues for an analytic approach that emphasizes the interrelatedness of researcher and researched. Here, intersubjectivity is understood as a dialectical relationship between research participants, including the researcher (in Duelli Klein, 1983, p. 94). Duelli Klein (1983, p. 94) suggests that "whenever possible, feminist methodology should allow for such intersubjectivity." Intersubjectivity creates a research situation wherein the researcher not only shares her experiences, but shares her research project with her participants (Duelli Klein, p. 94). That is, those about whom the researcher seeks understanding have the power to influence the production of knowledge within a given research study, and more generally, within the scholarly community.

The "how to" of feminist research is sometimes tedious, overwhelming, and of course, time consuming. Rewards often seem all too few and far between. At the same time, however, feminist research is exciting and challenging. The critical lens offered by feminism is empowering and enriching. Feminist research is inextricably entwined with the personal. Such scholarship ultimately frees us all to explore our own lives and the lives of others. Wherever we arrive, the journey is exhilirating.

REFERENCES

Addelson, K. P. (1983). The man of professional wisdom. In S. Harding & M. B. Hintikka (Eds.), *Discovering reality: Feminist perspectives on epistemology, metaphysics, methodology, and philosophy of science* (pp. 165–186). Dordrecht, Holland: D. Reidel Publishing Company.

Anderson, J. A. (1987). *Communication research: Issues and methods.* New York: McGraw-Hill.

Barnlund, D. C. (1973). Towards a meaning centered philosophy of communication. In J. Stewart (Ed.), *Bridges not walls: A book about interpersonal communication* (pp. 36–41). New York: Random House.

Benson, T. (Ed.). (1985). *Speech communication in the 20th century.* Carbondale, IL: Southern Illinois University Press.

Berlo, D. K. (1960). *The process of communication.* New York: Holt.

Bleier, R. (1984). *Science and gender: A critique of biology and its theories on women.* New York: Pergamon Press.

Bochner, A. P., & Eisenberg, E. M. (1985). Legitimizing speech communication: An examination of coherence and cohesion in the development of the discipline. In T. Benson (Ed.), *Speech communication in the 20th century* (pp. 299–321). Carbondale, IL: Southern Illinois University Press.

Bormann, E. G. (1980). *Communication theory.* New York: Holt, Rinehart & Winston.

Bowers, J. W., & Courtright, J. A. (1984). *Communication research methods.* Glenview, IL: Scott, Foresman and Company.

Brownmiller, S. (1984). *Femininity.* New York: Fawcett Columbine.

Campbell, P. N. (1975). The *personae* of scientific discourse. *Quarterly Journal of Speech, 61,* 391–405.

Cohen, H. (1985). The development of research in speech communication: A historical perspective. In T. Benson (Ed.), *Speech communication in the 20th century* (pp. 282–298). Carbondale, IL: Southern Illinois University Press.

Coyner, S. (1983). Women's studies as an academic discipline: Why and how to do it. In G. Bowles & R. Duelli Klein (Eds.), *Theories of women's studies.* London: Routledge & Kegan Paul.

Dance, F. E. X., & Larson, C. E. (1972). *Speech communication: Concepts and behavior.* New York: Holt, Rinehart & Winston.

Darnell, D. K. (1971). Toward a reconceptualization of communication. *Journal of Communication, 21,* 5–16.

Deetz, S. (1973a). An understanding of science and a hermeneutic science of understanding. *Journal of Communication, 23,* 139–159.

Deetz, S. (1973b). Words without things: Toward a social phenomenology of language. *Quarterly Journal of Speech, 59,* 40–51.

Deetz, S. (1976, December). *Philosophical and theoretical considerations in a sociology of knowledge.* Paper presented at the Speech Communication Association Convention, San Francisco, CA.

Delia, J. (1979). The future of graduate education in speech communication. *Communication Education, 28,* 271–281.

Du Bois, B. (1983). Passionate scholarship: Notes on values, knowing and method in feminist social science. In G. Bowles & R. Duelli Klein (Eds.), *Theories of women's studies* (pp. 105–116). London: Routledge & Kegan Paul.

Duelli Klein, R. (1983). How to do what we do: Thoughts about feminist methodology. In G. Bowles & R. Duelli Klein (Eds.), *Theories of women's studies* (pp. 88–104). London: Routledge & Kegan Paul.

Dworkin, A. (1987). *Intercourse.* New York: The Free Press.

Ferment in the Field. (1983). *Journal of Communication, 33*(3).

Fitzpatrick, M. A. (1983). Effective interpersonal communication for women of the corporation: Think like a man, talk like a lady.... In J. Pilotta (Ed.), *Women in organizations: Barriers and breakthroughs* (pp. 73–84). Prospect Heights, IL: Waveland Press.

Foss, K. A., & Foss, S. K. (1983). The status of research on women and communication. *Communication Quarterly, 31,* 195–204.

Gordon, R. (1983). Attitudes of researchers towards deception and communication research. *Communication Quarterly, 31,* 220–223.

Gordon, R. (1986). *What women can teach men about research.* Paper presented at the Gender Role Conference, Pennsylvania State University, College Park, PA.

Graham, H. (1983). Do her answers fit his questions? Women and the survey method. In E. Gamarnikow, D. Morgan, J. Purvis, & D. Taylorson (Eds.), *The public and the private* (pp. 132–146). London: Heinemann.

Griffin, S. (1981). *Pornography and silence: Culture's revenge against nature.* New York: Harper Colophon.

Harding, S. (1986). *The science question in feminism.* Ithaca: Cornell University Press.

Hart, R. (1985). The politics of communication studies: An address to undergraduates. *Communication Education, 34,* 162–165.

Hawes, L. C. (1973). Elements of a model for communication processes. *Quarterly Journal of Speech, 59,* 11–21.

Hawes, L. C. (1975, November). *The naturalistic study of human communication.* Paper presented at the Speech Communication Association, Houston, TX.

Henley, N. (1977). *Body politics: Power, sex, and nonverbal communication.* Englewood Cliffs, NJ: Prentice-Hall.

Janeway, E. (1980). Who is Sylvia?: On the loss of sexual paradigms. In C. R. Stimpson & E. S. Person (Eds.), *Women: Sex and sexuality* (pp. 4–20). Chicago: University of Chicago Press.

Jonas, H. (1963). The practical uses of theory. In M. Natanson (Ed.), *Philosophy of the social sciences* (pp. 119–142). New York: Random House.

Keller, E. F. (1982). Feminism and science. *Signs, 7,* 589–602.

Keller, E. F. (1985). *Reflections on gender and science.* New Haven, CT: Yale University Press.

Kuhn, T. (1962). *The structure of scientific revolutions.* Chicago: University of Chicago Press.

Lange, L. (1983). Woman is not a rational animal: On Aristotle's biology of reproduction. In S. Harding & M. B. Hintikka (Eds.), *Discovering reality: Feminist perspectives on epistemology, metaphysics, methodology, and the philosophy of science* (pp. 1–15). Dordrecht, Holland: D. Riedel Publishing.

Lather, P. (1982, June). *Notes toward an adequate methodology in doing feminist research.* Paper presented at the National Women's Studies Association Conference, Bloomington, IN.

Levin, D. (1985). *The body's recollection of being: Phenomenological psychology and the deconstruction of nihlism.* London: Routledge & Kegan Paul.

MacKinnon, C. A. (1982). Feminism, Marxism, method, and the state: An agenda for theory. *Signs, 7,* 515–544.

Miller, G. (1983). Taking stock of a discipline. *Journal of Communication, 33,* 31–41.

Oakley, A. (1981). Interviewing women: A contradiction in terms. In H. Roberts (Ed.), *Doing feminist research* (pp. 30–61). London: Routledge and Kegan Paul.

Pearson, J. C. (1985). *Gender and communication.* Dubuque, IA: Wm. C. Brown.

Pearce, W. B. (1985). Scientific research methods in communication studies and their implications for theory and research. In T. Benson (Ed.), *Speech communication in the 20th century* (pp. 255–281). Carbondale, IL: Southern Illinois University Press.

Pearce, W. B., Cronen, V. E., & Harris, L. M., (1982). Methodological considerations in building human communication theory. In F. E. X. Dance (Ed.), *Human communication theory: Comparative essays.* New York: Harper & Row.

Phillips, G. M., & Wood, J. T. (1983). *Communication and human relationships: The study of interpersonal communication.* New York: Macmillan.

Rakow, L. (1986). Rethinking gender research in communication. *Journal of Communication, 36,* 11–26.

Reinharz, S. (1979). *On becoming a social scientist.* San Francisco: Jossey-Bass Publishers.

Rosenfield, L. (1987). Review of *The Pornography of Representation.* By Susanne Kappeler. *Quarterly Journal of Speech, 73,* 257–259.

Sereno, K. K., & Mortensen, C. D. (Eds.). (1970). *Foundations of communication theory.* New York: Harper and Row.

Spender, D. (1981). The gatekeepers: A feminist critique of academic publishing. In H. Roberts (Ed.), *Doing feminist research* (pp. 186–202). London: Routledge and Kegan Paul.

Spender, D. (1982). *Invisible Women: The schooling scandal.* London: Writers and Readers Publishing.

Spender, D. (1985). *Man made language.* (2nd ed.) London: Routledge and Kegan Paul.

Spitzberg, B., & Cupach, W. R. (1984). *Interpersonal communication competence.* Beverly Hills, CA: Sage Publications.

Spitzack, C. (in press). Under the knife: Self knowledge through effacement. *Quarterly Journal of Ideology.*

Spitzack, C., & Carter, K. (1987). Women in communication studies: A typology for revision. *Quarterly Journal of Speech, 73,* 401–423.

Stanley, L., & Wise, S. (1981). 'Back into the personal' or: Our attempt to construct 'feminist research'. In G. Bowles & R Duelli Klein (Eds.), *Theories of women's studies II* (pp. 98–118). Berkeley: Women's Studies, University of California.

Stewart, J. (Ed.). (1973). *Bridges not walls: A book about interpersonal communication.* New York: Random House.

Stewart, L., Cooper, P. J., & Friedley, S. A. (1986). *Communication between the sexes: Sex differences and sex-role stereotypes.* Scottsdale, AZ: Gorsuch Scarisbrick.

Thorne, B., Kramarae, C., & Henley, N. (1983). Language, gender, and society: Opening a second decade of research. In B. Thorne, C. Kramarae, & N. Henley (Eds.), *Language, gender and society* (pp. 7–24). Rowley, MA: Newbury House.

Trask, H. K. (1986). *Eros and power: The promise of feminist theory.* Philadelphia: University of Pennsylvania Press.

Treichler, P. A., & Wartella, E. (1986). Interventions: Feminist theory and communication studies. *Communication, 9,* 1–18.

Trenholm, S. (1986). *Human communication theory.* Englewood Cliffs, NJ: Prentice-Hall.

Tunstall, J. (1983). The trouble with U.S. communication research. *Journal of Communication, 33,* 92–95.

Tucker, R. K., Weaver, R. L., & Berryman-Fink, C. (1981). *Research in speech communication.* Englewood Cliffs, NJ: Prentice-Hall.

Unger, R. K. (1983). Through the looking glass. No wonderland yet! (The reciprocal relationship between methodology and models of reality). *Psychology of Women Quarterly, 8,* 9–32.

Westkott, M. (1979). Feminist criticism in the social sciences. *Harvard Educational Review, 49,* 422–430.

Williams, K. R. (1973). Reflections on a human science of communication. *Journal of Communication, 23,* 239–250.

Wyatt, N. (1986). Cherished illusions: Mistaken notions about research techniques. *The Pennsylvania Speech Communication Annual, 17,* 17–28.

2

Exposing Masculine Science: An Alternative Feminist Approach to the Study of Women's Communication*

KATHERINE HAWKINS
Department of Speech Communication
Texas Tech University

In November of 1986, *Spectra*, the newsletter of the Speech Communication Association, published a guest editorial on "Communication Theory in the 1990's," authored by Ronald D. Gordon. In his editorial, Gordon reports on his attendance at the 1986 Penn State Conference on Gender and Communication. One of the impressions Gordon came away with is that many female scholars in the discipline of speech communication feel that communication theory is male-dominated. As evidence of this, he noted the claims that certain topics and/or research approaches are difficult to publish, and that there is a dearth of female journal editors. He observes that a truly female research perspective remains to be developed, and he calls on female scholars to render assistance in this regard. What, he asks, do our eyes see that his (and other men's) do not?

As I read Gordon's words, I found that I agreed most heartily with the position that *most* research is male-dominated, not only research in speech communication. In addition, I had some probably naive notions of why this was the case. Subsequent readings on the subject of gender and science clarified my understanding of the genesis of male-dominated science, and I began to see the impact of the dominant male world view on my own research. This essay, then, is my response to Gordon's query. Here is what my eyes see that men's, perhaps, do not.

Specifically, the focus of this essay is twofold. First, I argue that the genderization of science (i.e., the association of masculinity with objectivity) encourages a masculinist bias in the conduct of research. Further, this

* The author wishes to thank John F. Deethardt for his thought-provoking contributions during the early stages of the development of this essay.

bias negatively affects gender research, in general, and the study of women's communication, in particular. Second, I posit an alternative approach to science, founded on feminist principles, that I believe is particularly well suited to the study of women's communication.

Before proceeding, I'd like to offer a brief caveat to the above. When I use the term, an alternative feminist approach to science, I do not mean to say that I am offering the "official" feminist approach to science. Rather, what I am about to offer is one alternative way of looking at science and at the conduct of research. The approach I offer is feminist in that the alternative approach I posit is grounded in what I believe to be feminist principles. The perspective I discuss is, therefore, *an* alternative approach to science that is feminist, not *the* alternative feminist approach to science.

To close the essay, I offer the study of sexual harassment as an illustrative example of the use of an alternative feminist approach to science. The investigation of sexual harassment is a revealing case in point for several reasons. First, sexual harassment is suffered almost exclusively by women (Clarke, 1981). Second, sexual harassment is a problem that is resistant to understanding or intervention. I will argue that the adoption of a male-oriented world view has prevented a clear understanding of the problem of sexual harassment, and that adoption of a female-oriented world view can offer valuable insights into the genesis of and intervention into the process of sexual harassment.

In my discussions of the masculinist bias in science, and of an alternative feminist approach to science, I often refer to the work of Evelyn Fox Keller. I do so not because there is a dearth of feminist critics of science, but because I think that Keller's critique, especially as it relates to the notion of static objectivity, is both novel and relevant to a discussion of the study of women's communication. In addition, her observations on the genesis of the masculinist bias are quite telling, and in explaining the persistence of the masculinist bias, offer clues to overcoming it.

THE MASCULINIST BIAS IN SCIENCE

In *Reflections on Gender and Science*, Evelyn Fox Keller (1985) argues that the concept of science has been overlaid by notions of gender. Specifically, she suggests that masculinity is associated with scientific objectivity. In addition, she notes that few have challenged this genderization of science. Keller (1985) states, "The historically pervasive association between masculine and objective, more specifically between masculine and scientific, is a topic that academic critics resist taking seriously" (p. 75). Keller observes that, although open acknowledgment of the intrinsic masculinity of scientific endeavor is no longer stylish, widespread belief in the association of masculinity with objective science remains.

Keller (1985) argues that the association of masculinity with objectivity begins with the evolution of gender identities. Gender identities are developed through experiences in the family, specifically, with parents. Initially, children bond with the primary caregiver, who is almost always a female. Therefore, the young child's identity is associated with that of the mother figure. The boundary between the identities of mother and child is blurred. Later in the process of development, the child attempts to forge a new separate identity of his/her own. As part of this process, the child must break away from the mother, developing a separate identity for him/herself that is uniquely "not-mother." The boundary between mother and child is now more clearly delineated. Internalization of the difference between "not-mother" and "mother," between "me" and "not me," is crucial to the development of the newly separate ego.

Keller (1985) suggests that the child, insecure in his/her new identity, turns to the father figure for protection from "reengulfment" into the mother, and loss of the newly separated identity. The father figure is seen as the standard bearer of individuality and separation, as protection from disintegration of the young and fragile ego. In addition, the father figure is representative of reality outside of the family unit, as that is his primary sphere of function. The father figure comes to represent objective reality for the child. As Keller (1985) states, "our earliest experiences incline us to associate the affective and cognitive posture of objectification with the masculine, while all processes that involve a blurring of the boundary between subject and object tend to be associated with the feminine" (p. 87).

The development of a separate gender identity is especially difficult and problematic for the male child, as he must not only develop a separate identity from the mother, but a separate gender identity as well (Chodorow, 1974, 1978; Gilligan, 1982; Keller, 1985). Due to the problematic nature of the development of the male gender identity, the male child tends to be especially fearful of that which is associated with the feminine; specifically, a merging of the self with another. Therefore, maintenance of a strict boundary between "mother" and "not mother," between "me" and "not me," between subject and object, becomes of crucial importance to the male child.

Whereas the male child must shift his gender allegiance to the father, the female child may maintain her gender association with her mother. Continuing identification with the mother, however, may interfere with the female child's development of a separate female identity (Chodorow, 1974, 1978; Gilligan, 1982). The female child may experience problems with individuation as separation from the mother represents a threat to her developing gender identity. The male and female child, therefore, experience gender identity development quite differently. Whereas the male child seeks to maintain distance between his mother and himself, "not me" and "me," the female child seeks to maintain some degree of closeness between the mother and the self, between "not me" and "me." Keller (1985) concurs that the process of development of gender identity may encourage males to be inclined toward excessive delineation of the self from others, and females to be inclined toward inadequate delineation of the self from others.

Difficulty in accepting closeness between the self and others may be manifested in an emotional state that Keller (1985) refers to as static autonomy. Static autonomy is a response to the fear of the violation of the boundary between "me" and "not me." The state of static autonomy is characterized by rigid division of "me" from "not me," a building up of defensive barriers between the self and others. Static autonomy "connotes a radical independence from others" (p. 97) and is based not so much on security of ego boundaries, but on fear of their vulnerability to violation by others. Static autonomy reflects

> not so much confidence in one's difference from others as resistance to (even repudiation of) sameness, not so much the strength of one's own will as the resistance to another's, not so much a sense of self-esteem as uncertainty about the durability of self. (Keller, 1985, p. 102)

Keller believes that the fear of loss of self or of self-control that characterizes static autonomy prevents the openness to the feelings and perceptions of others that generates the experience of empathy.

Static autonomy is the emotional counterpart to the cognitive state of static objectivity. Static objectivity is a means of generating knowledge characterized by a severance of subject from object (Keller, 1985). The fear of merging in static autonomy is manifested in the researcher's divorcing him/herself from the focus of study. There is no sense of connectedness between the researcher and the researched. Static objectivity begins by first creating a distancing barrier between subject and object, such that the researcher does not contaminate his/her investigation with personal feelings about the focus of study. Intuition, or the development of insight without conscious reasoning that is sometimes generated through close association with others, is rejected as biased and unscientific. An unfortunate consequence of static objectivity, according to Keller, is that the imposition of rigid barriers between the researcher and the researched leads to lost potential to generate valuable knowledge that could be gained through sharing of experience.

Keller (1985) argues that our cultural norms support and encourage static objectivity as a laudable goal. As evidence, she notes that the experiences that transcend the boundaries of subject and object, for example, art, love, and religion, are accorded feminine status in our culture. Experiences that preserve the boundary between subject and object, for example, science, are accorded masculine status.

What we have seen, then, is that the genesis of a masculinist bias in science occurs early in the life of the developing child because separation and objectivity are associated with the father figure, while a lack of preservation of a boundary between the self and others is associated with the mother figure (especially for the male child). Keller (1985) concludes, "The genderization of science—as an enterprise, as an intellectual domain, as a world view—simultaneously reflects and perpetuates associations made in an earlier, prescientific era" (p. 87).

The masculinist bias in science is perpetuated because individuals who are drawn to careers in science are those individuals who feel a need for static autonomy, and the protective isolation associated with it. As Keller (1985) states:

> It seems reasonable to suggest that such a selection mechanism ought inevitably to operate. The persistence of the characterization of science as masculine, as objectivist, as autonomous of psychological as well as of social and political forces, would then be encouraged, through such selection, by the kinds of emotional satisfaction it provides. (p. 90)

As is argued above, men are most likely to experience static autonomy. Small wonder then, that most of those drawn to science are male, a condition noted by a number of scholars (Graham & Birns, 1979; Keller, 1985). There are other factors, of course, that influence the underrepresentation of women in the field of science. The one I describe is contributory.

An escalating cycle appears to exist, in which the endeavor of science attracts as participants those who experience psychological comfort in the practice of static objectivity. Their ascendance in the discipline of science then institutionalizes static objectivity as the manner in which knowledge is generated, thereby attracting new recruits of the same psychological type.

How is the masculinist bias in science demonstrated? Keller (1985) points out that the genderization of science (i.e., the association of static objectivity with masculinity) is demonstrated in at least two ways: (a) preference for "hard" over "soft" science, and (b) devaluation of that which is feminine. Both effects have had profound implications for gender research, including the study of women's communication. Each effect will be discussed in turn.

In the former case, the preference for the so-called "hard" over the so-called "soft" sciences is illustrated in four ways. First, "hard" sciences are given higher prestige and status in research institutions than are "soft" sciences. Second, there is a bias against professional publication of "soft" science research. Third, quantitative, controlled methods seem to be favored over alternative, nonquantitative methods. Finally, a great deal of research tends to rely on the comparison of experimental groups to general population (i.e., male) norms.

In the first instance, the rewards for emphasizing "hard" over "soft" science are reflected in the prestige and high status associated with the "hard," supposedly more objective sciences (e.g., physical sciences), and relatively low status associated with the "soft," supposedly less objective disciplines (e.g., human sciences). For example, the College and University Personnel Association publishes yearly national faculty salary surveys (Howe, Gilliam, & Miller, 1986a, 1986b). From the survey, I combined two sets of disciplines into what I labeled "hard" and "soft" science. "Hard" science included biological and physical sciences (e.g., biology, physics, chemistry), engineering, and math. "Soft" science included social sciences (e.g., sociology, anthropology, history), communication, and letters. Aside from education, fine arts, and agriculture, my designations of "hard" and "soft" science represent the majority of the reported disciplines. When 1984–1985 salary factors were compared (ratio of the average salary across ranks per discipline to the total average salary across ranks for all institutions), I found the following: in public institutions (both union and nonunion), salaries for "hard" science faculty were five percent higher than salaries for "soft" science faculty, a difference in earnings of a little less than $2000 per year. In private institutions, the difference was much larger. Faculty salaries for those in the "hard" sciences were 17 percent higher than faculty salaries in the "soft" sciences, a difference in earnings of close to $6000 per year. If it is valid to assess prestige and status by salary, and I think many people do, it seems clear that "hard" scientists are rewarded more than are "soft" scientists.

Availability of research grant dollars may be one cause (or effect) of differences in prestige and status between the "hard" and "soft" sciences. The National Science Foundation (1986) reports that, in 1984, the United States government provided well over five billion dollars to universities and colleges in the United States for research and development expenditures. Of that huge sum, about $147 million went to what they refer to as the social sciences (e.g., sociology, linguistics, anthropology—"soft" sciences, in my taxonomy), less than three percent of the total money available. Almost $780 million, more than five times the amount spent on social sciences, was spent on the physical sciences e.g., astronomy, chemistry, physics—"hard" sciences, in my taxonomy). Some might critique this rough comparison as unfair, saying, "Yes, but there are far greater monies available for disciplines such as astronomy and physics for grants to be awarded from." True, but isn't that the point? My argument is that the large discrepancy in dollars available for, and awarded to, the "hard" versus "soft" sciences is indicative of a difference in the perception of the degrees of importance of the two branches of science. In other words, "hard" sciences are deemed more important than "soft" sciences.

A preference for "hard" science is also reflected in patterns of publication. For example, research involving quantitative methodology seems to be preferred over research involving qualitative methodology (Wood & Phillips, 1984). As Carter (1984) points out, "Quantification and cold observation (mark) the trail to Truth" (p. 2). In addition, some have argued that journals are reluctant to publish research that is seen by the male-dominated editorial hierarchy as political or faddish. Editors are "directed away from publishing material perceived to be biased or of short-term interest" (Bate, 1984, p. 102). Of particular importance to researchers of women's communication is the observation that research on the sexes and communication is seen by some as falling into these categories (Bate, 1984). Resistance to publication can be discouraging, as failure to publish can threaten chances for success (i.e., promotion and tenure) in an academic career (Foss & Foss, 1983; K. Foss, 1984). Researchers of women's communication may be right then, in their claim that "it is difficult to get published in the mainstream journals if certain topics are chosen, methodologies are used, or perspectives are adopted" (Gordon, 1986, p. 2).

Another result of the emphasis on static objectivity and "hard" science is a proliferation of the use of controlled, experimental research, and the concomitant use of inferential statistics (Carter, 1984). In addition, repeatability of findings (i.e., reliability) and generalizability of results to larger populations are emphasized (Namenwirth, 1986). A great deal of knowledge has been generated through controlled quantitative methods, and it is not sensible to abandon all such research. However, it is equally nonsensical to posit that controlled quantitative research is the only manner in which useful knowledge may be generated. For example, one result of the reliance on controlled quantitative research is the loss of that which is unique, not common to the larger population (commonly referred to as "Error" of one kind or another) (Sprague, 1984). Namenwirth (1986) observes that the stress on objectivity, repeatability, and verifiability leads to only one kind of knowledge:

> The knowledge that results is remarkably reliable and useful, not to mention interesting, but it is limited to the characteristics things share in common; the individual is excluded. The taste and smell and feel of full reality is jettisoned to preserve the general and predictable. (p. 33)

Some methodologies that lend themselves well to the study of women's communication do not conform to restrictions imposed in controlled quantitative research. An illustrative example is the use of the personal documents of women, for example, letters, diaries, journals, and so on. Personal documents, as well as art and other individual expressions, provide valuable insights into the human experience, in that personal documents reveal the feelings and responses of individuals as they encounter experiences in their lives (Selltiz, Wrightsman & Cook, 1976). Foss and Foss (1983) argue that more attention should be paid to these "informal formats for discourse" (p. 200), as women do not have the same access to more formal discussion arenas (e.g., print media, public forums) as do men. Kramer and her associates (Kramer, Thorne, & Henley, 1978) agree with the assertion that personal documents are especially rich sources of data about the experiences of women. Despite the value of these artifacts, restricted use of controlled quantitative methods would preclude their study, as such personal documents are neither replicable nor generalizable.

Another feature of the masculine approach to science, the focus on population norms, is especially germane to the study of women's communication. The population norm is more often than not conceived to be the male norm, so that which is masculine, or associated with the masculine, is seen as the standard by which all else is judged (Gilligan, 1982; Johnson, 1984; Rawlins, 1984; Smythe & Schlueter, 1987). An unfortunate adjunct to this association is that when differences between men and women are found, the female style is often termed the deviant or inferior style (Jackson, 1984; Sprague, 1984). There have been large numbers of studies that sought to identify differences in the communication of men versus women (Foss & Foss, 1983; Kramer, Thorne, & Henley, 1978; Solomon, 1984). Johnson (1984) warns, "to compare women to men is to reaffirm and perpetuate rather than to question the normative value of male behavior" (p. 80).

Let me use an historical example for illustration. Lakoff (1975) presented an argument that women's language was replete with features that rendered it unassertive and powerless; for example, tag questions, compound requests, superpolite forms. A number of studies followed, seeking to prove that women's language did indeed contain these features, and that inclusion of the features led to negative perceptions of the user (Dubois & Crouch, 1975; Newcombe & Arnkoff, 1979; Warfel, 1984). Results were mixed on both counts; that is, it was not consistently shown that women's language contained these features, while men's did not; nor was it shown that use of the language features led to consistently negative perceptions of the users. That the debate on the issue rages to this day (Smythe & Schlueter, 1987) is testimony to the strength of the desire to prove women's language both different from and inferior to men's. It seems to me that more interesting questions could be asked that are not limited by discussions of male versus female language style, for example does status influence language style? What functions do various language styles serve? Does perception of language style change across settings?

Namenwirth (1986) points out that the emphasis on differences between men and women precludes discussion of similarities between men and women, or differences within groups of men or of women, that might be equally interesting and important. In addition, she argues that the "near-obsessive" focus on discovering a biological basis for small male/female differences has distorted the study of the relationship of gender to other variables. Similar criticisms could be leveled at the emphasis in communication research on male/female differences. The communication of men, as a group, and the communication of women, as a group, can and should be legitimate areas for study without comparisons to one another. For example, Johnson (1984) asserts that regardless of any relationship to the communication of men, "the unique character and interactional patterns of women must be known so they can be saved" (p. 80). In short, a research focus on comparisons to population (i.e., male) norms tends to result in the labeling of differential features of women's speech as inferior, and militates against the study of women's communication as valuable in and of itself.

Turning to the second effect of the association of the masculine with static objectivity, Keller (1985) argues that the genderization of science in Western culture results in a devaluation of that which is feminine, or associated with that which is feminine:

> A circular process of mutual reinforcement is established in which what is called scientific receives extra validation from the cultural preference for what is called masculine, and, conversely, what is called feminine—be it a branch of knowledge, a way of thinking, or woman herself—becomes further devalued by its exclusion from the special social and intellectual value placed on science. (p. 92)

An effect of the genderization of science may be to devalue the study of women and that which is associated with women, for example, women's communication. For example, women's strengths in interpersonal relationship maintenance skills are often labeled weaknesses (Johnson, 1984). In addition, research methods that build on women's strengths in relationship maintenance, for example, participant observation, are often labeled unscientific, and therefore, undesirable.

The devaluation of things associated with women is compounded by male control of language and, thereby, perceptions of reality. The perception of reality is determined by the process of thinking. Thinking, in turn, is limited by language. Language, therefore, limits perceptions of reality. This perspective is known as the Sapir-Whorf hypothesis (Pearson, 1985). Those who control language, then, control perceptions of reality.

In Western culture, men control language. Several researchers note that men exercise power through their domination of language, and thereby, of reality (Fishman, 1983; Kramer, Thorne, & Henley, 1978; Spender, 1984). The powerlessness of women in structuring perceptions of reality deemphasizes the female experience:

> As self-appointed proprietors of language and naming practices, men have been able to structure and name a world that is amenable to their experiences and outlooks. Women and women's experiences have been negated and devalued as a result. (Rakow, 1986, p. 17)

Spender (1984) proposes that the female experience is ignored because the dominant group, men, have no interest in the particular concerns of women. Women constitute a muted group, according to Spender, in that their alternative world view is ignored, while the world view of men is given precedence. "No matter what women do or say, no matter how they represent their experience, in these terms, if it is not also the experience of men, it will be consigned to the realm of nondata" (p. 199). It is by virtue of men's power in controlling perceptions of reality that, according to Spender, sexual inequality is institutionalized and perpetuated.

The devaluation of things associated with women, for whatever reason, encourages the avoidance of the study of issues of particular interest to women, for example, women's experience, women's communication. It should be clear from the foregoing discussion that the masculinist bias in science has a marked influence on the conduct of research, and that that influence does not favor the study of gender and communication, nor, more specifically, the study of women's communication.

AN ALTERNATIVE FEMINIST APPROACH TO SCIENCE

In the preceding discussion, I argued that the genderization of science has led to two negative outcomes: a reliance on and preference for the tools of "hard" science, and a devaluation of things associated with women. I demonstrated that both of these factors militate against the successful conduct of gender research, in general, and of the study of women's communication, in particular. In this section, I posit the value of an alternative feminist approach to science. This approach differs from a masculinist approach in that it is characterized by dynamic, as opposed to static, objectivity, a research goal of understanding, as opposed to control, and finally, a conceptualization of the focus of study as active and sensitive, as opposed to passive and insensitive, to the researcher's chosen mode of inquiry. The following discussion of an alternative feminist approach to science draws on Fee's (1986) summary of the feminist critique of the natural sciences. I found her observations to be relevant to the conduct of research in the human sciences, as well, and can be easily adapted to communication research. The alternative feminist approach to research I posit, then, is most directly relevant to the human sciences and, I believe, to the study of women's communication.

According to Fee (1986), one feminist criticism of masculine-biased science decries the creation of a rigid boundary between the subject of knowledge (the researcher) and the natural object of that knowledge (the focus of study). This notion is quite similar to Keller's (1985) characterization of static objectivity provided earlier. The first distinction I'll draw, then, between a masculinist approach to science and an alternative feminist approach to science is that while a masculinist approach to science stresses static objectivity, the alternative feminist position I posit stresses what Keller (1985) refers to as dynamic objectivity.

Keller (1985) characterizes dynamic objectivity as a process not unlike empathy, in that there is a recognition of the commonalities between the researcher and his/her focus of study. These commonalities provide a basis for an enriched understanding. Balancing a recognition of commonalities with respect for the independent integrity of the focus of study fuels the generation of greater knowledge:

> Dynamic objectivity is thus a pursuit of knowledge that makes use of subjective experience . . . in the interests of a more effective objectivity. Premised on continuity, it recognizes difference between self and other as an opportunity for a deeper and more articulated kinship. The struggle to disentangle self from other is itself a source of insight—potentially into the nature of both self and other. (Keller, 1985, p. 117)

The cognitive stance of dynamic objectivity is based on the emotional state of dynamic autonomy, in which an individual's confidence in his/her own independence allows for the recognition of connectedness with others. In other words, the dynamically autonomous self is not threatened by a merging with others; rather, merging, or the empathic experience, is seen as an opportunity for the generation of new knowledge about both the self and about others.

I prefer the notion of dynamic objectivity over the notion of static objectivity for several reasons. First, even if the converse of dynamic objectivity, static objectivity, were desirable, it seems nearly impossible to attain. For example, the statically objective person believes that it is preferable to conduct research that is totally rational, objective, and value-free (Keller, 1985). In fact, several scholars have illustrated the fallacy of supposedly objective and value-free research. For example, Carter (1984) points out that the supposedly "value-free" research of traditional science is, in fact, "value-laden" in that it espouses logic and rationality as the only paths to knowledge, rejecting other ways of knowing, for example, experiential knowledge. For example, Rose (1986) argues that the knowledge that women gain through life experience, for instance, child rearing, is important and legitimate. Namenwirth (1986) concurs that total objectivity is impossible in her position that masculinist science is not neutral at all, and has, in fact, been used to rationalize and justify preservation of dominant social and political ideologies throughout history, for example, white male-dominated hierarchical social systems. Other scholars have noted the fallacy of a neutral (specifically, sex-neutral) science (Foss & Foss, 1983).

Another goal of the statically objective researcher is to create an isolating distance between him/herself and the focus of study. Some researchers have pointed out the futility of attempting to do so. In an example particularly relevant to the study of women's communication, Rawlins (1984) observes, "We can never leave the bodies we are born with no matter how significantly we may alter them, and we never can totally transcend our primary socialization" (p. 70). It is true that the distance between "self" and "not self" is tenuous in the case of the investigator of women's communication. The focus of study, women, are common to everyone's experience, either because the researcher is a woman, or, in the case of a male scientist, because women figure prominently in his life (e.g., coworkers, supervisors, wife, mother). In addition, neither men nor women can escape the influence of sex-role socialization. Whatever its character, sex-role socialization will influence the manner in which researchers think about and respond to other individuals, be they male or female. In short, static objectivity, in its pure form, hardly seems realizable.

Even if true static objectivity were attainable, in my view, static objectivity is not an appropriate perspective for all research goals. Keller (1985) argues that static autonomy and static objectivity do not facilitate the develop of close relationships between the self and others. Without the development of close relationships, the experiences of empathy and intuition are unlikely. For this reason, she points out, valuable information and insights about the focus of study and about the self may be lost. For example, I once conducted some informal research at a rape crisis center. My responsibilities included interviewing rape victims, often in the immediate aftermath of the attack. Although I had never shared their particular experiences, having been victimized by bullies of various sorts in my life (mostly male), I felt that I could empathize with their feelings of violation, powerlessness, and vulnerability. My experience was that communicating my empathy with the victim helped her to share more of her feelings with me, as a degree of commonality had been established between us. It seemed to me that it helped them to discuss their feelings, and I certainly learned more about the experience of violation through a sharing of their experiences. At least in this case, I learned more as a researcher because I was objective in a dynamic, as opposed to a static way.

The second feminist criticism of natural science, according to Fee (1986), is that a subject/object split in research is used to legitimize the control and domination of nature. Keller (1985) argues that the need for control springs from static autonomy, the precursor of static objectivity. Static autonomy is characterized by defensiveness based on the fear of loss of self or of self-control. The emotional state of static autonomy creates a drive to control external sources of threat as a means of minimizing danger to the self. Schachtel (1959) points out that a drive to control is illustrated in the use of some experimental research. Schachtel (1959) criticizes this kind of research as concentrating more on manipulating phenomenon than on understanding them because "modern natural science has as its main goal prediction, i.e., the power to manipulate objects in such a way that certain predicted events will happen" (p. 171). Schachtel is referring to natural sciences, but his critique is valid for the use of controlled experimental research in the human sciences, as well. According to Schachtel (1959), the key to understanding the fullness of the focus of study is to allow the understanding to emerge from a freer, less controlled interaction with it. The second tenet of the alternative feminist approach to science that I posit, then, states that the goal of science should be understanding rather than control.

In an alternative feminist approach to science, free and less controlled interactions are encouraged through the development of dynamic objectivity. Dynamic objectivity, based on dynamic autonomy, is not characterized by defensiveness, or by attempts to control the focus of study. Rather, openness to external stimuli, through the development of relationships with others, is maintained. Keller (1985) argues that the maintenance of close interpersonal relationships serves as a check on the desire to control or to harm others. The goal of research characterized by dynamic objectivity is a more complete understanding, an attempt to see things the way they really are, and not as a result of the forced imposition of some dominant paradigm that may or may not be appropriate. Rose (1986) argues that the feminist epistemology seeks knowledge through rejecting reductionist explanations of phenomenon and concentrating on holistic, complex definitions of events. Fee (1986) asserts that a feminist scientist should use science not as a tool of control or of domination, but as a tool of liberation, in that limiting assumptions about the nature of men and women are discarded.

In order to give precedence to understanding, as opposed to control, research approaches that emphasize understanding should be characterized by a minimization of a priori assumptions about the focus of study, so that a less restrictive comprehension can result. Some qualitative research methods are examples of a less restrictive approach to research, for example, participant observation, unstructured interviewing. Qualitative approaches can be used effectively in the study of women's communication. For example, Foss and Foss (1983) state that phenomenological methodologies and naturalistic inquiry offer the potential of gaining new insights into women's communication and women's experiences of reality. As has been stated, masculinist research methodologies are based on a priori assumptions about the world and about people that are masculine-biased. In order to gain greater understanding about the experience of women, these assumptions must be questioned. Perceptions of reality that are more reflective of the experiences of women can emerge from research methods that are not restricted by externally imposed frameworks for understanding, and more specifically, do not involve the imposition of masculine-biased a priori assumptions about women.

Fee (1986) reports that the third feminist criticism of natural science is that nature is treated as if it were passive and insensitive to the intrusions of science. I would adapt her critique to human sciences (particularly the study of communication) to say that human respondents must be treated as if they were active and sensitive to the researcher's chosen mode of inquiry, which they are. The third tenet of the alternative feminist approach to science, then, is that the focus of study is conceived of as active and sensitive, as opposed to passive and insensitive, to research methodology. Just as Fee (1986) contends that nature must be "conceptualized as active rather than passive, a dynamic and complex totality requiring human cooperation and understanding rather than a dead mechanism, requiring manipulation and control" (p. 47), so must human respondents be conceptualized. In the human sciences, and the study of communication in particular, the costs of an intrusive research methodology must be weighed against the benefits to be gained by its use. Shulamit Reinharz (1979) labels attempts to find totally unobtrusive research methods futile, suggesting instead that research methods be chosen that have a positive effect:

> Influence and reactivity are inevitable in interaction. Since this is true, then the researcher could abandon the search for nonreactive methods and select the desired effect. Attempting to avoid an effect is a form of subject manipulation just as is the attempt to influence in a particular direction. (p. 319)

In short, to conceive of human respondents as insensitive to research methodology is specious. Researchers must be aware of the effects of the intrusion of their inquiry and choose research methods that have a positive, rather than a negative effect, on the respondent.

Cognizance of the sensitivity of the respondent to the researcher's chosen mode of inquiry should be of particular concern to those who study the communication of women. For example, women are very sensitive to the nonverbal cues of others, and are more desirous of others' approval than are men, in part due to their traditionally lower status position vis-á-vis men (Pearson, 1985). In addition, Gilligan (1982) points out that women's moral concern for others makes women more sensitive to others' opinions and points of view. These characteristics make women especially vulnerable to the influence of experimenter bias, the confounding influence that results when respondents identify and proffer "appropriate" responses based on subtle verbal and nonverbal experimenter cues (West & Wicklund, 1980).

To show sensitivity to the need to minimize experimenter bias in interactions with female interviewees, for example, interviewers can structure questions in such as manner as to avoid communication of expectations for "correct" answers. One way to minimize the communication of expectations might be to reject the structured interview format altogether, in favor of an unstructured interview format. In unstructured interviews, or open-ended interview formats, the interviewer encourages the interviewee to speak freely and fully in response to open-ended questions, that is, questions not required to be answered by a limited list of stated alternatives (Selltiz, et al., 1976). In addition, there is no prescribed order of questions. The interviewer follows the topic lead of the interviewee, encouraging the interviewee to reveal what he or she feels is most important or relevant to the discussion. In this manner, experimenter bias may be minimized in that the interviewee controls the focus of the interview, not the interviewer. The interviewee decides what constitutes a correct answer, not the interviewer.

The point of this brief preliminary discussion is to show that the third tenet of the alternative feminist approach to science is especially germane to the study of the communication of women because women are not passive and insensitive to inquiry. Rather, they are active and sensitive beings and as such, will respond to the manner in which they are approached. Methodologies that encourage spontaneous and open interaction between the researcher and the respondent are more likely to result in sharing of information than are strategic and controlling interactions that might result in a defensive reaction on the part of the respondent. As I have argued above, this truism is especially relevant to researchers who study the communication of women.

In summary, then, the alternative feminist approach to science that I've proposed can be contrasted to a masculinist approach to science in that an alternative feminist approach is characterized by dynamic, as opposed to static objectivity, a research goal of understanding, as opposed to control, and a conceptualization of the focus of study as active and sensitive, as opposed to passive and insensitive, to chosen modes of inquiry. Some would argue that the alternative feminist approach to science described herein represents a total rejection of traditional research, including any notion of objectivity, in favor of some purely subjective approach to knowledge. Such is not the case.

The critique that is offered herein is aimed at masculine-biased approaches to science that reject all approaches to knowing other than their own as unscientific. To argue for rejection of one approach in favor of another would be to commit the same error that is being attacked in this essay; that is, closed-minded advocacy of one type of research approach, one way of knowing. The methodologies preferred by those espousing a masculinist approach (e.g., controlled experimental designs) are well suited for some avenues of research, and have generated a great deal of useful and interesting knowledge. So, too, have other research methodologies, and their value should not be ignored. What is being espoused is the consideration of alternative means of knowing, a more balanced approach to research that is more open to a female, as opposed to male world view. As Gordon (1986) suggests, "It may now be time to seek balance, greater completeness in our vision, to encourage additional and even unorthodox explorations, this time more heavily drawn from women's experience" (p. 2). I give the study of women's communication as an example of an area of investigation that would profit from greater use of alternative approaches to research. These alternative approaches to research are feminist in the sense that they are in line with my understanding of a feminist world view that rejects, at least in part, the supremacy of masculine-biased notions of reality.

In short, this essay is not a call to revolution. Rather, it is a call for openness to and acceptance of alternative methods of knowing as equally legitimate and capable of knowledge generation as methodologies favored by a masculinist approach to science. As Rose (1986) contends, a feminist theory of knowledge "builds on traditions that have always been present in science, though submerged within the dominant culture, and it joins hands with the critique of science as now practiced, which has developed within the new social movements" (p. 72). An alternative feminist approach to science, then, can be seen as a next step in the natural progression in the development of science as a means of generating knowledge.

AN ILLUSTRATIVE CASE: SEXUAL HARASSMENT

In the previous discussion, I offered an alternative feminist approach to human science. In the following section, I give an example of the use of an alternative feminist approach to research. The illustrative case I offer is that of sexual harassment, an issue particularly germane to women, as a vast majority of women, and only a small minority of men, have experienced sexual harassment in their lives (Clarke, 1981; Collins & Blodgett, 1981; Michigan Task Force on Sexual Harassment, 1979; Safran, 1976). Sexual harassment is a communication issue in that it is through the interaction of men and women that episodes are created that come to be labeled sexual harassment. While some excuse sexual harassment as an inevitable consequence of the interaction of men and women, sexual harassment is emerging as an issue of considerable importance and consequence, and is of great interest to those who study women's communication.

Sexual harassment is a particularly revealing example of a case where alternative approaches to research are needed, as the study of sexual harassment is hampered by the limitations imposed by masculinist research approaches. Obviously, controlled experimental designs are probably unethical, as one cannot randomly assign subjects to "harass" and "not harass" experimental and control groups. In addition, questions of motivation, pivotal to an understanding of how communication events come to be labeled sexual harassment, are extremely difficult to pursue with conventional methods of research, as the people involved in the event are sometimes vulnerable to civil or criminal charges, or may fear for their jobs or for their physical and mental well being. Finally, in a point that I elaborate in the "Participant Observation" section below, I believe that an understanding of the dynamics of sexual harassment is nearly impossible if one accepts a masculine world view. In order to come to some understanding of the complex dynamics of sexual harassment, more sensitive and flexible methods of research must be employed. As I argued above, such methodologies are encouraged in an alternative feminist approach to research.

What actions constitute sexual harassment? Although notions of the severity of harassment vary from individual to individual (an interesting area for study in and of itself), the definition of sexual harassment, as provided by the Equal Employment Opportunity Commission (1980) reads:

> Unwelcome sexual advances, requests for sexual favors, and other verbal or physical conduct of a nature which constitute harassment when (a) submission to the conduct is either explicitly or implicitly a term or condition of an individual's employment, (b) submission to or rejection of such conduct by an individual is used as the basis for employment decisions affecting that individual, and/or (c) such conduct has the purpose or effect of unreasonably interfering with an individual's work performance or creating an intimidating, hostile, or offensive work environment.

It seems to me that an understanding of the motivations, feelings, and interpretations of the individuals involved in communication events that are labeled sexual harassment is intrinsic to comprehending sexual harassment, as is knowledge of antecedent conditions that may precipitate harassment. I believe that the alternative methodologies described below are appropriate for the investigation of these factors. I've provided three illustrative examples of research methods for consideration: participant observation, unstructured (or semistructured interviews), and use of personal documents.

Participant Observation

Participant observation is one category of a larger group of observation techniques. Quite simply, observation involves the noting and recording of some phenomenon by an observer. Observation may be structured, as in the use of checklists, or it may be unstructured, as in participant observation. Unstructured methods of observation tend to provide richer and more varied sources of information; in that, as much as possible, the unstructured observer attempts to record events in the absence of any a priori assumptions about the genesis or progress of the event. These methods are, therefore, better suited to developing an understanding of the true complexities of an occurrence, especially in the early stages of research, when little is known about a phenomena, or when a priori assumptions about the focus of study may be in question. In addition, unstructured methods are more flexible, in that the definition of some act may be altered as new data warrants (Selltiz, et al., 1976).

Participant observation is a form of observation in which researchers immerse themselves in the ongoing dynamics of the setting, behaving and experiencing as one with other setting incumbents. Participant observation has long been used by anthropologists and sociologists in their studies of group and tribal interactions. In participant observation, descriptions and interpretations of ongoing activities are recorded unobtrusively by the participant observer during his/her period of participation. The investigator plays a dual role in this approach, that of participant, and that of observer (Jackson, 1984; Reinharz, 1979; Selltiz, et al., 1976). As participant, the investigator is able to merge with the observed, to become an actor in the events as they unfold. As observer, the investigator records his/her own intuitions and insights as to the motivations, feelings, and interpretations of fellow group members, as well as his/her own reactions to events.

In participant observation, the researcher's experiences and intuitions are perceived as a legitimate, and potentially rich source of data (Jackson, 1984; Reinharz, 1979). Goodall (1984) urges a rediscovery of the method of participant observation, "in which the researcher and the researched share more than papers and pencils—they share as well the experience and the unique knowing that direct experience and reflective thought can produce" (p. 91). The perspective of the participant observer, ideally, is one of dynamic objectivity, a cognitive stance described by Keller (1985) and detailed in earlier sections of this essay.

Several advantages make participant observation attractive to the researcher of women's communication in general, and sexual harassment, in particular. First, participant observation stresses the development of close relationships between the observer and the observed, and is, therefore, well adapted to studies involving women, such as sexual harassment, as some research suggests that women may be more comfortable disclosing in the context of close relationships (Treichler & Kramarae, 1983). In addition, Selltiz and his associates (1976) point out that unstructured methods such as participant observation are appropriate for investigations in which either little is known about a phenomenon, or in which what is known is suspect.

I think that the most important aspect of participant observation, as it regards sexual harassment, is in the opportunity to operate with minimal a priori assumptions. Acceptance of a masculine-biased perspective in the case of sexual harassment is problematic because a crucial difference in male and female world views may be a pivotal issue in sexual harassment. Goodall (1984) reports on a study he conducted on friendship and marriage, in which he discovered that men and women have vastly divergent perspectives on sex and friendship. Goodall and his associates found that less than five percent of the men they surveyed, and nearly eighty percent of the women they surveyed, thought that men and women could be friends without sex being an issue. How is this relevant to sexual harassment? Apparently, the vast majority of men feel that if they are friends with a woman, then sex is an issue (possibility?). We have already discussed that for most men, the male world view is *the* world view. If we can accept that most men feel this way, then most men must feel that if they think sex is an issue in their friendship with a women, then the woman must think that as well. It is conceivable, then, that a male may *mistake* a female's friendly overtures as an invitation to sex because he falsely assumes that she shares his views.

Recent studies confirm perceptual differences between women and men regarding "sexual" versus "friendly" behavior. Roberts (1986) describes a study conducted by Frank Saul which involved videotaping a male professor interacting with a female student in which the female student was asking for an extension on an assignment deadline. He showed the videotape to both male and female respondents, later asking them what attributions they would make about the intentions of the male professor toward the female student and vice versa. The majority of the male respondents reported that the female student was flirting with the professor, and would like to go out on a date with him. The professor was predicted to accept. The majority of the female students, conversely, reported that the student and the professor were being friendly, and that there was nothing sexual about their conversation. Saul repeated the study several times with different male/female interactions, and obtained similar results.

What's going on here? Without trying to overgeneralize, I think Saul's study suggests that many men have different definitions of sexual overture than do women. This awareness calls for a reframing of researcher questions. Is it conceivable that a male may mistake a female's friendly overtures as an invitation to sex? Could such a misunderstanding lead to accusations of sexual harassment? Might an accused harasser then charge that "she asked for it"? These are precisely the kinds of questions that someone immersed in the situation, such as a participant observer, could answer. The adoption of a male point of view, without cognizance of a female point of view, could easily lead to blaming the victim of sexual harassment for the incident because the male view takes precedence.

Unstructured Interviews

The second technique I'll discuss is the unstructured, or semistructured, interview. Essentially, interviews are question-and-answer sessions designed to elicit information from interviewees on a variety of subjects. As was the case with methods of observation, methods of interviewing may be either structured, with a specific chronology of questions asked to all interviewees, or it may be unstructured or semistructured, where specific questions may be planned in advance, but the interviewer is much less directive in his/her interactions with interviewees (Selltiz, et al., 1976). The unstructured method is particularly useful when the interviewer is not cognizant of the complexities of some event or topic, and so, is appropriate for situations in which the interviewee, as opposed to the interviewer, provides direction for the interview (Bogdan & Taylor, 1975; Van Maanen, 1983). This is especially true when the majority of questions asked are open-ended questions; that is, questions where there is no finite range of answers from which to choose.

Unstructured interviews provide a valuable tool to the researcher of sexual harassment, particularly in their interactions with female respondents. This is so for several reasons. First, women tend to develop topics gradually and progressively, rather than abruptly (Treichler & Kramarae, 1983). In unstructured interviews, respondents direct topic development at their own pace, and are not obliged to keep up with topic shifts introduced by an interviewer. In addition, women tend to see questions as part of conversational maintenance, not merely as requests for specific information (Treichler & Kramarae, 1983). Women might be more comfortable then, with an interview situation in which they, too, could ask questions, resulting in more of a dialogue with the interviewer than a monologic question-and-answer session. Unstructured interviews are flexible enough to accommodate this desire for interaction, as opposed to a direction imposed by a researcher's agenda. Finally, in the unstructured interview, the interviewer does not control the interviewee, as is more the case with structured interviews. Rather, the course of the interview emerges from a natural conversation between the two participants in the interview. The interviewee is allowed to decide what information is important, what to reveal and what not to reveal. This is especially important when interviewing women, as women tend to accept others' topic introductions in conversation (Kramer, Thorne, & Henley, 1978). In the case of sexual harassment, where the interviewer has little knowledge of the genesis of the event, valuable information could be lost through an interviewer's misdirection of the interview. In addition, it is essential that a supportive environment be created when interviewing a woman who has been sexually harassed, as many victims of sexual harassment report feelings of shame, guilt, and fear following harassment (Michigan Task Force on Sexual Harassment, 1979). Unstructured interviews provide a good forum for supportive interaction, as the role and responsibility of the interviewer in the unstructured format is to encourage disclosure by providing unconditional positive feedback to the interviewee. Disclosure is also encouraged because the interview is more of a spontaneous conversation than a strategic interrogation, thereby reducing defensiveness on the part of the interviewee.

Personal Documents

Personal documents are any of a class of personal productions or artifacts, such as letters, diaries, poetry, journals, works of art or literature, and so on. Personal documents must be tangible (recorded in some manner), produced on the individual's own initiative, and focus on the individual's personal life experiences (Selltiz, et al., 1976). Personal documents provide a commodity relatively rare in research, a glimpse of people as they see or once saw themselves. They reveal the author's perceptions of life, as he or she experienced the ongoing process. These artifacts reveal the life of the author as it was and is lived, and provide a unique window to the inner experience of the individual, often at critical junctures in their lives.

Many have argued that because of women's limited access to public forums of discourse and expression, more use should be made of the more informal and private works of women (Foss & Foss, 1983; S. Foss, 1984; Kramer, Thorne, & Henley, 1978). Attention should be turned to forums in which women feel or felt free to express themselves, such as art, or other individual productions. In addition, research use of personal documents, particularly diaries and journals, should prove to be immensely useful in determining the chronology of events leading up to sexual harassment episodes, as well as in providing insights into the interpretations and motivations of the actors involved in the episodes. Victims of sexual harassment are urged to maintain a diary or journal, describing all of their interactions with the alleged harasser, for use as evidence should a criminal or civil suit be filed (Clarke, 1981). Use of these personal documents can provide a wealth of data for the researcher of sexual harassment. For example, diary entries can show the state of mind of the victim of harassment before, during, and after the sexual harassment episode, as well as her perceptions of the relationship she shared with her harasser.

I have tried to make the case that the use of some alternative research methods, such as participant observation, unstructured interviews, and use of personal documents, can facilitate the study of sexual harassment as a communication phenomenon. The case I used to illustrate the efficacy of alternative investigative approaches, and the advantages of a balanced approach to research, was sexual harassment, but most programs of research could benefit from a rethinking of the match of research program to research goal.

The goal of this essay was twofold: to reveal the masculinist bias in existing science, and to suggest the value of an alternative feminist approach to science. The conclusion I drew was that a masculinist bias does exist in science, and is manifested in an apparent preference for "hard" over "soft" sciences, and a devaluation of that which is associated with women. I proposed an alternative approach to science, founded on feminist principles, that is characterized by dynamic objectivity, an emphasis on understanding, and a recognition of the reactivity of human beings as the focus of research.

I am calling for a modification in the manner in which research is conducted. Wood and Phillips (1984) note that research seems to be biased in favor of quantitative, controlled research, and simultaneously biased against nonquantitative methods. In its stead, Wood and Phillips call for "recognition of alternatives that honor rigorous standards for scholarship while being naturalistic, non-positivistic, non-quantitative, and not necessarily wedded to traditional research goals such as generalization and prediction" (p. 62). We should, then, continue to produce quality research based on the tenets of masculine science, and consider anew the value of research founded on the tenets of an alternative feminist approach to science. Science can only benefit from such a balance of perspectives.

REFERENCES

Bate, B. (1984). Submerged concepts in gender/communication research *Women's Studies in Communication, 7,* 101–104.

Bogdan, R., & Taylor, S. J. (1975). *Introduction to qualitative research methods: A phenomenological approach to the social sciences.* New York: John Wiley and Sons.

Carter, B. (1984, April). *Dancing away from the dance: Traditional versus passionate gender research.* Paper presented at the conference on Gender Role in Communication. Pennsylvania State University, University Park, PA.

Chodorow, N. (1974). Family structure and feminine personality. In M. Z. Rosaldo & L. Lamphere (Eds.), *Woman, culture, and society* (pp. 43–66). Stanford, CA: Stanford University Press.

Chodorow, N. (1978). *The reproduction of mothering: Psychoanalysis and the sociology of gender.* Berkeley, CA: University of California Press.

Clarke, E. (1981). *Stopping sexual harassment: A handbook.* Detroit, MI: Labor Education and Research Project.

Collins, E. G. C., & Blodgett, T. B. (1981, March–April). Sexual harassment: Some see it, some won't. *Harvard Business Review,* 76–95.

Dubois, B. L., & Crouch, I. (1975). The question of tag questions in woman's speech: They don't really use more of them, do they? *Language in Society, 4,* 289–294.

Equal Employment Opportunity Commission. (1980). *Interpretive guidelines on sexual harassment.* Washington, DC: Equal Employment Opportunity Commission.

Fee, E. (1986). Critiques of modern science. The relationship of feminism to other radical epistemologies. In R. Bleier (Ed.), *Feminist approaches to science* (pp. 42–56). New York: Pergamon Press.

Fishman, P. M. (1983). Interaction: The work that women do. In B. Thorne, C. Kramarae, & N. Henley (Eds.), *Language, gender and society* (pp. 89–101). Rowley, MA: Newbury House.

Foss, K. A. (1984). Research on communication and gender: Making the link to feminist theory. *Women's Studies in Communication, 7,* 83–85.

Foss, K. A., & Foss, S. K. (1983). The status of research on women and communication. *Communication Quarterly, 4,* 195–204.

Foss, S. K. (1984). A female perspective on the research process. *Women's Studies in Communication, 7,* 73–76.

Gilligan, C. (1982). *In a different voice: Psychological theory and women's development.* Cambridge, MA: Harvard University Press.

Goodall, H. L., Jr. (1984). Research priorities for investigations of gender and communication: Rediscovering the human experience of sexuality and talk. *Women's Studies in Communication, 7,* 91–97.

Gordon, R. D. (1986). Communication theory in the 1990's. *Spectra, 22,* 2.

Graham, M. F., & Birns, B. (1979). Where are the women geniuses? Up the down escalator. In C. B. Kopp (Ed.), *Becoming female: Perspectives on development* (pp. 291–312). New York: Plenum Press.

Howe, R. M., Gilliam, M. L., & Miller, S. S. (1986a). *1984–1985 national faculty salary survey: By discipline and rank in state colleges and universities.* Washington, DC: College and University Personnel Association.

Howe, R. M., Gilliam, M. L., & Miller, S. S. (1986b). *1984–1985 national faculty salary survey: By discipline and rank in private colleges and universities.* Washington, DC: College and University Personnel Association.

Jackson, L. M. (1984). Available research methods to study gender role in communication. *Women's Studies in Communication, 7,* 86–90.

Johnson, F. L. (1984). Positions for knowing about gender differences in social relationships. *Women's Studies in Communication, 7,* 77–82.

Keller, E. F. (1985). *Reflections on gender and science.* New Haven, CT: Yale University Press.

Kramer, C., Thorne, B., & Henley, N. (1978). Perspectives on language and communication. *Signs, 3,* 638–651.

Lakoff, R. (1975). *Language and women's place.* New York: Harper Colophon Books.

Michigan Task Force on Sexual Harassment in the Workplace. (1979). *Sexual harassment in the workplace: A report to the public.* Detroit, MI: Office of Women and Work: Michigan Department of Labor.

Namenwirth, M. (1986). Science seen through a feminist prism. In R. Bleier (Ed.), *Feminist approaches to science* (pp. 18–41). New York: Pergamon Press.

National Science Foundation. (1986). *National patterns of science and technology resources* (Report No. NSF 86-309). Washington, DC: National Science Foundation.

Newcombe, N., & Arnkoff, D. B. (1979). Effects of speech style and sex of speaker on person perception. *Journal of Personality and Social Psychology, 36,* 1293–1303.

Pearson, J. C. (1985). *Gender and communication.* Dubuque, IA: Wm. C. Brown Publishers.

Rakow, L. F. (1986). Rethinking gender research in communication. *Journal of Communication, 36,* 11–26.

Rawlins, W. K. (1984). Interpretive stance and gender-role research. *Women's Studies in Communication, 7,* 69–72.

Reinharz, S. (1979). *On becoming a social scientist: From survey research and participant observation to experiential analysis.* San Francisco, CA: Jossey-Bass Publishers.

Roberts, M. (1986). Understanding Rita? *Psychology Today, 20,* 14.

Rose, H. (1986). Beyond masculinist realities: A feminist epistemology for the sciences. In R. Bleier (Ed.), *Feminist approaches to science* (pp. 57–76). New York: Pergamon Press.

Safran, C. (1976, November). What men do to women on the job: A shocking look at sexual harassment. *Redbook,* 149–150, 217–224.

Schachtel, E. (1959). *Metamorphosis.* New York: Basic Books.

Selltiz, C., Wrightsman, L. S., & Cook, S. W. (1976). *Research methods in social relations*, (3rd ed.). New York: Holt, Rinehart, and Winston.

Smythe, M., & Schlueter, D. W. (1987 May). *Linguistic sex differences revisited: A meta-analytic review with implications for feminist theory.* Paper presented at the International Communication Association annual convention, Montreal, Canada.

Solomon, M. (1984). A prolegomenon to research on gender role communication. *Women's Studies in Communication, 7*, 98–100.

Spender, D. (1984). Defining reality: A powerful tool. In C. Kramarae, M. Schulz, & W. M. O'Barr (Eds.), *Language and power* (pp. 194–205). Beverly Hills, CA: Sage Publications.

Sprague, J. (1984 April). *Position paper on research priorities.* Paper presented at the conference on Gender Role in Communication. Pennsylvania State University, University Park, PA.

Treichler, P. A., & Kramarae, C. (1983). Women's talk in the ivory tower. *Communication Quarterly, 31*, 118–131.

Van Maanen, J. (1983). *Qualitative methodology.* Beverly Hills, CA: Sage Publications.

Warfel, K. A. (1984). Gender schemas and perceptions of speech style. *Communication Monographs, 51*, 253–267.

West, S. G., & Wicklund, R. A. (1980). *A primer of social psychological theories.* Monterey, CA: Brooks/Cole Publishing Company.

Wood, J. T., & Phillips, G. M. (1984). Rethinking research on gender and communication: An introduction to the issues. *Women's Studies in Communication, 7*, 59–60.

3

Incorporating the Feminist Perspective in Communication Scholarship: A Research Commentary*

KAREN A. FOSS
Department of Speech Communication
Humboldt State University

SONJA K. FOSS
Department of Speech
University of Oregon

" 'I am a woman'; on this truth must be based all further discussion." These words by Simone de Beauvoir, in the opening pages of *The Second Sex*, suggest the essence of the feminist perspective in research (1952).[1] The starting point of the feminist perspective is that there is no more fundamental issue to a culture than gender; the construction of gender on the basis of biological sex has implications for all of human experience.

Over the past several years, the potential of and need for the application of the feminist perspective in research has been acknowledged in the communication discipline. Convention programs have featured papers about the feminist perspective, conferences have been held to discuss its implications for research, and essays have called for its adoption.[2] Readers of

---

* We wish to thank Marlene G. Fine for her input on earlier versions of this chapter.

[1] While we are referring to the feminist perspective in the singular, we see it as a broad framework that incorporates a variety of feminist approaches. We prefer the label, "the feminist perspective," however, because we believe essential features are shared by the diverse frameworks that fall within the feminist perspective.

[2] Among the programs presented on the feminist perspective in research at recent conventions have been: "Feminist Studies: Issues in Theory and Practice," program presented at the International Communication Association conference, Montreal, Canada, May, 1987; "Contemporary Radical Feminist Theory: The Challenge of Finding New Rhetorical Tools," program presented at the Speech Communication Association convention, Chicago, Illinois, November, 1986; and "Gender and Communication Research: Four Perspectives," program

these essays or participants at these conferences and conventions might well believe that the feminist perspective is firmly established and clearly visible in the discipline of communication and that numerous models for the use of this perspective in research are available for emulation. On the contrary, the feminist perspective appears to be "muted" in communication research, just as women's voices are muted in our culture in general (Kramarae, 1981; Spender, 1980). Despite a great deal of talk and writing about the potential for the feminist perspective in research, that potential remains largely unrealized in the journals of our field.[3]

Our intent in this essay is to suggest how the feminist perspective has been and can be incorporated into the research that is published in communication journals. We will define the feminist perspective and describe the dilemma of publishing feminist research. Then, we will report the results of a survey of published research in six communication journals to discover how widely and in what form the feminist perspective appears in communication studies. Our goal is to promote and facilitate the increased use and acceptance of the feminist perspective in research. Until feminist research is recognized as a unique and legitimate perspective by traditional scholars, it will not become part of the conversation about research and theory in communication, and women's perceptions and experiences will remain apart from the substance of our discipline.

DEFINITION: THE FEMINIST PERSPECTIVE IN RESEARCH

Research paradigms provide frameworks for constructing knowledge and certify the acceptability of particular constructions. They are distinguished from each other by several metatheoretical questions and their answers, including what is the basic category of analysis, what are appro-

---

presented at the Western Speech Communication Association convention, Fresno, California, February, 1985. The first conference on Gender and Communication Research was held at the Pennsylvania State University in April, 1984. For a report on the conference and position papers from it, see *Women's Studies in Communication* 7 (Fall 1984). This conference also was held in 1985 and 1986. The Organization for the Study of Communication, Language and Gender also has held annual conferences since 1978. For one example of the many calls for research from the feminist perspective, see Karen A. Foss and Sonja K. Foss (1983).

[3] We have chosen journals as our focus here because we believe the scholarship published in journals generally represents the significant work in a discipline. In the academic community, what is published in journals determines the agenda and debates within a discipline and essentially constitutes "knowledge" in a discipline. While books clearly make substantial contributions to a discipline, they cannot be published as quickly or as frequently as journals. If the book is a textbook, there is the additional need to adapt to a student audience, a process that often demands simplification or at least generalization about ideas, a process unnecessary in journal essays.

priate data for analysis, what are the means for analysis, and what are the ends or goals of analysis. The feminist perspective differs from the current dominant research paradigm in each of these areas, offering a different framework for constructing knowledge and challenging the acceptability of current constructions of knowledge.

Basic to the feminist perspective is the notion that gender is a critical component of all dimensions of culture. This assumption is translated into efforts to understand gender as a basic category of analysis (Thorne, Kramarae, & Henley, 1983). When gender is seen as a category of analysis, it is not simply one of many variables that a researcher studies; instead, it is the major element studied. Gender is the focus because it is understood to be basic to all aspects of human experience; it functions as a lens through which all other perceptions pass. Further, gender is seen not as a biological given but as a social construction. The construction of gender so that women's experiences are subordinated and the implications of this subordination for both women and men constitute the focus of feminist inquiry.

The feminist perspective calls into question the very nature of the existing gender system and the nonfeminist research paradigm, in which traditional gender roles are taken for granted and are seen as having little impact on experience or on the research process. Consequently, the primary goal of the feminist perspective is the development of theory that unsettles or challenges common assumptions of the culture, raises fundamental questions about social life, and fosters reconsideration of what has been taken for granted (Gergen, 1982). The feminist perspective, then, constitutes a deliberate break with past research frameworks that did not see gender as central and requires that the scholar deliberately "forget" the way things are in previous frameworks (Belenky, Clinchy, Goldberger, & Tarule, 1986). Feminist scholars seek to reconceptualize the construct of gender by building on assumptions different from those of research frameworks biased toward men.

One way in which the feminist perspective challenges the existing research framework is by considering women's perceptions, meanings, and experiences as appropriate and important data for analysis. Rather than generalizing from men to create an explanation for the experience of both men and women, feminist inquiry incorporates the values and qualities that characterize women's experiences. Interdependence, emotionality, a sense of self-questioning or vulnerability, fusion of the private and public, wholeness, egalitarian use of power, focus on process rather than product, multiplicity, and paradox are among the qualities that have been suggested as common to women's experiences (Belenky, Clinchy, Goldberger, & Tarule, 1986; Gilligan, 1982; Kimball, 1981; Lippard, 1976; Schaef, 1981). Whether such qualities are seen as deriving from women's experiences of discrimination and isolation, the impact of women's bodies on their perceptions, the greater development of the right hemisphere in women, or some other source, feminist researchers acknowledge that women's experiences are different from men's (Ferguson, 1984; Kimball, 1981; Lippard, 1976; Shedletsky, 1982). In the development of constructs and theories within the feminist perspective, these qualities of women's experiences are taken into account, considered seriously, and valued.

Another way in which the feminist perspective constitutes a challenge to the existing research framework is in its formulation of new rules for how knowledge is constructed. Adoption of the feminist perspective does not mean simply grafting women's concerns onto the constructions and theories of men's knowledge that are already in place. Under such a plan, as Spender points out, women's "meanings, even if initially *positive*, would soon be pejorated and become negative" simply because they do not conform to the norm, which is defined as male (Spender, 1980, p. 65).

To integrate gender concerns into conceptions of knowledge, the way knowledge is constructed must be reconceptualized. Feminist scholars seek to change the rules for the construction of knowledge so they reflect women's experiences and incorporate women's values. When qualities of women's experience such as self-questioning and multiplicity are used to create rules for the construction of knowledge, very different kinds of knowledge result. Roberts (1976, p. 46) provides examples of such different knowledge: "But what if the masculist world view, which has depended on a logic of time lines, is also erroneous? What if the most fundamental error is the search for monocausation? What if the world is really a field of interconnecting events, arranged in patterns of multiple meaning? What if the search for simplistic 'orderliness' is, itself, the common problem . . .?"

Finally, the feminist perspective has a practical, activist dimension as well as an academic one. Adoption of a feminist perspective in research is inherently radical not only because it goes "to the root" of the basic constructs of masculinity and femininity but also because it asks that these fundamental concepts be changed (Campbell, 1973). Thus, the ultimate consequence of research informed by a feminist perspective is social change. In contrast to the current dominant research paradigm, which seeks to predict human behavior, the feminist perspective seeks to understand human behavior and through that understanding, to change social life. While scholars in many research traditions use their findings for pragmatic ends, feminist scholars focus on change related to gender. Feminist scholars see how gender has been constructed to denigrate women and seek to change such constructions. Feminist research, then, is done not just about women but for women.

THE FEMINIST PERSPECTIVE AND NEW-PARADIGM
SCHOLARSHIP

The effort to put the feminist perspective into practice is governed by several methodological principles that the feminist perspective shares with "new-paradigm" scholarship. Taking this label from Kuhn's (1970) work on how paradigm shifts occur in the scientific community, scholars who identify with the new paradigm exhibit a collective sense of dissatisfaction with the dominant research paradigm; many of them incorporate into their approaches to inquiry assumptions and methods consistent with the qualities of women's experiences that are fundamental to the feminist perspective.[4]

Specifically, new-paradigm scholars challenge the application of the beliefs and practices of science to human beings and human behavior. Harré and Secord (1973) characterize the old paradigm as grounded in mechanistic, causal, and logical positivist assumptions, resulting in a conception of the human being as "a complicated mechanism whose behavior can be fully explained, in principle, by a combination of the effects of external stimuli and prevailing organismic states. People are viewed as objects which are passively affected by events in their environment" (p. 30). Bochner (1985), writing about the old paradigm in interpersonal communication, describes the paradigm as characterized by efforts to represent reality, to discover covering laws that explain stable relationships among observables, and to represent scientific progress as linear and cumulative.

The feminist perspective and the new paradigm share five fundamental assumptions that distinguish them from the old paradigm. They emphasize wholes rather than parts, process rather than structure, knowledge as a process of interconnection rather than hierarchy, approximate descriptions rather than absolute truth, and cooperation rather than competition

---

[4] The new paradigm is not an easily identifiable and cohesive group of scholars who share a singular purpose and methodology. In fact, the movement is multidisciplinary and manifest in a variety of formats and vocabularies. Clifford Geertz (1972) in anthropology, Rom Harré (1984) and Kenneth Gergen (1982) in psychology, Richard Rorty (1979) in philosophy, and Peter Berger and Thomas Luckmann (1966) in sociology are identified with various aspects of new-paradigm thinking in the social sciences. Within the discipline of communication, new-paradigm thought assumes equally diverse forms, ranging from Pearce and Cronen's (1980; also Pearce & Foss, 1987) coordinated management of meaning to Brockriede's (1985) perspectivism and Bochner's (1985) pragmatism. Critical theory is considered by some to be a branch of new-paradigm inquiry as well; critical theorists assume that reflection is a legitimate basis for knowledge and direct their efforts toward understanding and proposing alternatives to underlying value systems rather than uncovering objective knowledge. For an overview of critical theory, see David Held (1980). The link between feminist and new-paradigm scholarship is suggested by Charlene Spretnak (1986).

(Capra, 1986). In combination, these factors result in the use of certain methodological practices in research. In our elaboration of these characteristics below, we do not mean to suggest that a feminist perspective and the new paradigm are identical. While the two perspectives share the five methodological assumptions, the ends of research are different: feminism is distinguished by its focus on the deconstruction of gender.

Methodological Assumptions

Wholeness.   Within the traditional research paradigm, researchers seek to understand the whole by breaking it into parts, analyzing those parts, and then reconstructing the whole. Researchers within a feminist perspective or within the new paradigm, however, assert that the properties of parts only can be understood in relation to the dynamics of the whole and that ultimately, there are no parts—only patterns in an inseparable web of relationships. Attention to wholeness, for example, would encourage a researcher seeking to understand an organization to study the communication not only of the managers and key employees but of all organizational members.

Process.   A search for fundamental structures, which then give rise to certain processes, characterizes the conceptualization of knowledge in the old paradigm. But structure is considered inseparable from process by feminist and new-paradigm researchers; structure is not seen as preceding process but as intricately tied to it in a variety of ways. Thus, the process by which something comes to be is seen as more important than the static elements of its structure. A focus on process would suggest, then, that researchers not study a phenomenon such as women's role in organizations alone but also examine the process by which those roles are constructed.

Interconnectedness of knowledge.   In the old paradigm, knowledge is hierarchical; once fundamental laws, principles, and structures are uncovered, scholars can construct the layers of information that arise from them, ultimately arriving at an accurate and complete understanding of the phenomenon under investigation. The feminist perspective and new-paradigm scholarship, in contrast, operate from a "network" metaphor to suggest that knowledge is a process of lateral interconnection that is not necessarily uncovered by a linear, systematic progression. Scholars who pursue a line of research such as communication apprehension, which is based on a particular instrument, generally build knowledge hierarchically. Each new study is based on and incorporates the findings of the previous studies in which the selected instrument for measuring apprehension was used. A scholar who approaches the same topic laterally, however, might deliberately generate alternative conceptions of communication apprehension and choose to enter the study of communication apprehension from a new starting point. For example, a scholar might ask a group of self-defined communication apprehensives to define communication apprehension themselves and use their definitions to construct a new approach to the study of communication anxiety.

Approximation.   The certainty of scientific knowledge—Descartes' legacy to the West—is replaced in feminist thinking by the understanding that knowledge, like everything else, is a process of construction. Feminist scholars posit that scientific descriptions do not exist independently of the process of knowing. Thus, all knowledge is limited, approximate, and relative. Rather than asserting that they "know" the nature of a phenomenon such as the qualities that constitute leadership, feminist scholars would suggest they have provided one perspective on or a glimpse into one dimension of leadership.

Concomitant with a view of knowledge as approximate is acknowledgment of the role of the source in the process of knowledge construction. Rather than attempting to divorce knowledge from the source of knowing, the researcher is seen as central to and necessarily involved in the process. As feminist scholar Eisenstein (1983) explains: "But I do not subscribe to the belief that knowledge necessarily stems from detachment and measurement, carried out from some fictive Archimedean point 'outside' of the reality under consideration. Rather, I side with those who believe that understanding springs from empathy, involvement, and commitment" (p. xx).

Cooperation.   An implicit characteristic of the old paradigm is its dominating approach to knowledge, subjects, and the world in general. In much social scientific research, the researcher stands apart from the subjects and data in order to control them. Feminist and new-paradigm thinkers believe, in contrast, that in order for the world to survive, we no longer have the prerogative to assert our superiority over the things and processes of the world. Thus, feminist scholarship is characterized by methods that rely on cooperation rather than competition—cooperation among researchers and cooperation between the researcher and the participants in a study.

To summarize, the feminist perspective is a research stance that begins with the assumption that the division of the world in terms of gender is significant. This assumption is the basis for challenging existing theoretical frameworks by incorporating as data women's experiences and developing rules for the construction of knowledge based on the qualities that characterize these experiences. While it is the only theoretical tradition that takes gender as a basic category of analysis, the feminist perspective shares with other new-paradigm forms of scholarship a number of principles that govern its methodology.

When applied to communication research, the feminist perspective involves the asking of questions about the construction of our gender system through communication and about how gender informs communication (Putnam, 1982; Rakow, 1986). In communication inquiry, a feminist scholar seeks to discover how to change the conception of gender that is constructed and maintained through communication. Changes are suggested in theories of communication that have been created through the lens of gender without an acknowledgment of the importance of that lens. In communication research, the key communication activities of women's experiences—their rituals, vocabularies, metaphors, and stories—are an important part of the data for study. How women use these activities to make sense of their experiences and how they contribute to the construction of particular notions of gender are central concerns in feminist scholarship in communication.

We hope that our explanation of how we understand the feminist perspective makes clear that it is not a perspective that can be adopted only by women. Male researchers do not have to have experienced womanhood in order to incorporate women's experiences, accord them positive value, and seek to construct knowledge by taking them into account. Anyone who attempts to integrate women's voices into research in order to question the construction of gender is adopting a feminist stance. Likewise, the feminist perspective is not a perspective held by all women engaged in processes of research. Simply because researchers are women does not mean they utilize this perspective. The rewards are great for working within the old paradigm, and women who are trained in the methods and standards of this male-biased framework may choose to create and understand knowledge within its confines. Nor are we suggesting that traditional scholarship be eliminated: it provides a useful perspective and can be used to answer particular kinds of research questions. We simply seek pluralism in research perspectives—a pluralism that would include a feminist perspective.

THE DILEMMA OF THE FEMINIST PERSPECTIVE

To define the feminist perspective in research is much easier than to design and complete research projects that employ the perspective fully. Because the perspective looks to women's experience for data, research that is done from a feminist perspective often must move beyond the laboratory to gather those data. Because the perspective rejects many of the values and assumptions that frame the methods of the dominant research paradigm, researchers who use the feminist perspective must create new methods that are consonant with the values of feminism. Many of these methods are time consuming and difficult, and some force the researchers to confront serious ethical and personal dilemmas—gathering oral histories from women who share their experiences as abused children or battered adults, for example.

Completing a research project from the feminist perspective, however, is easier than publishing the results of the research. We believe that the issue of publishing feminist research creates a dilemma for scholars. To gain visibility and ultimately acceptance for the feminist perspective, scholars must find a way to present this perspective in the accepted publishing outlets of the field. Yet, research done from a feminist perspective uses data and methods that are not only unacceptable within the dominant research paradigm but also are often inimical to that paradigm. Feminist scholars, then, often are pressured to conduct studies within the old-paradigm research mode—in which gender constructions are taken for granted—since these kinds of studies are more likely to be accepted for publication.

While feminist scholars recognize that a feminist theoretical perspective on research constitutes a true challenge to the dominant research mode, they also recognize that the challenge is dissipated when the research is presented in terms acceptable to that framework. Yet, they also know that if they do not present their research in acceptable terms, it will not be disseminated in outlets that will provide the opportunity and audience to mount a true challenge to the existing paradigm. Thus, the dilemma is how to challenge and simultaneously to gain visibility and legitimation for such a perspective in the publications of the discipline that may be unsupportive or unaware of it.

Given the dilemma of challenge versus legitimation, we would expect to find that the feminist research that has been published makes accommodations to the traditional framework. To be published in a mainstream journal, the reputation of which is based on publication of research derived from a nonfeminist framework, a scholar likely will have had to alter the presentation of feminist notions to secure publication of the essay. Of course, accommodations to journal reviewers and editors are not unique to the feminist perspective. Indeed, at the most basic level, the process of publishing is one of accommodation to reviewers' and editors' varying expectations and demands. Furthermore, the introduction of any new perspective to a discipline—whether something relatively minor such as the use of a new critical method or something as major as a paradigm shift—involves accommodation to the status quo in order to gain an initial hearing for that new viewpoint.

We believe, however, that the feminist perspective constitutes a major challenge to the existing research tradition of the communication discipline because it challenges both the content and form of that tradition. It demands not only that the experiences of women be given a voice in the substance of the discipline but also that this substance be presented via methodologies that are consistent with women's experiences—deliberate involvement of the scholar with the participants of the study, for example. The challenge of the feminist perspective is total and all-encompassing and has the potential to alter the discipline in fundamental ways; thus, presenting this perspective in essays designed for publication is particularly difficult (Nielsen, 1982; Raymond, 1982; Spender, 1982).

USE OF THE FEMINIST PERSPECTIVE IN COMMUNICATION RESEARCH

To determine the nature and extent of use of the feminist perspective in published research in communication, we surveyed the essays concerning gender and women published in five mainstream communication journals for the past 10 years (1977–1987): the *Quarterly Journal of Speech, Communication Monographs, Human Communication Research,* the *Journal of Communication,* and *Critical Studies in Mass Communication.* These journals were chosen because they are the research journals associated with the two major national associations in speech communication. The *Quarterly Journal of Speech, Communication Monographs,* and *Critical Studies in Mass Communication* are published by the Speech Communication Association; *Human Communication Research* and the *Journal of Communication* are associated with the International Communication Association. We also surveyed the essays in *Women's Studies in Communication,* a journal published by the Organization for Research on Women and Communication that is devoted exclusively to issues of gender and communication. We chose 1977 as the starting date for our survey because that was the year *Women's Studies in Communication* began publication. The creation of a journal devoted to issues of women and gender suggests that these topics had become significant enough to warrant a special forum for their presentation. The exception to the 1977 starting date was *Critical Studies in Mass Communication,* which began publication in 1984.

We selected from these six publications the essays in which issues of gender or women were central; the essays are listed in the appendix. Centrality of gender to a study was determined by noting whether terms such as "sex," "gender," or "women" appeared in the title of the article; we were not interested in those essays in which sex was one among many variables studied but was not a focus of the study. In all of the studies published in *Women's Studies in Communication,* gender was judged to be central. Thus, all of the essays published during the 10-year period were included except for one issue, which was devoted to proceedings of a conference and was not subjected to the usual blind-review process.

Our interest in these essays was to identify the kinds of accommodations made to the dominant research paradigm in order for feminist research to be published. Our survey revealed seven basic ways a feminist perspective has been incorporated in these studies, each of which involves some kind of accommodation to the traditional research framework: (a) using old-paradigm, nonfeminist methods to conduct a study in which gender is an important topic of investigation; (b) highlighting features of women's experience in the study; (c) using women's experiences as data but employing traditional methods for their analysis; (d) Citing nongender-related literature as a theoretical base for a study; (e) using the conclusion section of an otherwise traditional essay to challenge old-paradigm notions; (f) criticizing gender research; and (g) suggesting standards of evaluation for the feminist perspective.

We see each of these categories as suggesting strategies feminist researchers can use to increase the chances for publication of their essays. We use the term "strategy" guardedly. While we maintain that these features can be used consciously, we are not arguing that these authors did so. We are applying the term a posteriori, looking back at the essays for patterns that—whether apparent or not to the authors—may be useful in the future to those writing from a feminist perspective. We are using these published essays, then, as starting points for us to speculate about strategies that seem to be available to help secure publication of research from a feminist perspective. In the next section, we will describe essays from the journals surveyed that exemplify each of these seven categories of accommodation.

Using Old-Paradigm Methods

One kind of accommodation made to facilitate publication of feminist research is to take the construct of gender as a starting point but then to use old-paradigm approaches to conduct and report a study. The scholar acknowledges that gender functions as a filter for experience and believes that gender provides a valuable perspective from which to approach knowledge. The study itself, however, is conducted using traditional methods consistent with the old paradigm. Patricia Hayes Bradley's study of folk linguistics is one example of this strategy (1981). She describes the sometimes-contradictory literature that posits a connection between the devaluation of women's speech and the lack of status accorded women in society, thus acknowledging that gender is both a function and reflection of status in our culture. She then conducts a traditional laboratory study of the qualifying devices used by women and men when presenting arguments in small group discussions in order to test the relationship between women's speech and status.

Another example is Robert Johnson's (1980) study of the use of the phrase, "blacks and women," to refer to the hostages released early during the Iran hostage crisis. He notes that the phrase was "comfortably applied by American journalists to a specific group of black men and white women" and that it "may be symptomatic of a deeply rooted cultural notion that for males race is the crucial factor while for females it is their sex" (p. 62). This direct acknowledgment of the way both gender and race unconsciously permeate society is very much in line with the feminist perspective. Johnson then proceeds to show the high percentage of use of the phrase, "blacks and women," in several newspapers, using traditional techniques of content analysis. Both Bradley's and Johnson's studies deal with gender as the critical issue but then explore it using old-paradigm methods.

Highlighting Features of Women's Experience

Another category of essays brings to attention one or two features of women's experiences not typically acknowledged, valued, or even studied by the dominant research framework. Such studies make readers aware of aspects of women's experience that are not featured in traditional communication studies. Sandra Ragan and Victoria Aarons' (Ragan & Aarons, 1986) essay suggests that by examining how silence functions in works of fiction, we can uncover some functions served by silence that have not yet been explored in studies of actual relationships. They describe two stories in which the female protagonists' " 'silent' marriages paradoxically allow them to 'speak' forcefully" (p. 69). Thus, they suggest a reconceptualization of the notion that women are manipulated more through men's noncommunicativeness or silence than the inverse—that men more often than women use silence to control conversation. They also raise the issue of paradox, a quality often attributed to women's experiences, in their discussion of how women may use silence in order to "speak."

A second essay that brings to the foreground a feature of women's experience is an essay by Robert Scott and James Klumpp (Scott & Klumpp, 1984) on Ellen Goodman's newspaper columns. They begin by admitting that their interest in Goodman's writing is her focus on the point "where public meets private" (p. 68); the fusion of the public and private has been seen as a feature of women's experience. Ferguson (1984), for example, suggests that the public and private realms are more alike than we previously have recognized:

They are alike in that the relation of self to others sustained in personal, face-to-face encounters provides the grounds for the experience of community in the larger arena, for the recognition of connections and commonality with those who are strangers but who are still human, like oneself, and thus not easily discarded as enemies. Similarly, the experience of risk and loss that the nurturance of freedom entails can prepare us for the encounter with the unfamiliar, the unknown, and the dangerous that public life requires. (p. 201)

Scott and Klumpp show how the public and private realms are brought together in Goodman's columns. Unlike Ragan and Aarons, Scott and Klumpp do not acknowledge the connection with women's experience that their essay suggests nor do they acknowledge the feminist perspective in their essay; nonetheless, their article incorporates and illuminates a dimension of women's experience—a fusion of the private with the public—and thus serves as a partial model for feminist research.

Using Women's Experiences as Data

Other essays use as data women's communication experiences that are different from men's—data that generally have not been considered worthy of investigation because of the devaluation of women in our culture and research tradition. Fern Johnson and Marlene Fine (1985), studying sex differences in obscenity use, acknowledge that obscenity has been considered outside the linguistic domain of women. They explore differences in the obscenities that occur in the linguistic environments of women and men and sex differences in standards of appropriateness for obscenity. By studying the actual use of obscenity among women—a double taboo in that obscenity generally is not studied, but especially not its use by women—they provide information about women's experiences and forms of communication. They also illuminate the paradox women face in terms of language use and power—obscenity may be used in an effort to counter male verbal violence, but it may generate male violence instead.

Lana Rakow concludes her essay, "Rethinking Gender Research in Communication," with a reference to another neglected form of data associated with women's experience—telephone use (1986). Not only is women's use of the telephone unusual as data, but Rakow suggests that we need to ask different questions about these data than we normally would:

> For example, if we are interested in understanding the relationships between gender and communication technologies, we would be wise not to start by looking for differences in women's and men's behavior with a technology, as if gender itself, as some individually possessed essence, causes behavior.

Instead, we might look for the ways in which a technology is used to construct us as women and men through the social practices that put it to use. (pp. 23–24)

The use of data connected to women's lives but regarded as unimportant in the traditional research framework is a way to introduce a feminist perspective and to begin to ask different research questions as well.

Citing Nongender Research

Another way the studies in our survey seem to have accommodated the prevailing research tradition is evident in the theoretical literature cited as backdrop for the studies. The authors often cite literature already accepted within the discipline of communication. In her study of the debate on the Equal Rights Amendment (ERA), Sonja Foss (1979) makes use of fantasy-theme analysis and the theory of symbolic convergence. Martha Solomon (1979) uses Northrup Frye's notions of the *mythoi* of romance to study the ERA, and traditional literature on persuasion provides the background for Charles Montgomery and Michael Burgoon's study of androgyny and resistance to persuasion (1980). While linking a study with an already established tradition is expected in research of any kind, what is distinctive about the practice in these essays is that the theories cited typically are not connected with gender research. In other words, gender issues are presented via connection to theories in which gender is not central, a strategy that clearly grants more credibility to an essay, as far as the mainstream is concerned, than one in which only feminist or gender-related literature is cited.

Using Conclusions to Challenge

The use of the conclusion section of an essay to raise issues germane to the feminist perspective and thus to highlight that perspective was another strategy that emerged from our survey of communication journals. Usually, the conclusion section of a research report provides a summary of the study and its limitations. In feminist research, the conclusion can be used to perform a much more important function: to acknowledge the role of the feminist perspective in research, despite the traditional features of the study.

An example of how the conclusion can be used to challenge is Myra Isenhart's study (1980) of sex and the decoding of nonverbal cues, in which she found that women were better decoders than men of nonverbal cues. She also found that femininity, as measured by the BSRI, and ability to decode nonverbal cues are negatively related. As a result of her findings, she suggests that previous research about gender roles and communication be questioned: "Interpretation of the surprising negative correlation between femininity and decoding ability is better grounded in a hard look at previous assumptions and arguments than in regret for the problems posed by these tests and this sample" (p. 316). Thus, her study suggests another possibility for the conclusion of an essay: to address how the traditional research framework limits the findings of the study. Such a discussion could be followed by a description of the feminist perspective and how its use might have altered the conduct of the study and the insights gained. For example, a scholar might explain that she chose to use feminist interviewing techniques, in which she revealed personal information to the interviewees and came to know them well. She then could discuss the benefits and drawbacks of using feminist interviewing techniques.

Katherine Warfel's study (1984) of the relationship between Bem's gender-schema theory and perceptions of power in speech also revealed results at odds with traditional expectations about powerless speech. She, too, raises questions about our definition of power in her conclusion, questions in line with the feminist perspective. For instance, she recognizes that power is assumed to be a positive quality but, in fact, this may be a questionable assumption: "The results of this study reveal that there is some kind of tradeoff involved with the use of power.... Although a generic style does seem to lead to perceptions of dominance, objectiveness, and professionalism, it may also produce perceptions of incompetence" (p. 265). The use of the conclusion to question traditional assumptions and to offer the feminist perspective as an alternative way to frame research, then, increases the visibility of the feminist perspective in research.

Criticizing Gender/Feminist Research

Other essays in our survey reveal the use of self-critique as a means of both accommodating the traditional research framework and presenting the feminist perspective. To criticize the perspective from which one's research is conducted allows readers to see that the perspective is just that—a perspective—with particular constraints and limitations.

Putnam's critique of gender research suggests that gender researchers may have fallen into some of the same pitfalls as mainstream researchers, such as looking for and considering differences as more significant than similarities (1982). She also questions the assumption of many researchers that gender is socially and collectively defined and asks how such research would differ if it were individually defined. In addition, she suggests that we not confine our research to how gender influences communication but also that we look at how communication affects gender.

Phyllis Randall, in "Re-Examining the Smiles of Women," summarizes the literature on women's smiles and criticizes the fact that "all smiles have been treated alike, although in everyday life, people are very well aware of such variations as the nervous smile (noted by Henley), the pasted-on smile, the wry smile, the tentative smile, the self-satisfied smile, and the smile of pleasure" (Randall, 1985, p. 6). She then suggests the range of meanings that can be attributed to smiling and calls for a rethinking of our basic premises in regard to smiling:

> Is it not possible for a woman's smile to mask inward emotion just as much as man's non-expressive face can—a different response to the same technique of not divulging private information? If so, then the smile, too, can be related to power. Is not a major part of the allure of the Mona Lisa her enigmatic smile? And is not that kind of allure related to power in a personal relationship? Further, is it not possible that some of the "appeasement" smiles are really equivalent to the "rolling eyes" behavior of young black girls . . . [described] as "a gesture of insubordination"? True, both are expressions used by the powerless, but insubordination is very different from appeasement. (Randall, 1985, p. 8)

One dimension of the feminist perspective is its grounding in vulnerability and self-questioning; feminist scholars do not conceive of themselves as "right." The strategy of self-critique may be one way to deal explicitly with objections of mainstream reviewers to feminist scholarship.

Generating Standards of Evaluation

A final way to highlight the feminist perspective in research while making accommodations to the traditional research framework is to spell out the standards by which it is to be assessed. Until studies centered in the feminist perspective become common, feminist scholars should suggest criteria by which the data or procedures used can be judged. A common criticism of and reason for discounting feminist research is the failure of feminist scholars to distinguish good from bad feminist research. By suggesting criteria for judging their research, feminist scholars can begin to develop, discuss, and refine a body of standards that can be used to judge their scholarship.

Suppose, for example, that a scholar conducts a study using as data women's quilts. At the conclusion of the study, the author undoubtedly can say much about the difficulties of working with such forms of communication, the temptations to be avoided, the limitations of the data, and the kinds of insights they are likely to reveal. She then can utilize the experience with those data to propose standards of adequacy for dealing with such forms of communication from a feminist perspective. Or, suppose a researcher consciously conducts a study not as a disinterested, objective, and detached scholar but as a passionately involved participant who acknowledges personal and social change as goals of the study (Treichler, Kramarae, & Stafford, 1985). He might collect data through personal involvement with and caring for the individuals who are the subject of the study and with the aim of discovering insights useful to women as they live their lives. Once such procedures have been used to conduct the research, the author undoubtedly can suggest standards to guide feminist research.

While none of the studies we examined in our survey directly posit standards of evaluation, one moves in this direction. Karlyn Kohrs Campbell's essay (1980) on Elizabeth Cady Stanton's farewell address to the National American Woman Suffrage Association offers an example of an essay in which standards of evaluation are implicit. Campbell suggests that inherent in the speech are principles of humanism that lie behind feminism. These features of Stanton's speech could serve as categories by which to understand and evaluate other feminist discourse: "Philosophically, it [Stanton's speech] reminds us of the conditions of every human life: that each of us is unique, responsible, and alone. These conditions entail the republican principle of natural rights and the religious principle of individual conscience. If women are persons, they merit access to every opportunity that will assist them in the human struggle" (pp. 311–312). While Campbell's essay does not specifically suggest standards for evaluating the feminist perspective per se, it is a step in that direction in its presentation of fundamental principles underlying the women's movement—principles that could become criteria for evaluating essays about women.

CONCLUSION

This survey of the current visibility of the feminist perspective in published research in communication confirms that a process of accommodation occurs when a new perspective of any kind is introduced into an existing research tradition. In order to gain initial visibility and begin to be acknowledged as an alternative research frame, the challenging perspective must find its way into publication, a process that requires adjustments to the expectations of the status quo. We uncovered seven such accommodations of the feminist perspective to the traditional research framework in the published essays in communication over the past 10 years. Even in *Women's Studies in Communication,* where one might expect to see the feminist perspective fully realized in research, this was not the case. The same kinds of accommodations were evident in this journal as in the mainstream journals. The first step toward full implementation of the feminist perspective in research has been taken, and the strategies suggested can be used deliberately by other scholars writing from a feminist perspective to facilitate publication of their research. But the process must not stop here.

While we understand the need for adaptation in order to succeed in making the feminist perspective an accepted and valued research framework, there is little evidence in the journals of movement beyond accommodation to a phase where the *challenge* of the perspective takes precedence over *accommodation.* A plateau seems to have been reached with the feminist perspective; it is visible only when it accommodates in major ways. In fact, one could argue that, after 10 years at this particular stage, the accommodations have become institutionalized patterns for publishing feminist research. Whether or not such institutionalization has occurred, feminist scholars will continue to have difficulty remaining "sufficiently radical" (Pearce & Freeman, 1984, p. 65) to challenge the old-paradigm research framework; yet, this challenge is the essence and purpose of the feminist perspective.

We hope this essay will serve as a catalyst for the discipline in moving the feminist perspective to the next stage of development. By offering a definition of the feminist perspective, making explicit the dilemma it entails, and pointing out the accommodations that have been made to the status quo in the publication of essays that incorporate it, we hope the perspective becomes a topic of discussion among more than just a minority of scholars in the discipline. Only then can it become a fully realized—rather than just a partially expressed—voice in the discipline of communication.

APPENDIX

Quarterly Journal of Speech

Sarah Trenholm and William R. Todd de Mancillas, "Student Perceptions of Sexism," 64 (October 1978).

Pattie P. Gillespie, "Feminist Theatre: A Rhetorical Phenomenon," 64 (October 1978).

Martha Solomon, "The 'Positive Woman's' Journey: A Mythic Analysis of the Rhetoric of STOP ERA," 65 (October 1979).

Sonja K. Foss, "The Equal Rights Amendment Controversy: Two Worlds in Conflict," 65 (October 1979).

Alexis Tan, Jack Raudy, Cary Huff, and Janet Miles, "Children's Reactions to Male and Female Newscasters: Effectiveness and Believability," 66 (April 1980).

Julia T. Wood and W. Barnett Pearce, "Sexists, Racists, and Other Classes of Classifiers: Form and Function of '... ist' Accusations," 66 (October 1980).

Karlyn Kohrs Campbell, "Stanton's 'The Solitude of Self': A Rationale for Feminism," 66 (October 1980).

Charles Conrad, "The Transformation of the 'Old Feminist' Movement," 67 (August 1981).

Robert L. Scott and James F. Klumpp, " 'A Dear Searcher into Comparison': The Rhetoric of Ellen Goodman," 70 (February 1984).

Celeste Condit Railsback, "The Contemporary American Abortion Controversy: Stages in the Argument," 70 (November 1984).

Randall A. Lake, "Order and Disorder in Anti-Abortion Rhetoric: A Logological View," 70 (November 1984).

Phyllis M. Japp, "Esther or Isaiah?" The Abolitionist-Feminist Rhetoric of Angelina Grimke," 71 (August 1985).

Karlyn Kohrs Campbell, "Style and Content in the Rhetoric of Early Afro-American Feminists," 72 (November 1986).

Communication Monographs

Charles L. Montgomery and Michael Burgoon, "An Experimental Study of the Interactive Effects of Sex and Androgyny on Attitude Change," 44 (June 1977).

Ernest G. Bormann, Jerie Pratt, and Linda Putnam, "Power, Authority, and Sex: Male Response to Female Leadership," 45 (June 1978).

John E. Baird, Jr. and Patricia Hayes Bradley, "Styles of Management and Communication: A Comparative Study of Men and Women," 46 (June 1979).

Michael Calvin McGee, "The Origins of 'Liberty': A Femininization of Power," 47 (March 1980).

Charles L. Montgomery and Michael Burgoon, "The Effects of Androgyny and Message Expectations on Resistance to Persuasive Communication," 47 (March 1980).

Patricia Hayes Bradley, "Sex, Competence and Opinion Deviation: An Expectation States Approach," 47 (June 1980).

Anthony Mulac and Torborg Louisa Lundell, "Differences in Perceptions Created by Syntactic-Semantic Productions of Male and Female Speakers," 47 (June 1980).

Patricia Hayes Bradley, "The Folk-Linguistics of Women's Speech: An Empirical Examination," 48 (March 1981).

Barbara M. Montgomery and Robert W. Norton, "Sex Differences and Similarities in Communicator Style," 48 (June 1981).

Michael J. Cody and H. Dan O'Hair, "Nonverbal Communication and Deception: Differences in Deception Cues Due to Gender and Communicator Dominance," 50 (September 1983).

Katherine A. Warfel, "Gender Schemas and Perceptions of Speech Style," 51 (September 1984).

Sandra Petronio, Judith Martin, and Robert Littlefield, "Prerequisite Conditions for Self-Disclosing: A Gender Issue," 51 (September 1984).

Anthony Mulac, Torborg Louisa Lundell, and James J. Bradac, "Male/Female Language Differences and Attributional Consequences in a Public Speaking Situation: Toward an Explanation of the Gender-Linked Language Effect," 53 (June 1986).

B. Christine Shea and Judy C. Pearson, "The Effects of Relationship Type, Partner Intent, and Gender on the Selection of Relationship Maintenance Strategies," 53 (December 1986).

Michael D. Miller, Rodney A. Reynolds, and Ronald E. Cambra, "The Influence of Gender and Culture on Language Intensity," 54 (March 1987).

Critical Studies in Mass Communication

Karen K. List, "Two Party Papers' Political Coverage of Women in the New Republic," 2 (June 1985).

David L. Eason, "On Journalistic Authority: The Janet Cooke Scandal," 3 (December 1986).

H. Leslie Steeves, "Feminist Theories and Media Studies," 4 (June 1987).

Human Communication Research

Lynda Greenblatt, James E. Hasenauer, and Vicki S. Freimuth, "Psychological Sex Type and Androgyny in the Study of Communication Variables: Self-Disclosure and Communication Apprehension," 6 (Winter 1980).

Myra W. Isenhart, "An Investigation of the Relationship of Sex and Sex Role to the Ability to Decode Nonverbal Cues," 6 (Summer 1980).

Margaret L. McLaughlin, Michael J. Cody, Marjorie L. Kane, and Carl S. Robey, "Sex Differences in Story Receipt and Story Sequencing Behaviors in Dyadic Conversations," 7 (Winter 1981).

B. Aubrey Fisher, "Differential Effects of Sexual Composition and Interactional Context on Interaction Patterns in Dyads," 9 (Spring 1983).

Michael Burgoon, James P. Dillard, and Noel E. Doran, "Friendly or Unfriendly Persuasion: The Effects of Violations of Expectations by Males and Females," 10 (Winter 1983).

Anthony Mulac, James J. Bradac, and Susan Karol Mann, "Male/Female Language Differences and Attributional Consequences in Children's Television," 11 (Summer 1985).

Mark A. deTurck, "A Transactional Analysis of Compliance-Gaining Behavior: Effects of Noncompliance, Relational Contexts, and Actors' Gender," 12 (Fall 1985).

Patricia Hayes Andrews, "Gender Differences in Persuasive Communication and Attribution of Success and Failure," 13 (Spring 1987).

Kathryn Dindia, "The Effects of Sex of Subject and Sex of Partner on Interruptions," 13 (Spring 1987).
Anthony Mulac, Lisa B. Studley, John W. Wiemann, and James J. Bradac, "Male/Female Gaze in Same-Sex and Mixed-Sex Dyads: Gender-Linked Differences and Mutual Influence," 13 (Spring 1987).

Journal of Communication

Muriel G. Cantor, "Women and Public Broadcasting," 27 (Winter 1977).
Virginia P. Richmond and D. Lynn Robertson, "Women's Liberation in Interpersonal Relations," 27 (Winter 1977).
Alexander Rysman, "How the 'Gossip' Became a Woman," 27 (Winter 1977).
Jeannette M. Haviland, "Sex-Related Pragmatics in Infants' Nonverbal Communication," 27 (Spring 1977).
Susan Franzblau, Joyce N. Sprafkin, and Eli A. Rubinstein, "Sex on TV: A Content Analysis," 27 (Spring 1977).
Richard A. Dienstbier, "Sex and Violence: Can Research Have It Both Ways?," 27 (Summer 1977).
Judith Lemon, "Women and Blacks on Prime-Time Television," 27 (Autumn 1977).
Wendy Martyna, "What Does 'He' Mean—Use of the Generic Masculine," 28 (Winter 1978).
Barbara Bate, "Nonsexist Language Use in Transition," 28 (Winter 1978).
Sandra E. Purnell, "Politically Speaking, Do Women Exist?," 28 (Winter 1978).
William J. O'Donnell and Karen J. O'Donnell, "Update: Sex-Role Messages in TV Commercials," 28 (Winter 1978).
Jeanne Marecek, Jane Allyn Piliavin, Ellen Fitzsimmons, Elizabeth C. Krogh, Elizabeth Leader, and Bonnie Trudell, "Women as TV Experts: The Voice of Authority?," 28 (Winter 1978).
Denise Warren, "Commercial Liberation," 28 (Winter 1978).
Charles Lazer and S. Dier, "The Labor Force in Fiction," 28 (Winter 1978).
Matilda Butler and William Paisley, "Magazine Coverage of Women's Rights," 28 (Winter 1978).
Jennie Farley, "Women's Magazines and the ERA: Friend or Foe?," 28 (Winter 1978).
Janet S. Sanders, "Talking and Not Talking About Sex: Male and Female Vocabularies," 29 (Spring 1979).
Renate L. Welch, Aletha Huston-Stein, John C. Wright, and Robert Plehal, "Subtle Sex-Role Cues in Children's Commercials," 29 (Summer 1979).
Katherine Meyer, John Seidler, Timothy Curry, Adrian Aveni, "Women in July Fourth Cartoons: A 100-Year Look," 30 (Winter 1980).
Robert C. Johnson, " 'Blacks and Women': Naming American Hostages Released in Iran," 30 (Summer 1980).
Bradley S. Greenberg, Robert Abelman, and Kimberly Neuendorf, "Sex on the Soap Operas: Afternoon Delight," 31 (Summer 1981).
Dennis T. Lowry, Gail Love, and Malcolm Kirby, "Sex on the Soap Operas: Patterns of Intimacy," 31 (Summer 1981).

Gerald U. Skelly and William J. Lundstrom, "Male Sex Roles in Magazine Advertising, 1959–1979," 31 (Autumn 1981).

Dolf Zillmann and Jennings Bryant, "Pornography, Sexual Callousness, and the Trivialization of Rape," 32 (Autumn 1982).

Barbara Bate and Lois S. Self, "The Rhetoric of Career Success Books for Women," 33 (Spring 1983).

Daniel Linz, Edward Donnerstein, and Steven Penrod, "The Effects of Multiple Exposures to Filmed Violence Against Women," 34 (Summer 1984).

Barry L. Sherman and Joseph R. Dominick, "Violence and Sex in Music Videos: TV and Rock 'n' Roll," 36 (Winter 1986).

Jane D. Brown and Kenneth Campbell, "Race and Gender in Music Videos: The Same Beat but a Different Drummer," 36 (Winter 1986).

Ferrel Christensen, "Sexual Callousness Revisited," 36 (Winter 1986).

Dolf Zillmann and Jennings Bryant, "Response," 36 (Winter 1986).

Ellen Seiter, "Stereotypes and the Media: A Re-Evaluation," 36 (Spring 1986).

Lana F. Rakow, "Rethinking Gender Research in Communication," 36 (Autumn 1986).

Women's Studies in Communication

(*Women's Studies in Communication* was published intermittently between 1978 and 1981; all issues published were included in our survey. We have not included vol. 7, Fall 1984 here because that issue was devoted to conference proceedings and was not a refereed issue.)

Michael J. Schneider and Karen A. Foss, "Thought, Sex, and Language: The Sapir-Whorf Hypothesis in the American Women's Movement," 1 (Spring 1977).

Susan B. Shimanoff, "Sex as a Variable in Communication Research 1970–1976: An Annotated Bibliography," 1 (Spring 1977).

Susan B. Shimanoff, "Man ≠ Human: Empirical Support for the Whorfian Hypothesis," 1 (Summer 1977).

Nancy Wood Bliese, "Sex-Role Stereotyping of Adjectives: A Hopeful Report," 1 (Summer 1977).

Kathleen Ansell, "Current Research on Women in Management/Administration," 2 (Summer 1978).

Sandra E. Purnell, "Women's Studies in Communication: Status Report," 2 (Summer 1978).

Audrey A. Nelson, "Sex and Proxemics: An Annotated Bibliography," 2 (Summer 1978).

Cynthia J. Huyink, "A Dramatistic Analysis of *Sexual Politics* by Kate Millett," 3 (Summer 1979).

Sonja K. Foss, "Feminism Confronts Catholicism: A Study of the Use of Perspective by Incongruity," 3 (Summer 1979).

Sheila J. Gibbons, "Covering Women: Women's Publications and the Mass Media," 3 (Summer 1979).

Kenneth K. Sereno and Janet L. Weathers, "Impact of Communicator Sex on Receiver Reactions to Assertive, Nonassertive, and Aggressive Communication," 4 (Fall 1981).

Audrey A. Nelson, "Women's Nonverbal Behavior: The Paradox of Skill and Acquiescence," 4 (Fall 1981).

Elizabeth Berry, "Emma Goldman: A Study in Female Agitation," 4 (Fall 1981).

Judy C. Pearson, "Sex and Speech Criticism in the Classroom: An Annotated Bibliography," 4 (Fall 1981).

Linda L. Putnam, "In Search of Gender: A Critique of Communication and Sex-Roles Research," 5 (Spring 1982).

Leonard J. Shedletsky, "The Relationship Between Sex Differences in Cerebral Organization and Nonverbal Behavior," 5 (Spring 1982).

Celeste Condit Railsback, "Pro-Life, Pro-Choice: Different Conceptions of Value," 5 (Spring 1982).

Thomas Baglan and Doris J. Nelson, "A Comparison of the Effects of Sex and Status on the Perceived Appropriateness of Nonverbal Behaviors," 5 (Spring 1982).

Janice Schuetz, "Secular and Sectarian Conflict: A Case Study of Mormons for ERA," 5 (Fall 1982).

Myra Isenhart, "A Review of Critical Issues in the Measurement of Psychological Gender Role," 5 (Fall 1982).

Johnny I. Murdock and Catherine W. Konsky, "An Investigation of Verbosity and Sex-Role Expectations," 5 (Fall 1982).

Donald G. Ellis, "Relational Stability and Change in Women's Consciousness-Raising Groups," 5 (Fall 1982).

Rita Braito and Robert B. Schafer, "Self-Concept and Perceived Power Utilization: The Case of Husbands and Wives," 5 (Fall 1982).

Julie Yingling, "Women's Advocacy: Pragmatic Feminism in the YWCA," 6 (Spring 1983).

Katherine Kurs and Robert S. Cathcart, "The Feminist Movement: Lesbian-Feminism as Confrontation," 6 (Spring 1983).

Martin S. Remland, Carolyn McK. Jacobson, and Tricia S. Jones, "Evaluations of Sex-Incongruent Nonverbal Communication for Male and Female Managers," 6 (Spring 1983).

Helen M. Newman, "Concealing Sexual Identity Through Verbal and Nonverbal Communication," 6 (Spring 1983).

Gail A. Siegerdt, "Communication Profiles for Organizational Communication Behavior: Are Men and Women Different?," 6 (Fall 1983).

Mary Anne Fitzpatrick and Julie Indvik, "Me and My Shadow: Projections of Psychological Gender Self-Appraisals in Marital Implicit Theories," 6 (Fall 1983).

Mildred S. Myers, "Mary Cunningham and the Press: Who Said What and How?," 6 (Fall 1983).

Noreen Wales Kruse, "The Myth of the Demonic in Anti-ERA Rhetoric," 6 (Fall 1983).

Emil Bohn and Randall Stutman, "Sex-Role Differences in the Relational Control Dimension of Dyadic Interaction," 6 (Fall 1983).

Michael Burgoon, James P. Dillard, Randall Koper, and Noel Doran, "The Impact of Communication and Persuader Gender on Persuasive Message Selection," 7 (Spring 1984).

Virginia Eman Wheeless, "A Test of the Theory of Speech Accommodation Using Language and Gender Orientation," 7 (Spring 1984).

Tricia S. Jones and Claire C. Brunner, "The Effects of Self-Disclosure and Sex on Perceptions of Interpersonal Communication Competence," 7 (Spring 1984).

James J. Bradac, Michael O'Donnell, and Charles H. Tardy, "Another Stab at a Touchy Subject: Affective Meanings of Touch," 7 (Spring 1984).

Phyllis Randall, "Re-examining the Smiles of Women," 8 (Spring 1985).

Fern L. Johnson and Marlene G. Fine, "Sex Differences in Uses and Perceptions of Obscenity," 8 (Spring 1985).

William R. Todd-Mancillas and Ana Rossi, "Gender Differences in the Management of Personnel Disputes," 8 (Spring 1985).

Belle A. Edson, "Bias in Social Movement Theory: A View from a Female-Systems Perspective," 8 (Spring 1985).

Robert Abelman, "Sex Differences in Parental Disciplinary Practices: An Antecedent of Television's Impact on Children," 8 (Fall 1985).

Judi Beinstein Miller, "Patterns of Control in Same-Sex Conversations: Differences Between Women and Men," 8 (Fall 1985).

Andrew S. Rancer and Kathi J. Dierks-Rancer, "The Measurement of Psychological Gender Orientation: A Summary and Review," 8 (Fall 1985).

Gary A. Copeland and R. C. Adams, "Procedural Questions and Theoretical Issues Surrounding the Gender Orientation Scales," 8 (Fall 1985).

Lawrence R. Wheeless and Virginia Eman Wheeless, "Gender Orientation: Procedural and Theoretical Issues Redressed," 8 (Fall 1985).

Lawrence B. Nadler and Marjorie Keeshan Nadler, "The Role of Sex in Organizational Negotiation Ability," 9 (Spring 1986).

Laree S. Kiely and Dan Crary, "The Solution That Has No Name: Application of the Social Value Model to Friedan's *The Second Stage*," 9 (Spring 1986).

Lynne Webb, "Eliminating Sexist Language in the Classroom," 9 (Spring 1986).

Barbara Luebke, " 'First Woman' Stories: A Sign of Progress or More Special Treatment?," 9 (Spring 1986).

Melanie Booth-Butterfield, "Recognizing and Communicating in Harassment-Prone Organizational Climates," 9 (Fall 1986).

Michael R. Hemphill and Angela Laird Pfeiffer, "Sexual Spillover in the Workplace: Testing the Appropriateness of Male-Female Interaction," 9 (Fall 1986).

Sandra L. Ragan and Victoria Aarons, "Women's Response to Men's Silence: A Fictional Analysis," 9 (Fall 1986).

Jacqueline Taylor, "Encoding and Decoding Nonverbal Gender Display in Cross-Gender Performances," 9 (Fall 1986).

Deborah Weider-Hatfield, "Differences in Self-Reported Leadership Behavior as a Function of Biological Sex and Psychological Gender," 10 (Spring 1987).

William Foster Owen, "The Verbal Expression of Love by Women and Men as a Critical Communication Event in Personal Relationships," 10 (Spring 1987).

Virginia Eman Wheeless, Donald C. Hudson, and Lawrence R. Wheeless, "A Test of the Expected Use of Influence Strategies by Male and Female Supervisors as Related to Job Satisfaction and Trust in Supervisor," 10 (Spring 1987).

Craig Johnson and Larry Vinson, " 'Damned if you Do, Damned if you Don't?': Status, Powerful Speech, and Evaluations of Female Witnesses," 10 (Spring 1987).

REFERENCES

Belenky, M. F., Clinchy, B. M., Goldberger, N. R., & Tarule, J. M. (1986). *Women's ways of knowing: The development of self, voice, and mind.* New York: Basic Books.

Berger, P. L., & Luckmann, T. (1966). *The social construction of reality.* Garden City, NY: Doubleday.

Bochner, A. P. (1985). Perspectives on inquiry: Representation, conversation, and reflection. In M. L. Knapp & G. R. Miller (Eds.), *Handbook of interpersonal communication.* Beverly Hills: Sage.

Bradley, P. H. (1981). The folk-linguistics of women's speech: An empirical examination. *Communication Monographs, 48,* 73–90.

Brockriede, W. (1985). Constructs, experience, and argument. *Quarterly Journal of Speech, 71,* 151–63.

Campbell, K. K. (1973). The rhetoric of women's liberation: An oxymoron. *Quarterly Journal of Speech, 59,* 74–86.

Campbell, K. K. (1980). Stanton's "The Solitude of Self": A rationale for feminism. *Quarterly Journal of Speech, 66,* 304–12.

Capra, F. (1986). The concept of paradigm and paradigm shift. *ReVision, 9,* 11–12.

de Beauvoir, S. (1952). *The second sex.* (H. M. Parshley, Trans. and Ed.). New York: Vantage.

Eisenstein, H. (1983). *Contemporary feminist thought.* Boston: G. K. Hall.

Ferguson, K. E. (1984). *The feminist case against bureaucracy.* Philadelphia: Temple University Press.

Foss, K. A., & Foss, S. K. (1983). The status of research on women and communication. *Communication Quarterly, 31,* 195–204.

Foss, S. K. (1979). The equal rights amendment controversy: Two worlds in conflict. *Quarterly Journal of Speech, 65,* 275–88.

Geertz, C. (1972). *The interpretation of culture.* New York: Basic Books.

Gergen, K. J. (1982). *Toward transformation in social knowledge.* New York: Springer-Verlag.

Gilligan, C. (1982). *In a different voice: Psychological theory and women's development.* Cambridge: Harvard University Press.

Harré, R. (1984). *Personal being: A theory for individual psychology.* Cambridge: Harvard University Press.

Harré, R., & Secord, P. (1973). *The explanation of social behaviour.* Totowa, NJ: Littlefield, Adams.

Held, D. (1980). *Introduction to critical theory: Horkheimer to Habermas.* Berkeley: University of California Press.

Isenhart, M. W. (1980). An investigation of the relationship of sex and sex role to the ability to decode nonverbal cues. *Human Communication Research, 6,* 309–18.

Johnson, F. L., & Fine, M. G. (1985). Sex differences in uses and perceptions of obscenity. *Women's Studies in Communication, 8,* 11–24.

Johnson, R. C. (1980). Blacks and women: Naming American hostages released in Iran. *Journal of Communication, 30,* 58–63.

Kimball, G. (Ed.). (1981). *Women's culture: The women's renaissance of the seventies.* Metuchen, NJ: Scarecrow.

Kramarae, C. (1981). *Women and men speaking: Frameworks for analysis.* Rowley, MA.: Newbury.

Kuhn, T. S. (1970). *The structure of scientific revolution* (2nd ed.). Chicago: University of Chicago Press.

Lippard, L. (1976). *From the center: Feminist essays on women's art.* New York: E. P. Dutton.

Montgomery, C. L., & Burgoon, M. (1980). The effects of androgyny and message expectations on resistance to persuasive communication. *Communication Monographs, 47,* 56–67.

Nielsen, L. L. (1982). Alchemy in academe: Survival strategies for female scholars. In M. L. Spencer, M. Kehoe, & K. Speece (Eds.), *Handbook for women scholars.* San Francisco: Center for Women Scholars, Americas Behavioral Research Corporation.

Pearce, W. B., & Cronen, V. (1980). *Communication, action, and meaning: The creation of social realities.* New York: Praeger.

Pearce, W. B., & Foss, K. A. (1987). The future of interpersonal communication. *ACA Bulletin, 61,* 93–105.

Pearce, W. B., & Freeman, S. (1984). On being sufficiently radical in gender research: Some lessons from critical theory, Kang, Milan, and MacIntyre. *Women's Studies in Communication, 7,* 65–68.

Putman, L. L. (1982). In search of gender: A critique of communication and sex-roles research. *Women's Studies in Communication, 5,* 1–9.

Ragan, S. L., & Aarons, V. (1986). Women's response to men's silence: A fictional analysis. *Women's Studies in Communication, 9,* 67–75.

Rakow, L. F. (1986). Rethinking gender research in communication. *Journal of Communication, 36,* 11–26.

Randall, P. (1985). Re-examining the smiles of women. *Women's Studies in Communication, 8,* 1–10.

Raymond, R. (1982). Mary Daly: A decade of academic harassment and feminist survival. In M. L. Spencer, M. Kehoe, & K. Speece (Eds.), *Handbook for women scholars.* San Francisco: Center for Women Scholars, Americas Behavioral Research Corporation.

Roberts, J. L. (1976). Pictures of power and powerlessness: A personal synthesis. In J. L. Roberts (Ed.), *Beyond intellectual sexism: A new woman, a new reality.* New York: David McKay.

Rorty, R. (1979). *Philosophy and the mirror of nature.* Princeton: Princeton University Press.

Schaef, A. W. (1981). *Women's reality: An emerging female system in the white male society.* Minneapolis: Winston.

Scott, R. L., & Klumpp, J. F. (1984). "A dear searcher into comparison": The rhetoric of Ellen Goodman. *Quarterly Journal of Speech, 70,* 69–79.

Shedletsky, L. J. (1982). The relationship between sex differences in cerebral organization and nonverbal behavior. *Women's Studies in Communication, 5,* 10–15.

Solomon, M. (1979). The positive woman's journey: A mythic analysis of the rhetoric of STOP ERA. *Quarterly Journal of Speech, 65,* 262–74.

Spender, D. (1980). *Man made language.* Boston: Routledge & Kegan Paul.

Spender, D. (1982). *Invisible woman: The schooling scandal.* London: Writers and Readers Publishing.

Spretnak, C. (1986). Female thinking. *ReVision, 9,* 37–39.

Thorne, B., Kramarae, C., Henley, N. (1983). Language, gender and society: Opening a second decade of research. In B. Thorne, C. Kramarae, & N. Henley (Eds.), *Language, gender and society.* Rowley, MA.: Newbury.

Treichler, P. A., Kramarae, C., & Stafford, B. (1985). Section 3: On boundaries. In P. A. Treichler, C. Kramarae, & B. Stafford (Eds.), *For alma mater: Theory and practice in feminist sholarship.* Urbana, IL: University of Illinois Press.

Warfel, K. A. (1984). Gender schemas and perceptions of speech style. *Communication Monographs, 51,* 253–67.

II

Theoretics of Feminism and Communication Studies

4

Challenging the Patriarchal Vision of Social Science: Lessons from a Family Therapy Model

SHEILA McNAMEE
Department of Communication
University of New Hampshire

This essay addresses the idea that there are "appropriate" methods for examining human interaction and highlights an alternative way to merge a feminist perspective within the domain of social scientific research. My argument has been addressed by other noted feminist scholars such as Harding (1986), Belenky, Clinchy, Goldberger, and Tarule (1986), Treichler and Wartella (1986), Mies (1983), Du Bois (1983), and Stanley and Wise (1983) who question the goals of what Haraway (1981; 1985) and others have critiqued as "androcentric science." In feminist theory and research, attention is focused on the question: What constitutes "science"? The debate, itself, is certainly not new. The questions representing both sides of the argument point to the research dichotomy of "natural" versus "human" sciences. Should science be built upon the assumptions of objectivity, generalizability, and control? Or should science embrace alternative assumptions such as subjectivity (or the awareness that there is no one Truth but a constructed view of truth), plurality, and intervention? The latter premises are attempts to avoid polarization by focusing on how difference constructs a relationship (Bateson, 1972, pp. 271–2).

In this chapter, I introduce a model of family therapy and translate this model into a method for conducting social scientific research. My purpose in making this translation/connection is based upon my assumption that social science, as an area of inquiry like therapy, has understanding and improving the human condition as its goal. What we can learn from a clinical context that emphasizes the varied difficulties people have adapting to and interacting in the world is more than anecdotal. What we can learn from this context can inform our research in a productive and creative manner.

In addition, the clinical model I describe—the Milan model of systemic family therapy (Selvini-Palazzoli, Boscolo, Cecchin, & Prata, 1978, 1980; Tomm, 1984a, 1984b; Campbell & Draper, 1985; Boscolo, Cecchin, Hoffman & Penn, 1987)—is epistemologically consistent with feminist theory. Both the Milan model and feminist theory encourage us, as researchers, to break from our tendencies to polarize what we study and how we study it.

For example, the therapeutic context and the research context are traditionally seen as different. A clinician's interviews with clients are rarely (if ever) considered as "research" *per se.* Many social scientists believe that there is not enough "rigor" or "control" in a clinical setting to allow for an "objective," "generalizable" view of the social order. Conversely, research is rarely considered therapeutic. Even policy research which is conducted for the primary purpose of setting social agendas (and thus, is interventive), is constructed in accordance with the criteria of objectivity, control, and generalizability.

One of the key distinctions between therapy and research is that therapy is often focused on *facilitating* change while research is concerned with *accounting* for change. For example, communication researchers are often interested in determining how a change in communicative style or strategy will influence interpersonal competence, media impact, and so on. Therapists, on the other hand, are in the business of helping people change undesirable patterns.

However, a clinician must have an understanding or a way of accounting for expected changes before he or she can facilitate change. A clinician has a theory which guides his or her observations and the subsequent interventions he or she makes. A researcher, on the other hand, has a method or technique, in the form of a research design and research instruments that ultimately facilitate change (e.g., the construction of manipulated conditions designed to produce various differences in the phenomena under investigation). The position of accounting for change in the therapeutic context and the position of facilitating change in the research context remain unexamined aspects of each respective domain. Just as a clinician is less aware of the ways in which he or she *accounts* for change in a system, the researcher tends to be blinded to the ways in which his or her work can fulfill a goal of *facilitating* change.

Blurring the distinction between research and therapy provides a way of meeting the interventive goal of feminist theory (Treichler & Wartella, 1986). By "interventive," Treichler and Wartella refer to the ways in which two (or more) disciplines can inform each other such that they have some effect on one another. Treichler and Wartella are specifically interested in the connection between feminist theory and communication studies. They see this connecton as an "intervention." In therapeutic literature and practice, intervention is standard terminology used to describe the behavior of the clinician. That is, clinicians are trained to intervene in (to come between) their clients' dysfunctional behavioral routines or cognitive constructions and their clients' desires to function effectively in the world. The Milan systemic model of family therapy developed by Selvini-Palazzoli and her colleagues (1978, 1980) is introduced here in an effort to underscore intervention in communication and feminist research.

WHY A CLINICAL MODEL FOR RESEARCH?

I have suggested, above, why clinical and research models should be seen as mutually informative. Specifically, my use of a clinical model in a social scientific research context stems from three lines of argument: (a) there are epistemological consistencies between feminist theory and the theory of systemic family therapy; (b) the act of employing a clinical model as a research model emphasizes the arbitrary distincton between social control and social intervention; and (c) family is a "natural" context. While different cultures and subcultures hold different definitions of "family" experience, the metaphor of family is commonplace and is one used to orient a great deal of thinking about gender, politics, and economics.

I do not offer the systemic family therapy model as the "best" model because it is precisely this kind of polarization that feminism attempts to avoid. But I do believe that a model based on the study of the socially contructed notion of "family"—adopted to study communication—offers *one* alternative to the positivistic, lineal models of science so heavily criticized by feminists (see, Harding, 1986; Stanley & Wise, 1983; Mies, 1983). A therapy model that emphasizes intervention can serve as a model for conducting social research. In this chapter, I will show how this model reveals the common assumptions and goals of systemic and feminist perspectives.

Taking a therapy model that emphasizes intervention and translating it into a model for conducting social research places intervention at the forefront of research activity. Researchers borrowing from a context which legitimates, celebrates, and emphasizes intervention recognize that research can be social intervention.

In order to understand why a systemic model of family therapy has something to offer feminist scholars, it is necessary to consider the forum in which systemic family therapy arose.

Family therapy has hitherto presented itself as an antipsychoanalytic reaction. The therapists of this persuasion deny the determinism of intrapsychic forces and the transparency of symbols, treating meaningful action as messages flowing through communicative channels. (Maranhao, 1986, p. xi)

It is first important to realize that family therapy, as a movement, shifted attention from individually-oriented to relationally-oriented descriptions of problem behavior. This is a major shift because it requires abandoning, for the most part, explanations of problem behaviors that are based on internal, causal mechanisms. However, even within the family therapy field, there is still great disparity between those models assuming lineal[1] causes of problems among family members (e.g., the husband withdraws *because* his wife is a nagging kind of person) and models which focus on identifying patterns which connect behavior, ideas, and people in a way that is dysfunctional (e.g., the more the husband withdraws, the more his wife nags, which increases his withdrawl which increases her nagging, etc.).

Even within the reactionary movement of family therapy, radical epistemological differences among family therapy models have evolved. Maranhao (1986, p. xi) describes these differences as a distinction between focus on models of the family vs. a focus on "communicative matrices." Specifically, the distinction Maranhao refers to is between simply stating that "family" is the context with which a therapist works (which leaves room for lineal, causal explanations) versus an orientation toward understanding and describing the patterned ways in which the behaviors of one person connect to the behaviors of another in the formation of redundant, interactive sequences.

Hoffman (1985, p. 382) summarizes the major distinction between various family therapy models using Howe's and von Foerster's (1974) distinction between first-order cybernetics (the study of observed systems) and second-order cybernetics (the study of observing systems). Von Foerster's distinction, in particular, is an important one because the distinction underscores the respective positions vis á vis the assumption of objectivity. Those who adopt what Maranhao calls a focus on models of the family assume that the family can be observed and the therapist/observer remains "outside" the system. Those who adopt a focus on communicative matrices assume that their own behaviors co-construct (with the family) the system being studied and thus provide useful information about that system and the interactive patterns that maintain it in a generative or dysfunctional manner.

In first-order cybernetics there is a belief that the observer can remain distant and distinct from the phenomena being observed. Second-order cybernetics, on the other hand, recognizes the recursive relationship between observer and observed. The latter position shares an epistemological orientation with feminism, which I discuss later. The idea of construct-

---

[1] Using the term "lineal" rather than "linear" is purposive and based on Bateson's (1979) observation that "lineal" refers to a sequence of ideas or propositions that does not return to a starting point, while "linear" is a term used in reference to geometry.

ing a system through interaction does not exempt the researcher or theorist from recognizing his/her own social responsibility.

THE MILAN SYSTEMIC MODEL

The Milan model (Selvini-Palazzoli,et al., 1978, 1980), developed in Italy, is based upon Bateson's cybernetic epistemology (1972, p. 309), which has commonly come to be called "systemic" (Keeney, 1983, p. 14). Detailed descriptions of the Milan model have been provided by Tomm (1984a, 1984b) and Campbell and Draper (1985).

In brief, the Milan model accepts the recursivity between meaning and action and focuses on patterns that connect ideas, behaviors, events, and people, which distinguish it from other clinical models where analytic focus is placed on the individual and/or family and a logic of lineal causality. Consistent with the pluralistic nature of feminist theory (Spender, 1980, p. 103) and systemic epistemology, the Milan associates developed what they call "guiding principles" for a clinician using their model. The term "guiding principles" carries markedly different implications than the strict "technique-orientation" of some more traditional clinical models.

Most schools of therapy identify specific techniques designed to flow logically from the model's foundational premises. The clearest example of this is Minuchin's structural family therapy model (1974). Minuchin's model is based on several assumptions. One assumption states that altering a person's position in a system alters his or her experience which alters the way he or she thinks. In practice, a structural family therapist might physically orchestrate the position of family members during a therapy session. The clinician may do this by moving people (e.g., a child sitting between feuding parents may be directed to sit elsewhere while the parents are directed to move their chairs closer to one another), by directing who will talk to whom (e.g., "Tell you wife, not me, how you interpreted her question."), and indicating who can speak for whom (e.g., "I do not want to know what *you* think about your brother's stealing, I want to know what *he* thinks.").

In contrast to Minuchin's model, the Milan model simply suggests orienting principles and makes no statement about what a clinician should or should not do, specifically. The guiding principles suggested by the Milan team are hypothesizing, circularity, and neutrality. Each of these principles guides the analysis of and intervention into a social system.

Hypothesizing

Hypotheses address the function of behaviors, ideas, and interactions rather than treating information as fact or truth. Importantly, hypotheses are not devised independently of the specific interaction they are attempting to explain. Hypotheses typically focus on behavioral sequences and any known interpretations and/or evaluations of these sequences made by those who are part of the system. "The therapist must provide reasons for behaviours that contrast with explicative schemas and the intentionality assumed by members of the family system, and yet that are as plausible to them as their own" (Ugazio, 1985, p. 26). A systemic hypothesis allows for the possibility of change while avoiding the risk of the therapist's idea being rejected by the family. The practice of hypothesizing suggests that a variety of competing explanations for a "symptom" may be useful. They serve as frames through which the therapist can direct questions and connect data to produce information.

To clarify this principle, suppose that a therapist is presented with the following information about a family she is about to interview for the first time. Charles and Linda are a young couple with a teenaged son, John. John is having problems in school. His teacher has informed Charles and Linda that John has difficulty completing his assignments, although he appears to be very bright as well as very conscientious about working on the assignments. Charles has a difficult time understanding John's problem because of his own reputation as an efficient, organized, and very prompt person. Linda feels that John is like her. He has difficulty completing his school work because he wants to do his best and impress his teacher, his parents, and his peers. It is this pressure to perform, she thinks, that keeps John from finishing any project. Because Linda also struggles with this problem, she is sympathetic toward John's situation. Thus far, neither Charles nor Linda have been able to help John change his work style and they are concerned that this problem, if unattended, will present larger obstacles for him in the future.

Several systemic hypotheses can be constructed about this family. The following two are only suggestions.

> By being so different from the rest of his family, Charles is able to help both John, his son, and Linda, his wife, see that there is a different way to approach work. Simultaneously, Linda and John help Charles by providing yet another context in which he can be seen as efficient and organized. This helps John and Linda recognized the importance and benefits of their work style.

Or,

> Charles and Linda help John take his school work seriously by showing concern with his performance. John, in turn, helps his parents feel like they are "good parents" by presenting them with a problem to work on.

The Milan team suggests the development and use of several alternative hypotheses. In this way, a clinician can remain systemic and contextually sensitive in his or her thinking about the system rather than adopting and thereby reifying only one way to punctuate the system. A clinician can only construct alternative punctuations of a system (i.e., alternative ways to sequence and label the system as illustrated in the two hypotheses above) if a view of "pragmatic truth" as opposed to classical truth (Tomm, 1984a) is adopted.

Pragmatic truth refers to the clinician's acceptance that the "story," logic, or explanation offered by family members at a given time is more useful than other stories and thus the story becomes "true." The story serves a pragmatic function. It helps members orient and make sense out of their own behaviors, as well as the behaviors of others. Pragmatic truth refers to the *selections* people make based on the distinctions they draw (i.e., the stories they construct).

Classical truth, on the other hand, refers to the idea that there is (or could be) one correct story, logic, explanation for any particular behavior. The distinction between pragmatic and classical truth is subtle yet significant. With an idea of pragmatic truth, clinicians and researchers develop a sense of respect and awe for the unique ways in which people conduct their lives. Classical truth imposes a lineal, judgmental, monolithic sense of superiority and discrimination. The clinical effect of classical truth can be seen when a clinician believes his or her hypothesis. It is very difficult, if not impossible, to construct alternative hypotheses that provoke useful interventions/connections because the clinician is trying too forcefully to impose his or her view of what is right or wrong on the system.

Circularity

As a guiding principle, circularity is based on Bateson's logic of coherence where a difference can be a combinatory relationship (Bateson, 1972, pp. 271–2). At the methodological level, the Milan team develop circularity as a technique for interviewing clients. "Circular questioning" or "circular interviewing," asks questions that address a difference or define a relationship as opposed to questions of facts and feelings that require a judgment of difference by (digital) distinction.

The most common form of circular question focuses on differences in time, or differences between ideas, people, or events. Using the two systemic hypotheses about Charles, Linda, and John, different circular questions can be developed. A clinician using the first hypothesis might be interested in asking the following circular questions:

Who believes most strongly that Charles is really different from the rest of the family?

Was Charles more or less efficient before John started having difficulties with his school work?

If Charles were to stop acting in such an organized and efficient manner, who would take his place, Linda or John?

If John were to stop having difficulties in school, what other problems might he have?

Or, for the second hypothesis:

Who, between Charles and Linda, shows more concern for John's problem?

When do you think John will be able to take his school work seriously without procrastinating so much? (to parents)

Do you think that John would be more or less likely to have problems with school if you were more concerned? ... less concerned? (to parents)

If John were not having school problems, how would you show him that you are concerned and good parents?

Both sets of circular questions illustrate the principle of circularity. By asking John's parents about his behavior, a systemic clinician can potentially gain more useful information because John's parents have less interest in persuading the clinician to adopt John's story about or explanation of his problem. Also, Linda's and Charles' answers to the therapist's questions about what John thinks, for example, provide new information to John about how his parents see him as well as themselves.

Circular questions such as these depart from the stories or logic (i.e., explanations) that family members exchange daily. They provide an opening for new information which often is not radically different from what the family members already believe. A well thought-out circular question is provocative in a subtle way. To design useful circular questions, it is important to devise systemic hypotheses that are circular (as opposed to lineal and causal) in their orientation. Circularity avoids a blameful approach as illustrated in the questions above where *each* family member is seen as contributing in benevolent ways to the creation of a pattern.

As an example from a nontherapeutic context, let's suppose a researcher is studying perceptions of women managers in small businesses. Rather than asking the manager, Ann, how she gets along with those working for her, a systemic interviewer will gather more useful information by asking a third person, Susan, how Ann gets along with her employees (e.g., "Susan, would you describe Ann's relationship with her employees as more formal or informal?"). Susan might be another manager from a different department in the business or some other close observer. The interviewer might also ask Susan if Ann and her colleagues get along better now than they did before some specific event such as the reorganization of management.

Circular questioning can avoid the generation of stereotypic information that is based, for instance, in depictions of "ideal" managers. Ann, for example, has much invested in commenting on her relationship with those working for her. She is more likely than Susan to present the interviewer with her "preferred" picture. This preferred picture may be Ann's intended consequent of her behavior yet tells nothing of how her behavior is perceived by others. That is, Ann's self-report provides little information regarding the *systemic* implications of her behavior.

Although asking one of Ann's employees, Elinor, the same questions asked of Susan might yield a different interpretation, the process would produce much the same result because Elinor, too, has a vested interest in convincing the interviewer (as well as her colleagues) to see the situation or relationship as she does. Thus, using the technique of circular questioning to interview a third person involved in the system might provide information that makes a difference in the system and is, therefore, useful. In a circular fashion, asking all members the same kind of questions highlights the potential of different ways to label or punctuate the situation.

Circular questioning allows the interviewer (whether therapist or researcher) to gather information about the various ways in which people interpret the behaviors and ideas of each other within particular contexts. By answering circular questions in the context of the entire system being analyzed, involved members come to see how their own actions are interpreted by others. This is often called "gossiping in the presence" by the Milan team (Tomm, 1984b, p. 260). The technique of circular questioning often illuminates a "difference that makes a difference" (Bateson, 1972, p. 271–272) to the overall performance of persons within a system.

The divergencies of interpretations become interesting information as opposed to a traditional researcher's or clinician's interest in discovering one logical explanation. In this way, the observer and the observed have available a new set of connections/relationships. The data gathered through this questioning method is transformed into information about connections between people, ideas, relationships, and time—and thus, into additional hypotheses about patterns. The beauty of this technique is that it reminds clinicians that all punctuations are equally logical within the frames of reference that different people use. The Milan clinician is more likely to remember that his or her own punctuation or interpretation of a situation is simply one more—not the "right" one.[2] Hypothesizing and asking circular questions encourage the clinician to remain flexible; neutrality encourages him or her to remain curious.

Neutrality

Neutrality is described as "the ability to escape alliances with family members, to avoid moral judgements, to resist all linear traps and entanglements" (Hoffman, 1981, p. 303). To remain in a neutral position vis-á-vis the system does not imply inactivity. Instead, a neutral position is a clinician's attempt to remain curious. "Curiosity leads to exploration and invention of alternative views and moves, and different moves and views breed curiosity" (Cecchin, 1987). Everything is accepted at face value but rejected as truth. It should be noted, however, that neutrality is an ideal.

Once a therapist acts, he or she loses any neutral stance because all behavior, in interaction, contributes to the continual formation of power relationships (Foucault, 1980). Neutrality is not used in the traditional, sterile sense that it is used to describe the position of the "objective," distanced researcher or the position of the "clinically detached" psychoanalyst. The Milan team recognize that any act is contrained by and helps to organize the possible patterns of social interaction (Watzlawick, Beavin, & Jackson, 1967). Thus, the best we can do is acknowledge our responsibility in contributing to the construction of ongoing interactive patterns and simultaneously avoid accepting any one position as more correct than another (including our own position). This is neutrality from the Milan systemic model.

Neutrality, in the Milan model, actually means maintaining a stance or a frame of curiosity about the system being studied as well as about the clinician's (or researcher's) own role in constructing and/or intervening in that system. From a position of curiosity, a plurality of perspectives can be entertained. An observer who is not curious stops asking questions because he or she is satisfied with the answers and thus, he or she has (at least temporarily) accepted one explanation as "true." In consequence,

---

[2] It is interesting to note that the Milan method of working involves use of a therapeutic team where one or two therapists actually conduct the interview with the family, and the remainder of the team (approximately 2–5 people) observe from behind a one-way mirror. The format for conducting a Milan systemic interview includes what is called an "intersession" where the clinicians interviewing the clients reunite briefly with the clinicians behind the mirror. During this intersession, all members of the therapeutic team share their hypotheses with one another. At this time, a variety of views of the same system are exposed, reminding the clinicians that their constructed hypotheses of the system (family) are only punctuations—not "truths." Comparing the differences between competing hypotheses continues and mirrors the circular process employed in the clinical interview.

losing curiosity encourages objectivity. If a clinician is not curious, he or she stops asking questions. When there are no more questions to ask, it is because the clinician thinks he or she "knows" what is going on (what is wrong with) the system/family. Asking questions means interacting with the family. When a clinician and family are interacting with a sense of curiosity, the clinician is less likely to look on that family as an understandable "object" because the process of questioning actively involves the clinician in an experience that is "real" and very subjective. Here, again, "subjective" describes the active, co-construction of a logic/explanation.

Among other things, curiosity or neutrality for a researcher means addressing why particular research questions and analyses of data are the selected ones. As long as a researcher or clinician remains curious, he or she does not accept any punctuation or explanation as real, inevitable, or expected. Each act, including his or her own, becomes an opportunity for curiosity. A plurality of perspectives and a recognition of the researcher's own signature help to maintain this systemic principle.

The examples of hypothesizing and circularity presented earlier illustrate the notion of neutrality. The questions asked of family members are attempts to show a keen sense of curiosity about their beliefs and actions. It is difficult to portray here the dynamic nature of this kind of questioning. With each response, further avenues heightening the clinician's curiosity are exposed. Systemic neutrality is based upon the idea of respect for the system. This is the kind of respect that fosters a continual *questioning* of premises underlying the beliefs people hold as opposed to the kind of questioning that *challenges* family members' premises.

In sum, the Milan model focuses on connections in a family's or individual's belief system. In practice, the focus is maintained by employing a circular questioning style to collect data about beliefs concerning relationships between people, events, behaviors, and meanings. Circular questions also add a temporal dimension by accessing individuals' perceptions of sequences of behaviors and potential future states (e.g., "Was Ann a different kind of manager before this research began?" or "If Ann were to stop being understanding, would those working for her be less productive?"). By focusing on relational and temporal connections within and among logics, we have a way to attend to the historical features of those logics without adopting a deterministic, lineal perspective.

The guiding principles of hypothesizing, circularity, and neutrality are rooted in the belief that it is helpful to understand the different reasons/causes given by people involved in the system (including the clinician's own explanations) so that connections or relations may be drawn among explanations. Simply put, a systemic therapist is not trying to find one reason to explain why the system is as it is. He or she tries to connect all of the "personal epistemologies" (Bateson, 1972, pp. 309–37) in a way that is novel, yet somewhat consistent with family members' ideas and thus might facilitate the system in finding its own solution. For example, let's suppose that Ann learns through the systemic interview that Susan defines Ann's relationship with her employees as formal. This may be very different from the description Ann, herself, would give. Hearing this information, whether it is a "true" or "false" description of Ann's *experience*, provides Ann with information about how another (Susan) *sees* her relationships. She may then consciously act in ways that might bring her experience and Susan's observation closer together. Ann will find her own solution.

The notion of pragmatic truth (i.e., ideas that are believed to be true by a person because those ideas work and they allow that person to maintain his/her logic/explanation) provides a context where the questions asked become interventive strategies that imply new punctuations and labels by exposing equally plausible yet competing realities. Intervention strategies provide new connections for all members of the system (including the clinician). The notions of a dynamic system, the absence of a knowing or objective position from which to stand, and the use of circular causality (which also allows for the lineal ways in which individuals *may* punctuate their experiences) are the conceptual tools that distinguish the Milan model from other systems-based models of social interaction.

THE SYSTEMIC MODEL IN THE RESEARCH CONTEXT

In the activity of scholarly research, survey or interview questions serve the same function as a clinician's questions. Questionnaires, observations, and measurements are research tools, just as a therapist's questions are his/her clinical tools. From traditional research perspectives, as well as traditional clinical perspectives, questions and instruments are not seen as necessarily provoking new connections. In general, the most highly esteemed clinical models (e.g., the psychoanalytic model, behavior modification) place heavy emphasis on diagnosis—that is, *accounting* for change or lack of change. It is only after diagnosis that clinicians working with these models move toward directing change. There is a traditional belief that the therapist's tools provide information concerning the state of affairs. Diagnostic tools and research instruments are not typically seen as social interventions, but rather as necessary or useful tools for "discovering."

In systemic epistemology, and in the Milan model specifically, questions themselves are viewed as social interventions. Questions in research and therapy indicate the distinctions drawn by a researcher. Particular theoretical or conceptual orientations facilitate specific kinds of distinctions. For example, a feminist approach, which is oriented to the ideas of subjectivity, plurality of perspective, and intervention will promote "looking for" a variety of orientations to any given interaction. Accepting the ideas of subjectivity, plurality, and intervention means avoiding the imposition of a view that articulates—and then leads to confirmation of—the observation that, for example, women do X and men to Y in particular kinds of interactions. Instead, researchers are likely to adopt a perspective similar to Kramarae's strategies approach (1981), which defines speech as "socially situated action" (p. 118) that demands an understanding of individuals' perceptions of context and intended goals.

The strategies approach avoids categorizing behaviors into types (perhaps masculine and feminine types). Instead, women and men are viewed as acting with particular images of context and with specific intentions. A person's conceptualizations of context and intentions constitute a logic—a way of acting and thinking about acting—that makes sense to him or her. The implication is that while an observer may see many people as using the same type of strategy, each person is actually employing and expressing a different strategy based on his or her unique logic.

Inquiring about these logics is consistent with the feminist goals of subjectivity, plurality, and intervention because they allow understanding of the varied and diverse ways (plurality) in which people come to make sense of their worlds. People do this through their own unique constructions of context, their present interpretations of past experience, and their intentions (subjectivity). The process of asking about these aspects of interaction has the potential to alter (intervene in) a person's logic simply by calling attention to previously unattended to aspects of interaction (e.g., unintentional behavior might become intentional or new punctuations might be introduced).

A systemic epistemology provides the conceptual tools for analyzing the processes of research—tools which focus on the social, political, and ethical ramifications of interpretations of data as well as the social, political, and ethical ramifications of conducting research. To recognize the researcher's activity in terms of the interventions provoked in social systems is to take on the role of social responsibility and recognize the researcher's inevitable self-reference, autonomy, and immersion in the system he or she hopes to understand.

Adopting the systemic epistemology in the study of communication changes the research focus in two ways: (a) it keeps researchers from examining concepts in a reified manner (e.g., starting from a view of women's speech as different from men's speech and thus seeking out those differences, consequently *making* these differences real), and (b) it continually reminds researchers that they are not exempt from intervening in the process of conducting research. These changes demand an examination of the content of study and the processes which inform research.

TOWARD A FEMINIST/SYSTEMIC EPISTEMOLOGY

Oakley (1981), Frye (1985), and Spender (1985) are feminist theorists who have addressed the issue of alternative methodologies for social science. The Milan systemic model offers alternatives to traditional research methods—a model where the dichotomy between observer and observed is rejected. This model shares three central issues with feminist theory: (a) subjectivity, (b) plurality of perspective, and (c) a focus on intervention.

Subjectivity

The idea of subjectivity is distinguishable from, and simultaneously in relation to, the positivistic idea of an objective science. With objectivity comes the idea of truth-conditional or criterion-indexed approaches and/or observations, a belief in the lineality of events, and the notion that the researcher is separate from the process of researching.

On the other hand, feminist theory celebrates subjectivity but not at the expense of objectivity.

> Feminist science-making ... reject[s] the dichotomies between science and the maker of science, between observation and experience; we reject the idea that the task of science is to examine a given, fixed reality of which we are observers, not participants. The challenge for feminist science will be to see, name, describe, and explain without recreating these dichotomies ... (Du Bois, 1983, p. 112)

Du Bois goes on the describe her self-doubt about her ability to be "objective," honest, unbiased, unmanipulative in designing, reporting, and interpreting her research (p. 113). She is not interested in tossing the *idea* of objectivity aside. "Our doubts and uncertainties are not only natural, they are even desirable. They keep us honest ... by obliging us continually to question our purposes, our motives, our values, our integrity, our scholarship" (p. 113). These uncertainties hold "the beginnings of the *synthesis* of subjectivity and objectivity that is the source of intellectual power and responsibility—and truth" (p. 113).

An understanding of Bateson's work, upon which the systemic model of family therapy is developed, also involves recognizing that subjectivity cannot be discussed devoid of objectivity, that circular causality can only be conceptualized in counter-relation to lineal causality, and that evolutionary change can only be seen in light of the idea of homeostasis or stability. The centrality of Bateson's idea that understanding is the process of seeing difference (1972, p. 271–1) entails an active acknowledgement of the particular distinctions drawn by individuals. Such distinctions are evaluated by a criterion of ethics (Keeney, 1983, p. 80) in human practice as opposed to a criterion of objective truth.

Traditional, positivistic models of science assume that a theory pictures the world as causally connected. If a theoretical proposition does not reflect the "real" world as assumed, it is meaningless. The criterion for evaluation of any theory is clear correspondence of concept and measure through observation (i.e., operationalized phenomena).

In discussing Bateson's systemic epistemology (1972; 1979), Keeney suggests a move beyond the objectivity/subjectivity distinction to the alternative he calls "ethics."

> From an ethical perspective we do not ask whether we are 'objective' or 'subjective.' Instead, we recognize the necessary connection of the observer with the observed, which leads to examining how the observer participates in the observed. (Keeney, 1983, p. 80)

As a criterion for science, ethics emphasizes responsibility and acknowledges intervention of the researcher/observer.

Because feminist scholarship emphasizes the personal aspect of theorizing (Frye, 1985; Harding, 1986, p. 23), the observer (the theorist, the researcher) is included in the process of observing. Most often, this perspective has been labeled "soft science" because its methods involve interviews, personal histories, and the like. Yet, one striking observation is that many feminist scholars are not "bothered" by the apparent lack of "objectivity" inherent in these methods.

For example, Mies (1983) proposes a methodology for feminist research which is designed to erradicate what she calls the schizophrenic situation women scholars are driven to if we depend upon positivistic social science.

> Women scholars have been told to look at their contradictory existence, i.e., at their subjective being as women as an obstacle and a handicap to 'pure' and 'objective' research. Even while studying women's questions they were advised to suppress their emotions, their subjective feelings of involvement and identification with other women in order to produce 'objective' data. (p. 120)

Mies introduces a methodology which purposively encompasses women scholars' experiences of sexist oppression. She articulates several methodological guidelines which, together, present a different orientation toward the issue of science as "objective." That is, we see little polarization and more of a "double consciousness" (p. 120). For example, Mies suggests that researchers accept, consciously, their partiality. She also suggests that the hierarchical relationship between researcher and researched be avoided. The double consciousness that Mies refers to implies an alternative view where dichotomies (such as subjective-objective) are rejected and all positions or perspectives become possible.

Bateson introduces a similar idea, that of "binocular vision" (1979, p. 147). If we have binocular vision, we recognize descriptions from each side of a relationship, both the researcher's description and the subject's description. In research on gender and communication, then, the conclusions which indicate, for example, that women's linguistic styles are evaluated less favorably than men's linguistic styles, tell as much about the personal epistemology of the researcher as it does about the objects of study. Epistemology (personal or collective) provides a frame for a researcher and that frame is the process of seeing difference (Bateson, 1972, p. 315) because epistemology distinguishes foreground from background. That is, the epistemological orientation that a researcher adopts is going to place some assumptions and beliefs in the forefront of all research activity and retire other views to the background. However, the researcher who accepts the idea of subjectivity as foreground is more likely to accept responsibility for the construction of discoveries (i.e., research results) through his or her use of theory. When the researcher also accepts the notion of plurality, he or she can abandon the idea that all researchers should share the same theoretical orientation.

Plurality of Perspective

Spender says, "The concept of multidimensional reality is necessary for it allows sufficient flexibility to accommodate the concept of equality" (1980, p. 103). Pluralism, as a theoretical criterion, suggests that multiple logics for making sense of the world are equally viable. This is not a relativist position. Instead, it accepts the validity of multiple realities and multiple ways of generating an answer. "Right and wrong are the foundation stones of hierarchical meanings and such dichotomies are not at all useful for feminism which is trying to structure nonhierarchical social organizations" (Spender, 1980, p. 104). The nonhierarchical plurality of feminist scholarship emphasizes drawing connections and seeing patterns. It avoids taking a perspective that unfairly values one method or perspective over another. As Spender says, the feminist perspective

requires us minimally to acknowledge that there is more than one reference system and that every reference system from political parties to personal friendships seems to have within it not only the means of legitimating itself but of discounting alternatives. (Spender, 1985, p. 308)

What we need is a methodology that allows us to tolerate and recognize different reference systems. The idea of plurality can guide us in this pursuit.

Many noted feminist theorists including Kelly (1984) and Spender (1985) describe feminist scholarship within a paradigm of "dual vision" which is consistent with the idea of plurality. In her definitional essay, "On Feminism and Propaganda," Spender discusses the problem of research as propaganda. She acknowledges that any scholar, in taking a position, insists on his/her "own impartiality while pointing to the partiality of others" (1985, p. 308). Similarly, Kelly (1984, p. 52) describes feminist thought and scholarship as consisting of a "unified 'doubled' view of the social order." Feminist and systemic theories attempt to construct methods that help us recognize our own partiality and maintain a unified double view of the world.

These theorists, like Bateson, attempt to chart a way of thinking that is dialectic, but not polemic. The goal is not to take the opposing position and present it as the "correct" perspective.

From my perspective ... it is just as misguided to accept either assertion [that patriarchy is compensatory or that it is natural] as the whole truth, as more than a partial view. As long as patriarchy begins with the premise that the male is the positive norm, and feminism begins with the premise that the female is the positive norm, then the war of propaganda simply continues to be waged. (Spender, 1985, p. 310)

The goal then becomes one of double vision.

If all frames of reference including our own are closed systems containing within themselves the means for their own legitimation and for the outlawing of the systems of others, then our minimal commitment should be to understand frames of reference. (Spender, 1985, p. 310)

Understanding frames of reference requires focusing on things in relation—whether those "things" be organizations, groups, people, ideas, acts, objects, or situations. Seeing "in relation" requires "both separation and full social participation" (Kelly, 1984, p. 56). It also requires avoiding an either/or frame because in order to build a relationship, both poles of a dichotomy must be considered. We have a clearer image of what "power" means to a person when we have a sense of that person's meaning for "impotence." Focus should be on the "more fascinating and comprehensive question, 'how do we converge different perspectives, whether they be fact and fiction, formal understanding and practical action or problem and cure?'" (Keeney, 1983, p. 3). Double description is one way to address this question. Double description juxtaposes descriptions from each side of the relationship to generate a sense of the relationship as a whole. The acceptance of the researcher's subjectivity and the awareness of multiple points of view help the feminist researcher to see research as interventive.

Intervention

The third issue central to this debate is the *celebration* of the idea of research as interventive. As discussed earlier, Treichler and Wartella (1986, p. 2) refer to the generative ways in which feminist theory and communication studies inform each other as "interventions." In a similar manner, research, theorizing, and everyday interaction are interventions to each other. The results of research influence and change people's lives and the problems and occurences of people's lives change and establish research agendas. The concept "intervention" is one not commonly used in traditional social science. The well-known studies of Rosenthal and Rosnow (1969) illustrated long ago that there are a variety of ways in which a researcher can have an effect on the data collected during scientific investigation. Yet the traditional interpretation of Rosenthal's and Rosnow's work has directed researchers to remain aware of the ways in which they must "control" the research environment so as to minimize demand characteristics. Commonly the attempt is to control intervention rather than accept it as a normal part of the scientific endeavor.

Intervention becomes the cornerstone for integrating a feminist epistemology with systemic epistemology. The particular translation of systemic epistemology that has emerged in the field of family therapy provides a useful model for alternative methods for social scientific research, particularly research in the area of communication studies.

IMPLICATIONS OF A FEMINIST/SYSTEMIC EPISTEMOLOGY

Feminist theory has much to offer social science. Treichler, Kramarae, and Stafford (1985), Belenky et al. (1986), and Harding (1986) are a few among many feminist writers who have illustrated that an alternative vision of science can offer a rich understanding of social processes. Yet, there has been little in the way of precise suggestions for action in implementing such an alternative view into traditional models. There are two reasons for the existence of this void, each of which will direct a researcher differently. The first is that the current paradigm shift (Kuhn, 1970) has not yet reached the stage where alternative methods have been constructed to coincide with the new paradigm. If Kuhn is accurate, then it can be assumed that such developments are "on the brink" and, consequently, scholarly activities should be devoted to filling this void.

Second, researchers and theorists may be accepting the leftover assumptions of positivistic science—the search for a unifying or "truth-giving" method—as they try to develop alternative paradigms. A feminist/systemic epistemology, using new questions, provides a different orientation to the study of social phenomena. Traditional perspectives ask how a researcher can discover the cause of certain phenomena. The alternative questions, asked from a feminist/systemic perspective, concern how a researcher can inquire about and make observations of phenomena that provoke new information and/or serve as useful social interventions into both the system being studied and the research's own system. In addition, instead of seeking one methodology, the feminist/systemic researcher acknowledges that data can still be collected in a wide variety of forms and they can be analyzed within a broad spectrum of techniques (e.g., empirical or interpretative). It is in the spirit of this second explanation that the systemic family therapy model developed by Selvini-Palazzoli and her colleagues is introduced. The intention is to offer a model that is useful in the study of social interaction. The model is not designed to become a "technique" but rather a way of thinking. The basic premise concerns the vision of communication research if thinking takes the form of a feminist/systemic epistemology.

In addition, this model accepts the interventional nature of observing and questioning. Once the myth of "objectivity" is removed, empirical interaction is all that remains. By seeing the research process as objective, researchers have mystified the normal, human interaction that occurs when, for example, a researcher gives a person a questionnaire. Embracing subjectivity demystifies the research endeavor by allowing the researcher's voice, not only the voice represented by data, to be heard.

The Milan model offers alternatives to traditional research methods, a model where the dichotomy between subject and observer is rejected. It takes as its foundation the same pluralistic stance as feminist theory. Viewing the domain of study (communication) from the systemic orientation of the Milan model means adopting the guiding principles in conducting research. In doing this, the researcher's active role as "social interventionist" is clarified. Recognizing how researcher and researched co-construct theories and research results inevitably must remind a researcher of his or her responsibility. Maintaining a stance of responsibility enhances the ability to see "truth" from a new frame; that is, as a construction arising out of the distinctions drawn. Those distinctions are influenced or brought about in interaction, whether that interaction be the focus of study or the process of studying (i.e., the interaction between the researcher and the researched).

In particular, Cecchin (1987) suggests that hypothesizing helps to maintain a stance of curiosity. He claims that when hypothesizing is thought of as "storytelling" an observer is more likely to generate hypotheses within a systemic epistemology. This is because when explanations are seen as stories, we are less likely, as social scientists, to treat them as "truth." It is easy to recognize that families come to the therapeutic context with tightly written scripts. The problem is that their scripts do not help them act as the family or individuals they would like to be. Clinicians offer new scripts which help families adjust their own stories. Recursively, the rewritten story of the family helps the clinician rewrite his or her own story and so on.

This process highlights the social construction of the therapeutic context. In the research context, the researcher is the only participant typically credited with constructed hypotheses. It is time to consider the elaborate stories (hypotheses) of subjects and the ways in which these hypotheses "fit" with the researcher's.

Hypotheses help to connect the stories of those being studied with the researcher's stories. Connection allows for seeing how the system maintains the pattern being examined. In these hypotheses the positive, logical contributions made by each member of the system can be recognized. This is a circular way to view the pattern. In framing these behaviors as benevolent and connected to others, researchers intervene by (a) acting in different ways towards that system (e.g., systems that may look "bad" to a psychoanalyst are seen as victims of *patterns* instead of victims to other people); and (b) by provoking the participants as well as themselves to see new connections (through circular questions), thereby changing dysfunctional patterns.

As a guiding principle, circularity implies not only the need to develop hypotheses about *connections* but, at a more pragmatic level, suggests new ways to ask questions in research. Instead of gathering lineal beliefs about the phenomenon (e.g., what "causes" what), questions of difference can be addressed. Circular questions may serve as useful interventions in that they have the potential to introduce information into the system in a new and provocative manner (i.e., in a way that connects past behavior to present behavior, one person to another, observation to experience, etc.)

Neutrality implies accepting nothing as "truth"; that an observer remain "curious." Recognizing the researcher's interventive role acknowledges the pragmatic truths and multiple constructions of a situation or variable.

Neutrality, as an idea, highlights the attempt to simply connect various forms of information as opposed to using them as competing alternatives (implying that one is correct).

SUMMARY

This overview should provide some cursory indication of how the Milan systemic model can help us meet the goals of a feminist/systemic epistemology in research. Data is accepted in its "traditional" form but also connected to the act of researching itself. Any given study is seen as a possible intervention in that the researchers, in conducting a circular interview, become aware of how they potentially provide new connections for subjects just as subjects provide new theoretical connections for researchers. Finally, results are not interpreted as "facts" but as alternative punctuations of patterns of interaction which may or may not facilitate change. Research, from this perspective, is more than a way of accounting for change or accounting for phenomena.

The systemic ideas of hypothesizing, circularity, and neutrality can serve as useful guides for researchers as well as clinicians. Employing these principles in research on communication does not mean abandoning experimental methods or statistical analyses. Rather, it means continuing an awareness of the researcher's role in *choosing* the methods and analytical techniques used. This awareness drastically alters the interpretations of social scientific work. Research becomes an alternative punctuation.

Seeing theoretical models and research methods as partial and open to correction, rather than complete and closed to correction, is an epistemological tool enabling generation and distinction of different orders of pattern (Keeney, 1983, p. 33). The goal of systemic therapy is to facilitate change in dysfunctional family systems. By asking questions about various observed or perceived connections between behavior and various influences on behavior, a researcher is able to facilitate a change in the way people (including him- or herself) think about these connections. Drawing a new conceptual distinction might aid in developing behavioral distinctions (that is, acting in different ways). Research serves the same function and, within the domain of communication studies, the use of the Milan systemic ideas helps to celebrate the goals of feminist scholarship and reorient research. This reorientation means rejecting the male tradition of positivistic science which necessarily includes a frame of objectivity where the male norm becomes the observer's unquestioned perspective (cf. MacKinnon, 1982; Harding, 1986).

It is syntactically and semantically correct to say that subjective statements are made by subjects. Thus, correspondingly, we may say that objective statements are made by objects. It is only too bad that these damned things don't make any statements. (von Foerster, 1976, p. 16)

REFERENCES

Bateson, G. (1972). *Steps to an ecology of mind.* New York: Ballentine.

Bateson, G. (1979). *Mind and nature: A necessary unity.* New York: Bantam Books.

Belenky, M. F., Clinchy, B. M., Goldberger, N. R., & Tarule, J. M. (1986). *Women's ways of knowing.* New York: Basic Books.

Boscolo, L., Cecchin, G., Hoffman, L., & Penn, P. (1987). *Milan systemic therapy.* New York: Harper and Row.

Campbell, D., & Draper, R. (Eds.). (1985). *Applications of systemic family therapy: The Milan approach.* London: Grune and Stratton.

Cecchin, G. (1987). Hypothesizing, circularity, and neutrality revisited: An invitation to curiosity. *Family Process, 26,* 405–414.

Du Bois, B. (1983). Passionate scholarship: Notes on values, knowing and method in feminist social science. In G. Bowles & R. D. Klein (Eds.), *Theories of women's studies* (pp. 105–116). Boston: Routledge and Kegan Paul.

Foucault, M. (1980). *Power-knowledge: Selected interviews and other writings, 1972–1977.* C. Gordon (Ed.), (C. Gordon, L. Marshall, J. Mephan, and K. Soper, Trans.). New York: Pantheon.

Frye, M. (1985). Arrogance and love. In P. A. Treichler, C. Kramarae, & B. Stafford (Eds.), *For alma mater: Theory and practice in feminist scholarship* (pp. 261–270). Chicago: University of Illinois Press.

Haraway, D. (1981). In the beginning was the word: The genesis of biological theory. *Signs, 6,* 469–481.

Haraway, D. (1985). A manifesto for cyborgs: Science, technology and socialist feminism in the 1980's. *Socialist Review, 80,* 65–108.

Harding, S. (1986). *The science question in feminism.* Ithaca, NY: Cornell University Press.

Hoffman, L. (1981). *Foundations of family therapy.* New York: Basic Books.

Hoffman, L. (1985). Beyond power and control: Toward a "second order" family systems therapy. *Family Systems Medicine, 3,* 381–396.

Howe, R., & von Foerster, H. (1974). Cybernetics at Illinois. *Forum, 6,* 15–17.

Keeney, B. (1983). *Aesthetics of change.* New York: Guilford Press.

Kelly, J. (1984). *Women, history, and theory.* Chicago: University of Chicago Press.

Kramarae, C. (1981). *Women and men speaking.* Rowley, MA: Newbury House.

Kuhn, T. S. (1970). *The structure of scientific revolutions.* Chicago: University of Chicago Press.

MacKinnon, C. (1982). Feminism, Marxism, method, and the state: An adenda for theory. *Signs, 7,* 515–44.

Maranhao, T. (1986). *Therapeutic discourse and Socratic dialogue.* Madison, WI: University of Wisconsin Press.

Mies, M. (1983). Towards a methodology for feminist research. In G. Bowles & R. D. Klein (Eds.), *Theories of women's studies* (pp. 117–139). Boston: Routledge and Kegan Paul.

Minuchin, S. (1974). *Families and family therapy.* Cambridge, MA: Harvard University Press.

Oakley, A. (1981). Interviewing women: A contradiction in terms. In H. Roberts (Ed.), *Doing feminist research.* London: Routledge and Kegan Paul.

Rosenthal, R., & Rosnow, R. L. (Eds.). (1969). *Artifact in behavioral research.* New York: Academic Press.

Selvini-Palazzoli, M., Boscolo, L., Cecchin, G., & Prata, G. (1978). *Paradox and counterparadox.* New York: Jason Aronson.

Selvini-Palazzoli, M., Boscolo, L., Cecchin, G., & Prata, G. (1980). Hypothesizing - circularity - neutrality: Three guidelines for the conductor of the session. *Family Process, 19,* 3–12.

Spender, D. (1980). *Man made language.* London: Routledge and Kegan Paul.

Spender, D. (1985). On feminism and propaganda. In P. A. Treichler, C. Kramarae, & B. Stafford (Eds.), *For alma mater: Theory and practice in feminist scholarship* (pp. 307–315). Chicago: University of Illinois Press.

Stanley, L., & Wise, S. (1983). 'Back to the personal' or: Our attempt to construct 'feminist research.' In G. Bowles & R. D. Klein (Eds.), *Theories of women's studies* (pp. 192–209). Boston: Routledge and Kegan Paul.

Tomm, K. (1984a). One perspective on the Milan systemic approach: Part I. Overview of development, theory and practice. *Journal of Marriage and Family Therapy, 10,* 113–125.

Tomm, K. (1984b). One perspective on the Milan systemic approach: Part II. Description of session format, interviewing style and interventions. *Journal of Marriage and Family Therapy, 10,* 253–271.

Treichler, P. A., Kramarae, C., & Stafford, B. (1985). *For alma mater: Theory and practice in feminist scholarship.* Chicago: University of Illinois Press.

Treichler, P. A., & Wartella, E. (1986). Interventions: Feminist theory and communication studies. *Communication, 9,* 1–18.

von Foerster, H. (1976). On where do we go from here? In K. Wilson (Ed.), *The collected works of the biological computer laboratory.* Peoria, IL: Illinois Blueprint Corporation.

Ugazio, V. (1985). Hypothesis making: The Milan approach revisited. In D. Campbell & R. Draper (Eds.), *Applications of systemic family therapy: The Milan approach* (pp. 23–32). New York: Grune and Stratton.

Watzlawick, P., Beavin, J., & Jackson, D. (1967). *Pragmatics of human communication.* New York: Norton.

5

Narrative Gender Differences: Orality and Literacy

MICHAEL PRESNELL
Department of Information and Communication Studies
California State University

Organizing experience into spoken and written narrative is an important process for human beings making sense of the world. Walter Fisher has proposed a narrative paradigm for the understanding of human communication (1984, 1985). He thereby echoes the recommendations of a host of scholars who see the production and interpretation of narrative as a fundamental human ability, in relation to which other dimensions of human experience and behavior are understood and explained (Heidegger, 1949, p. 278; MacIntyre, 1981; Ricoeur, 1976; White, 1981). A number of communication researchers have responded to Fisher's call for the development of a narrative paradigm for communication, most suggesting refinement of the model (Lucaites & Condit, 1985; McGee & Nelson, 1985; Warnick, 1987). I argue that current attempts to refine Fisher's proposed narrative paradigm tend to worsen gender biases at the heart of the paradigm. Specifically, Fisher relies on a model of narrative derived from written forms of communication, even though the paradigm supposedly models oral communication. Fisher's tendency to rely on written communication as a model for oral communication has its origin in the forced difference in literacy of men and women, whereby men have a longer history of participation in written styles of narratives than women, and women have a longer history of oral styles of narratives than men. I examine research on moral decision making as an example of how unexamined differences in narrative styles can influence research in areas that are only tangentially related to the study of narrative.

As in other areas of communication research, it is important that we do not assume that women and men perform and interpret narratives the same way. There is much evidence that women and men speak and write differently. For instance, men and women typically use different inflectional patterns, grammatical forms, adjectives, adverbs, and pronouns (Lakoff, 1975; Spender, 1980; Thorne & Henley, 1975). Less research has been conducted on gender differences in large units of discourse such as narrative form. The oral/literate distinction (Chafe, 1980; Goody, 1977; Havelock, 1982; Olson, 1977; Ong, 1982; Tannen, 1982) can aid in understanding more global gender differences in narrative structure, avoid a widespread bias in favor of men's forms of narrative, and suggest new approaches to understanding women's narratives.

My analysis of Gilligan's (1982) research on gender differences in moral decision making provides an example of how the oral/literate distinction can be employed to analyze gender differences in narrative. The oral/literate distinction helps to avoid gender bias in the narrative paradigm for communication, consequently allowing for a more inclusive treatment of narrative forms within Western culture. The oral/literate distinction provides a framework for understanding one version of gender bias in the practice and analysis of narrative, a bias that has limited the range of discursive expressions that have been understood as narrative.

Sensitivity to gender differences in narrative construction aids communication scholarship in at least three ways. First, an examination of gender differences in narrative reveals fundamental characteristics of narrative which might otherwise escape notice.[1] Second, narrative form may be a "confounding variable" in a variety of research methodologies. The use of narratives, a pervasive feature of communication, is sometimes an explicit part of a methodology, or at a minimum function in the arranging of experimental settings, giving instructions, and accomplishing the analysis. Narrative form may influence data collection, methodological design, and data interpretation in research topics not directly related to the study of narrative. Clarification of gender differences in narrative can provide a better understanding of different narrative styles and their influence on agenda setting for research, the way narrative functions as part of methodologies, and how narrative might influence data interpretation in the study of human communication. Third, broadening our understanding of variances in narrative style is necessary for a comprehensive development of the "narrative paradigm."

---

[1] Noticing features of narrative requires that the researcher's attention is drawn to the feature, either as topically "remarkable" or as significant within the structure of narrative. Robinson (1981) expands the characteristic of "remarkableness" in storytelling. Kalčik (1975) describes the use of "kernal stories" in women's narratives, and subsequently Deemer (1975), Jenkins (1982), and Langellier and Peterson (1984) see broader applications of the notion for narrative theory in general. Edelsky (1981) proposes a distinction between "floor" and "turn-taking" based on an analysis of interuptions in women's conversation.

To articulate a narrative paradigm, the first task might seem to be to narrow the concept of narrative. In fact, recent criticisms of Fisher's narrative paradigm have focused on the supposed need to narrow its formulation to provide more explicit criteria for evaluating narratives (Lucaites & Condit, 1985; Warnick, 1987). Although Fisher wants to provide such evaluative criteria, the narrative paradigm is, by Fisher's own account, ontological and descriptive rather than epistemological. Fisher claims that the narrative paradigm describes a way of being human rather than a method of knowing, and serves as the "master metaphor" that guides the development of specific narrative models (Fisher, 1984, p. 6). I take the development of the narrative paradigm to be the explication of a fundamental human capacity, setting a context for the development of more specific models of narrative performance that provide critical criteria. I examine specific approaches to narrative to make explicit the paradigmatic assumptions behind them, rather than arguing for the adoption of a "new" paradigm. In short, I take "paradigms" to be fundamental operative assumptions that are discovered and understood in terms of their function in guiding theory development rather than paradigms themselves specifying critical criteria for judging discourse. Thus, contrary to both Fisher's critics and Fisher himself, I will elaborate rather than narrow paradigmatic assumptions about narrative by examining existing criteria that have already been used to evaluate narrative. My elaboration of the paradigm serves a purpose similar to the uncovering of implicit ideologies, rather than proposing specific definitions of narrative that ought to be adopted.

NARRATIVE AND LEGITIMATION

The designation "narrative," independent of the existence of any systematic definition, typically legitimizes some kinds of communicative events as worthy of study at the exclusion of others. Like a political ideology, the designation "narrative" gives a discourse greater authority. The label automatically naturalizes the significance of the discourse, that is, makes it seem natural to understand the discourse as significant.

It has been effectively argued that women's communication tends to be ignored because it is not considered narrative (Langellier & Peterson, 1984; Spender, 1980; Stanley, 1979). Researchers also have suggested that the disregard of women's storytelling as a narrative form is partly responsible for the lack of research on women's experience in general (Deemer, 1975; Farrer, 1975; Langellier & Peterson, 1984). In the analysis of discourse, women's talk risks being described as "gossip" or "chit-chat" rather than "storytelling" or "narrative" (Langellier & Peterson, 1984; Spender, 1980). For a discourse to be considered narrative, it must be perceived as providing connections between episodes of communicative expression. The connections between episodes of women's discourse tend to be trivialized, ignored, or invisible to researchers. Any discourse that does not provide readily understood connections between its discursive episodes risks being excluded as part of human history. Commenting on the importance of narrative for traditional conceptions of history, White (1981) observes that:

> To raise the question of the nature of narrative is to invite reflection on the very nature of culture and, possibly, even on the nature of humanity itself. . . . The absence of narrative capacity or refusal of narrative indicates an absence or refusal of meaning. (p. 1)

A discourse described as nonnarrative is a discourse outside of the mainstream of human history, sometimes treated as an expression of dissent, risking the powerlessness of marginality.

Traditionally, history is either narrative or relegated to being "merely" annals, chronicles, lists, notes, fragments, or artifacts. For instance, White (p. 7) points out that a list of events such as a chronicle from the eighth century (Figure 5-1) might not be treated as constituting a historical account of the period since it seems to fail to tell the story of the events, but instead simply lists them in a partially filled out chronological order.

In the apparently nonnarrative list of events in Figure 1, White sees a continuity that can be understood if we have contextual information about how lists might function. We need to know more than that the sequence of events was recorded within the context of a religious world view. We need to know how the religious views of the time were expressed. Unlike our modern secularized sense of time, the dates themselves represent "the year of our Lord" and provide continuity. Seen as a secular chronology, the dates require explicitly stated associated content for the sequence of dates to be perceived as a continuity. Within the context of a medieval Christian temporal structure, the listing of the dates express continuity,

709.	Hard Winter. Duke Gottfried died.
710.	Hard year and deficient in crops.
711.	
712.	Flood everywhere.
713.	
714.	Pippin, Mayor of the Palace, died.
715. 716. 717.	
718.	Charles Devastated the Saxon with great destruction.
719.	
720.	Charles fought against the Saxons.

Figure 1. **Selection From** *Annals of Saint Gall*

while events occur on the backdrop of the Christian teleology that the dates signify. Hardships are understood as part of the story of moral trials serving as both punishment and redemption. Years left blank are filled with the intention of God to allow humanity to move toward its destiny. The cues for understanding the coherency of the "list" is extratextual, in this case theological beliefs contemporaneous with the production of the discourse.

Just as a non-Christian or modern Christian who has adopted a sense of secular time may not make sense of the "list" of events in White's example, the discourse of women may not make sense to men or to women who have accepted patterns of communication traditionally defined as masculine. The discourse may make perfect sense to those who are familiar with the discursive patterns and who do have the relevant contextual knowledge. For instance, Jones (1980) argues that gossip is a style of discourse typical of a woman's speech community and consequently requires an understanding of the roles and attitudes of women for interpretation. According to Jones, the diminution of discourse as "only" gossip rejects as significant a style of communication typical of women, a rejection based on the investigator's failure to understand women's speech culture.

The issue raised here is central to any theory of narrative. Given that some extratextual knowledge is required to interpret any given discourse, at what point is reliance on extratextual knowledge considered a process of constructing narratives *about* pieces of nonnarrative discourse rather than discovering a narrative discourse? In White's example, it might be argued that the narrative White discovers is the product of his reading and not the discovery of the list as a narrative.

Arguments for a completely text-based reading assume that narratives must be textually self-contained, and that reliance on extratextual information threatens a reader's ability to clearly identify a narrative[2] These assumptions block a reader's historical understanding of the mythic (ideological) function of narrative definitions. The notion that the study of narrative must be limited to textual evidence partially derives from a gender bias (one kind of cultural bias) and sets up barriers to a narrative theory appropriate for studying human communication. A reader fails to interpret White's list as a narrative because the reader is an outsider to the discourse in question. As a nonparticipant, it may be impossible for me to have the knowledge or make the inferences necessary to understand a segment of discourse as narrative, while the participants immediately grasp the segment as telling a story. The role that extratextual cues typically play in the interpretation of narrative by participants should be inves-

---

[2] By "text" I mean the spoken or written discourse taken as an object of study, not simply written discourse.

tigated by a look at the discourse as a holistic event, not by beginning with the assumption that a narrative must be maximally self-contained regarding its interpretive cues.

One line of research that provides empirical evidence that the identification of narrative cannot be limited to intratextual significations is research on the distinction between "oral" and "literate" discourse. The oral/literate differentiation has been a valuable tool for cultural anthropologists and linguists such as Cook-Gumperz and Gumperz (1981), Chafe (1980), and Scollon and Scollon (1981). As I will show, it is particularly useful for understanding recent findings of gender differences in narrative production and interpretation.[3]

THE ORAL/LITERATE DISTINCTION

There are clear systematic differences between spoken and written language structures in addition to the differences in expressive medium. Grammatical completeness and deviation from standard syntax, word choice, topical organization, and amount of repetition have been known to differ systematically between spoken and written language. Luria (1976), Vetter (1969), and others describe how these linguistic differences

---

[3] The concepts of literacy and orality do not, of course, *explain* anything themselves. They are names for a cluster of characteristics of discourse, setting an agenda for explanatory models. The low or high dependence of discourse on contextual cues, linear or episodic structure, and abstract or concrete word choice all are empirical characteristics of the literate/oral distinction. These (and other) empirical features which are clustered under the distinction, can provide explanation. The theoretical distinction is meant to group these empirical characteristics by virtue of their origin in the impact of written language on oral discourse, a phenomenon itself too complex to be explained by any single empirical model. The particular features of a discourse that are considered part of its "literacy" or "orality" rather than just a local feature of the language is a matter of how much evidence exists to justify associating the feature with the literate or oral discourse histories of the language. Thus, the distinction literate/oral itself is part of historical or "diachronic" discourse study, while the characteristics it clusters are largely a part of structural or "synchronic" discourse study. The oral/literate distinction is consistent with the traditional tendency to consider historical linguistics "descriptive" and structural linguistics "explanatory," emphasizing the role that description can play in theoretical model building. The oral/literate distinction itself cannot be directly tested or verified, but is more or less useful for guiding specific research and aiding understanding of global discourse features. A fully developed explanatory system of discourse processes would explain the links between the different clustered features rather than simply naming their rough correlations, a task I believe remains to be accomplished by a cognitive approach to communication sensitive to historical as well as logical, inferential, and biological factors. Such a massive undertaking, as far as I know, has not been even approximated, although both the field of semiotics and some versions of cognitive science have suggested this kind of comprehensive theory (Eco, 1976; Pylyshyn, 1986; Sperber & Wilson, 1986).

seem to correlate with cognitive and affective differences. Olson (1977), Goody (1977), Ong (1982), Tannen (1982), and others conclude it is possible to characterize language communities as primarily oral or primarily literate cultures, not on the basis of how much of the population is literate, but by considering the extent to which literate or oral forms of discourse permeate all modes of discourse.

The oral versus literate discourse distinction is not identical with the spoken versus written discourse distinction. Orality and literacy as names for different discursive styles can both be applied to spoken and written discourse. While all cultures have an oral cultural tradition, stemming from a period in the culture's history prior to the development of writing, cultures that have developed writing vary in the impact that writing has had on its discursive forms. Thus, one culture's traditions of spoken communication may be heavily influenced by the experience of writing, while another culture may not evidence a parallel impact. Likewise, written language may retain spoken discourse structures and lexical units. In other words, in cultures that produce even a small amount of written language, there is considerable variance in the degree to which literate *styles* of discourse begin to displace oral styles in *both* written and spoken language.

LITERATE DISCOURSE: LINEARITY, CONTEXT-INDEPENDENCE, ABSTRACTION

Literate discourse is typified in part by the linearity of its topical and thematic structure, along with a relatively complex syntactic structure (for instance, compound sentences and multiple prepositional phrases). The meaning of words and phrases are determined to a high degree by the position they have in the development of the discourse. The elaboration of topics tends to be organized according to logical hierarchies. In performance, the logical hierarchy tends to unfold in a more-or-less invariant linearity, for instance, following a temporal or causal ordering. While oral structures (not just structures spoken but discourse that is structured orally) largely depend on the context of an utterance for determining its meaning, literate structures (not just structures that are written) depend more on explicit discursive propositions that precede and follow an utterance/sentence to supply meaning. Literate discourse internally supplies each segment with a context. Discursive units contributing to topical and thematic development need minimal context outside of the discourse for interpretation. A literate *speaker* needs fewer gestures and artifacts to illustrate her or his points. Thus, literary discourse is an example of Hall's notion of a "low-context" message system (1977).

One advantage of the internal structuring of meaning in discourse is the resulting independence of the discourse from the context of its production. Relatively context-free, literate discourse requires less involvement on the part of interlocutors than does an oral discourse. In speaking or writing, the audience/readership are presented with information instead of being invited to respond. They are given few explicit cues about the producer of the discourse or the relationship between the sender and receiver. The reliance on implicit contextual cues along with explicit intratextual cues gives literate discourse the appearance, at least, of being more "objectively" interpretable. That is, an interpretation justified only by textually locatable cues gives the impression that the interpretation is objectively verified. This impression is only possible, of course, on the background of implicit knowledge about the discursive event, ignoring the associative dimensions of language in favor of the explicit textual cues. Goody (1977) and Goody and Watt (1968) provide some support for the notion that the modern concept of objectivity is historically tied to the development of literacy. They argue that the acquisition of written language fostered analytic thinking, that is, noncontextual thinking based on propositional form rather than concrete or associative reasoning.

A literate structure of discourse, then, can be characterized by these three interrelated tendencies: (a) literate topics are linearly developed and hierarchically ordered, (b) a literate structure relies primarily on intratextual cues as its interpretive context; consequently (c) literate discourse can be abstracted from its original situation of performance and still communicate its topically-relevant propositional meaning.

ORALITY: SITUATIONALITY, EPISODES, HIGH-CONTEXT

Oral discourse structures require a more complex understanding of the situation of the discourse than do literate discourse structures. The structure of oral discourse is partially shaped by the significance of depicted events and speaker-listener relationship rather than primarily the propositional logic internal to the discourse. For instance, a definition of a chicken in an oral culture might include "something to eat," "they wander onto the road and get killed," and "they're usually white and can be seen at a distance." A literate discourse would more consistently organize descriptions according to one or more comparative or classificatory logics, for instance, they are domesticated birds, larger than most wild birds, and one kind of commonly eaten bird.

Oral narrative structures follow an episodic development rather than a beginning-middle-end development. This is also a feature of women's storytelling noted by Kalcik (1975). She describes how women's storytelling consistently returns to "kernel stories" of larger stories, elaborating the theme from different points of view rather than developing the story linearly toward a climax which signals the end. Similarly, oral structures follow pragmatic associations rather than an abstract schema of logical development. The climax or main point of a story might be told in the middle of the story. Episodes might be connected by their relative entertainment value to a perceived changeable audience rather than by a noncontextual, causal, temporal, or formal logical sequence. The stories might return to parts of the story already told to amplify points and fill in details which become significant only later in the story. Oral discourse presents us with a collection of episodes that circle back on one another depending on the context of interpretation.

Thus, the context of production and interpretation is extremely important for understanding oral discourse. In Hall's (1977) terminology, oral discourse is a *high-context* discourse, requiring an understanding (implicit or explicit) of a wide range of factors specific to the situation within which it takes place. Moreover, oral discourse cannot easily be abstracted from its context without inducing a failure of understanding. Oral discourse, then, can be characterized by these three interrelated tendencies: (a) oral discourse relies on extratextual cues for its interpretive context (it is a high-context message system), (b) oral discourse is episodic and nonhierarchical in structure, and (c) oral discourse cannot be abstracted from its original situation of performance and still communicate a topically relevant propositional meaning.

ORIGINS OF THE ORAL/LITERATE GENDER DIFFERENCE

The oral/literate distinction as a gender difference can be explained by a number of interrelated historical circumstances. I will briefly discuss three: (a) women's forced illiteracy and their consequent preservation of oral traditions, (b) gender specific socialization patterns within the traditional nuclear family, and (c) the subordination of women in interpersonal encounters.

Ong (1982) points out that Learned Latin (a literate discourse), was a sex-linked language for over 1000 years. Only men learned Latin, and they learned it primarily in all-male groups outside of the home. Women did not have access to Learned Latin, and were thereby excluded from training in theology and rhetoric. For centuries, competency in Learned Latin was a prerequisite for involvement in public affairs. Women, if educated at all, were educated in vernacular schools, allowing them to maintain oral traditions more consistently than men who studied a primarily nonspoken language. The language derivatives of ancient Latin became "mother tongues" (language used by mothers in the home in everyday discourse) while Learned Latin developed as a second, written language, available almost exclusively to men for economic, political, and religious discourse.

Training in classical rhetoric stressed the persuasive dimensions of discourse, outlining techniques and strategies to achieve a goal. This goal-orientation carried over to general educational strategies when educators began to see the pedagogical usefulness of persuasion. The logical ordering of ideas and their presentation appeals to the authority of the academy and its representatives, and demonstrations of the usefulness of information to the students (as status marker as well as to aid in earning a living) has increased over the centuries. Revisions in education by rhetoricians such as the sixteenth century reformer, Peter Ramus, helped shape education into a more analytic and textbook-oriented process (Ong, 1958). The more dialogically-oriented Sophistic methods of the early Greeks tended to be left behind. The exclusion of women from education became more systematic as education became more institutionalized. Examining the impact of the spread of literacy in Western culture, Meyrowitz (1985) concludes that

> there are many indications in various sources that the spreading of literacy during the sixteenth and seventeenth centuries may have widened the gap in male and female rights and enhanced the dominance of men over women. (p. 218)

With the increased emphasis on textual interpretation of religious documents, the discourse strategies of rhetoric became part of the process of learning to read and write. Originally an oral tradition, the study of rhetoric is now associated with the study of writing skills as often as the study of oral discourse. While rhetoricians from Aristotle to the present stress the need to adapt to audiences, the fundamental discursive strategies and assumptions of rhetoric (and communication in general) have remained fairly stable. The model of rhetoric as an aid in the contest of ideas has not fundamentally altered. Only in the current century have women participated in public discourse in significant numbers, and even now they are virtually forced to adopt traditional (masculine) models of discursive style in order to have a voice in public affairs (Spitzack & Carter, 1987).

Traditional education as influenced by the male-dominated rhetorical tradition stresses a hierarchical status relationship between teacher and student, education as a tool for gaining social control and power, and command of disputational strategies that can be employed in a wide variety of situations. Testing of disputational skills is still an explicit part of every graduate program in the form of a required "oral defense" of master's theses and Ph.D. dissertations. Training in the ability to take any side of an issue and argue effectively is still a major part of training in debate. In other words, the rhetorical tradition has reinforced the tendency to accept formal education as a status marker and means of gaining power, and supported the ability to effectively engage in disputation regardless of the content of the issue. These are some of the values that underpin Western public discourse to which women have had limited access.

Gender differences in discourse structure influence a variety of cognitive, affective, and communicative dimensions. For instance, Gilligan's (1982) research describes gender differences in moral decision making. She challenges Kohlberg's (1958, 1981) influential theory of moral development. Kohlberg outlines a hierarchy of moral development with the notion of justice presented as the highest moral principle by which people can act. He concentrates on moral decision making as a process of principled decision making. That is, morality is traditionally understood as the consistent and reasoned application of noncontextual moral principles (axioms). The principles are viewed as the abstract arbiter of human situations, like a disinterested third party who can apply principles of reason impartially. Correct moral decision making, in Kohlberg's model, requires reflective distance, formal reasoning abilities, and above all, the unambiguous application of specific moral principles. Morality is treated as a rule-governed behavior, protecting participants from the self-interests of others and preserving the rights of the individual. Investigating moral development, then, means listening for evidence of moral principles and their application.

According to the findings of Gilligan and others, women do not typically hold the principled reasoning approach to moral decision making. Instead, women are guided morally by a motivation to maintain relationships and protect their social partners. Instead of using logical inference to determine correct moral response to a situation—as men typically do—women situationally determine a moral response by seeking to minimize harm to all persons within the social context. The process of decision making involves unfolding ramifications of possible actions, a process that looks much like women's storytelling. Themes are reiterated in multiple forms, situational factors play a significant role, and a high degree of involvement is apparent. These correspond to the episodic structure, high-context coding, and high involvement of oral discourse style that I have described.

Men, on the other hand, argue linearly to solve the "problem" of a moral conflict, generally arriving at a definitive conclusion. Situational features are minimized since moral action is understood as action following non-situationally-defined principles, and distance ("objectivity") is established to distance oneself from personal involvement in the decision-making process itself. Involvement is limited to the results of the decision rather than figuring into the making of the decision. These features of moral decision making observed by Kohlberg correspond to the linear structure, low-context coding, and high abstraction features of literate discourse. As Gilligan (1982, p. 18) points out, Kohlberg's original data base is only derived from male subjects, yet he generalized his findings to the entire population.

Gilligan's work, in conjunction with the oral/literate distinction, can be used to understand how gender bias can mislead data collection and analysis. The primary means of data collection for both Kohlberg's and Gilligan's studies were interviews. The interview process used to conduct research is itself a social interaction. The moral individual, in Kohlberg's model, is precisely the individual who would be the most able to comfortably describe the moral decisions to a stranger or brief acquaintance, since moral decision-making requires the ability to distance oneself from social situations. A more formal interview situation would tend to reinforce the tendency for subjects who are used to distancing themselves from social situations to make judgments based on nonsituational principles and generalized axioms. Thus, a male style of moral decision-making is reinforced by a formal interview process that is a low-context, literate discourse structure. A more personalized informal interview situation that operates according to a high-context, oral discourse structure typical of women's communication cannot be expected to yield responses that are noncontextual and axiomatic, but rather situational and open to discussion. Thus, both the preconceived view of moral decision-making and formal interviewing strategies are reinforced. When formal interviews are used, data seem to indicate that men are more developed in moral decision-making than women, thereby making an exploration of alternative views less likely. The traditional model appears to be confirmed by empirical results discovered through the application of a scientifically "objective" method.[4] Use of a formal interview technique would be simply an example of an appropriate method chosen for the research topic, if the preconception of moral decision making is correct for the entire population. But as Gilligan and others point out, such is not the case. Gender bias is reinforced both through content of the research assumptions and the method employed.

Observations of everyday communication help explain how oral/literate discourse structures are supported within specific communicative episodes as gender specific. As already described, oral discourse is typified by a greater reliance on nonverbal cues. Research in nonverbal communication consistently reveals that women are more sensitive to situational nonverbal cues than men (Hall, 1978; Rosenthal, Hall, Archer, DiMatteo, & Rogers, 1979; Trotter, 1983). Henley (1977, p. 181) correlates numerous

---

[4] Keller (1985) provides valuable insight into the history of the scientific concept of "objectivity" and gender differences relevant to theory and methodology building.

subordinate/superior status cues with women/men gender differences. She argues that the greater ability of women in nonverbal perception and expression is the product of women coping with their subordinate status by paying greater attention to their environment. Davis and Weitz (1981) suggest that women adjust to their partner's nonverbal cues more than men and that some nonverbal gender differences are status-linked. In other words, women seem to be both more sensitive and responsive to nonverbal dimensions of their situation than men, partly in response to women's traditionally lower status level.

Contrary to popular myth, men talk more than women (Pearson, 1985). Recall that literate cultures are typified by a greater reliance on verbal rather than nonverbal context. Women also use language that facilitates positive interaction more than men by interrupting conversations less than men, and avoid conflicts in conversation more than men (Pearson, 1985, p. 179–181). Women take primary responsibility for both internal family relationship cohesion and maintaining extended family ties (Galvin & Brommel, 1986, p. 106–109). Ong notes that "For an oral culture learning or knowing means achieving close, empathetic, communal identification with the known" (1982, p. 45). "Oral cultures tend to use concepts in situational, operational frames of reference that are minimally abstract in the sense that they remain close to the living human lifeworld" (1982, p. 49). Hall (1977) describes High Context cultures as tending to avoid protagonist-antagonist conflict (p. 111), as promoting social unity and cohesion (p. 101), and as more concerned with an everyday understanding of social situations than Low Context cultures (p. 111–112). In other words, a variety of women's communicative patterns parallel oral, high-context cultural tendencies. These cultural patterns seem to be related to the subordinate status of women and stereotypic gender role definitions.

THE NARRATIVE PARADIGM OF COMMUNICATION

Researchers developing narrative as a paradigm for communication, while acknowledging some of the above-mentioned research, typically ignore the oral/literate distinction, equivocating storytelling and conversation with narrative in general (Cutbirth & Metts, 1985; Fisher, 1984, 1985; Lucaites & Condit, 1985). While storytelling is often cited within communication literature as the paradigm example of narrative, the features of narrative that are thought generally to characterize storytelling are sometimes more compatible with literate discourse than with oral discourse. Not only does this confuse and limit a narrative paradigm for communication studies, but it poses a serious threat to the study of women's communication patterns. If a *literate* model is adopted to study women's *oral* traditions, distinctive characteristics of women's communication could be systematically overlooked.

Fisher, the major proponent of the narrative paradigm, states:

> The narrative paradigm sees people as storytellers—authors and co-authors who creatively read and evaluate the texts of life and literature.... [I]t stresses that people are full participants in the making of messages, whether they are agents (authors) or audience members (co-authors). (1985, p. 86)

Fisher maintains that the narrative paradigm "can be considered a dialectical synthesis of two traditional strands in the history of rhetoric: the argumentative, persuasive theme and the literary, aesthetic theme" (1984, p. 75; 1985, p. 2). Lucaites and Condit, however, attempt to elaborate Fisher's approach by functionally distinguishing among poetic, dialectic, and rhetorical discourse. While Fisher "challenges the notions that human communication—if it is to be considered rhetorical—must be an argumentative form" (1984, p. 2), Lucaites and Condit claim that

> the underlying context of all rhetorical discourse is its nature as contested.... Rhetoricians are advocates ... and the functional oppositionality inherent to the contexts in which they operate imposes on the narratives they enact two unique formal requirements: unity of direction and unity of purpose.... The oppositionality inherent to rhetorical contexts requires that advocates take one side or another in a dispute. The reasons and evidence that they offer must therefore be directed at providing a single interpretation of a claim to fact, value or policy. (1985, p. 84)

Lucaites and Condit split Fisher's proposed synthesis of rhetorical and aesthetic themes in favor of retaining a persuasive, advocative definition of rhetorical narrative. The "functional" definition of rhetorical narrative by Lucaites and Condit clearly reflects the goal-directed, linear, noncooperative discourse style typical of literate discourse in general and men's discourse in particular. According to Lucaites and Condit's version of rhetorical narrative, women's discourse would only be included within rhetorical study if it conformed to the masculine style of literate discourse. Their definition (reflecting traditional definitions of rhetoric) would limit the study of rhetoric to discourse patterned after writing more than speech, and potentially exclude women's typical discourse style as a focus of research.

Both Fisher, and Lucaites and Condit, stress the use of the narrative paradigm to examine "public knowledge oriented toward decision making and civic action" (Fisher, 1985, p. 79), risking the exclusion of everyday discourse as a legitimate focus of attention and instead focusing on a domain of discourse dominated by men. The same combination of definitional and methodological exclusion of women can occur as that discovered by Gilligan (1982) in moral development research. The rhetorical narrative paradigm proposed by Lucaites and Condit defines a domain of research which by definition excludes women, then confirms its definition as valid by discovering in masculine discourse (literate discourse) the kind of structure and function posited in the theory. A nongender-biased and comprehensive narrative paradigm should encompass both literate and oral discourse styles, thereby including the discourse styles and functions of women. Only a narrative paradigm that can generate models of women's discourse as well as men's can hope to provide us with an understanding of "homo narrans," the narrative dimension of being human.

Cutbirth and Metts (1985) also attempt to elaborate on Fisher's narrative paradigm. While the authors recognize Fisher's attempt to "question the prevailing philosophy underlying rhetorical theory: that human beings are influenced primarily through formal logical argument" (p. 1), they apparently take Fisher to mean that it is rhetoric's stress on strictly *formal* argument to which Fisher objects. Cutbirth and Metts remark that "rather than seeking the resolution of opposing arguments, Fisher urges that the critic should explore the competition of narrative" (p. 2). Later they conclude: "Given Fisher's dictum that stories compete with one another, it seems logical that a given story will only compete with similar or relevant stories" (p. 18). The notion that a *rhetorical* approach to narrative must begin with the assumption that narrative is competitively argumentative is not only retained but extended to imply that all stories compete with one another. Coming close to building in competition as a definitional quality of narrative, the authors summarize "rules" of narrative based on an analysis of 182 narratives derived from 16 conversations. One of the characteristics supposedly true of "all narratives" is the "underlying hierarchical structure or story schema" (p. 9). They refer to the work of Labov and Waletzky (1966) to provide evidence for the rigidity of this hierarchical structure as ordering the sequence of the narrative, contrasting hierarchical structure with "free" clauses, that is, clauses that are not core to the narrative and which can be moved through the story. Thus, the episodic structure of women's narrative (perhaps, as described by Kalcik (1975), employing kernel stories variously placed through the narrative) is eliminated as a legitimate narrative form in favor of the linear, noncontextualized sequencing of literate discourse).

Although Cutbirth and Metts (1985) acknowledge the importance of cooperative and politeness principles in discourse, they go on to describe "spontaneous" narratives as follows:

> The teller stresses the centrality of his/her action in the event, and makes known his/her assessment of the actions of others. This is essentially what

Sacks (1978) means when he talks about the teller figuring "as the hero" of the story.... [T]he teller casts the "self" of the narrative in the best possible light. (p. 14)

The assumptions about the necessarily competitive egocentric nature of narrative reflect literate styles of narrative and potentially exclude consideration of oral structures by implying that nonhierarchical, episodic, cooperative, and other-centered narratives are simply poorly formed. Such findings are at variance with research on oral cultural discourse, women's narratives, and women's decision-making processes about social situations. Proposing that such a definition of narrative could serve as a paradigm for communication studies risks a dismissal of oral structures in general and women's narratives in particular, all under the illusion of providing a model for oral discourse.

SEXUAL POLITICS AND THE ORAL/LITERATE DISTINCTION

Some women with whom I have discussed the oral/literate distinction and Gilligan's research have suggested that such arguments entrench debilitating stereotypes of women as less logical, less able to distance themselves emotionally, less principled, and less able to deal with abstractions than men. Gilligan's findings that women typically apply the notion of care in moral decision making, and the reported tendency of women to conversationally attend carefully to cooperation and politeness, can be construed as reinforcing the "nurturing" and "helping" role of women, potentially distracting from the role of women as forceful leaders and individuals capable of self-determination. I believe that placing these issues in cultural perspective can help to sort out the conflict between the scholarly project of acknowledging women's communicative styles and the desire to promote constructive images of women which move beyond restraining traditional stereotypes.

There is nothing inherent in oral styles of narrative that limits the ability of individuals to excel in analytic tasks and to maintain a strong sense of personal goals. The notion that concern for group cohesion, personal involvement in decision making, and cooperative attitudes is dysfunctional in the modern world is itself a prejudicial belief. The primary commercial competitor of the United States in the development of technology, Japan, is predominantly an oral culture. Not only have the Japanese outdistanced the United States in several key technologies, they have done so in part by the strength and tenacity of their cooperative efforts.

The women's movement has promoted both the "mainstreaming" of women into typically masculine styles of discourse, and the cooperative efforts of women within social contexts that support their own communicative styles. If the oral/literate distinction is valid as a gender distinction, it suggests that women constitute a parallel culture to men's, and that an understanding of women's issues could benefit from the exploration of women's own cultural propensities *in women's own terms.*

The discovery of gender difference where none was thought to exist not only reveals a social bias but is as significant as the discovery of cross-cultural differences in phenomena once thought universal, or twin studies verification of learned differences that were thought to be inherited. In short, issues of gender differences and sexual politics are not special interests but necessary components of our full understanding of humanity.

REFERENCES

Chafe, W. (Ed.). (1980). *The pear stories: Cultural, cognitive, and linguistic aspects of narrative production.* Norwood, NJ: Ablex.

Cook-Gumperz, J., & Gumperz, J. J. (1978). From oral to written: The transition to literacy. In M. Farr (Ed.), *Variation in writing.* Hillsdale, NJ: Erlbaum.

Cutbirth, C., & Metts, S. M. (1985, November). *The conversational bases of narrative rationality: An extention of Fisher's narrative paradigm.* Paper presented at the Speech Communication Association Convention, Denver, CO.

Davis, M., & Weitz, S. (1981). Sex differences in body movements and positions. In C. Mayo & N. M. Henley (Eds.), *Gender and nonverbal behavior* (pp. 81–92). New York: Springer-Verlag.

Deemer, P. D. (1975). Response. In C. Farrer (Ed.), *Women and folklore.* Austin: University of Texas.

Dijk, T. A. van (1976). Philosophy of action and theory of narrative. *Poetics, 5,* 287–338.

Eco, U. (1976). *A theory of semiotics.* Bloomington: Indiana University Press.

Edelsky, C. (1981). Who's got the floor? *Language in society, 10,* 383–421.

Farrer, C. (1975). *Women and folklore.* Austin: University of Texas.

Fisher, W. R. (1984). Narration as a human communication paradigm: The case of moral argument. *Communication Monographs, 51*(1), 1–22.

Fisher, W. R. (1985). The narrative paradigm: In the beginning. *Journal of Communication, 35*(4), 74–89.

Galvin, K. M., & Brommel, B. J. (1986). *Family communication: Cohesion and change.* Glenview, IL: Scott, Foresman and Co.

Gilligan, C. (1982). *In a different voice: Psychological theory and women's development.* Cambridge, MA: Harvard University Press.

Goody, J. R. (1977). *The domestication of the savage mind.* Cambridge, MA.: Cambridge University Press.

Goody, J., & Watt, I. (1968). The consequences of literacy. In J. Goody (Ed.), *Literacy in traditional societies* (pp. 27–84). Cambridge, England: Cambridge University Press.

Hall, E. T. (1977). *Beyond culture.* Garden City, NY: Anchor Books.

Hall, J. A . (1978). Gender effects in decoding nonverbal cues. *Psychological bulletin, 85,* 845–857.

Havelock, E. A. (1982). *The literate revolution in Greece and its cultural consequences.* Princeton, NJ: Princeton University Press.

Heidegger, M. (1949). *Existence and being.* Chicago: Henry Regnery.

Henley, N. M. (1977). *Body politics: Power, sex, and nonverbal communication.* Englewood Cliffs, NJ: Prentice-Hall.

Jenkins, M. M. (1982). The story is in the telling: A cooperative style of conversation among women. In S. Tromel-Plotz (Ed.), *Gewalt durch Sorache: Die vergewaltinguing von frauen in gesprachen.* Frankfurt am Main: Fisher Taschenbuch Verlag (ERIC Document Reproduction Service No. ED 238 083).

Jones, D. (1980). Gossip: Notes on women's oral culture. *Women's Studies International Quarterly, 3,* 193–198.

Kalcik, (1975). . . . like Ann's gynecologist or the time I was almost raped. In C. R. Farrer (Ed.), *Women and folklore.* (pp. 3–11). Austin: University of Texas.

Keller, E. F. (1985). *Reflections on gender and science.* New Haven, CT: Yale University Press.

Kohlberg, L. (1958). *The development of modes of thinking and choices in years 10 to 16.* Unpublished doctoral dissertation, University of Chicago, Chicago.

Kohlberg, L. (1981). *The philosophy of moral development.* San Francisco: Harper & Row.

Labov, W., & Waletzky, J. (1967). Narrative analysis: Oral versions of personal experience. In J. Helm(Ed.), *Essays on the verbal and visual arts* (pp. 12–44), Seattle: University of Washington Press.

Langellier, K. M., & Peterson, E. E. (1984, November). *Spinstorying: A communication analysis of women's storytelling.* Paper presented to the Speech Communication Convention, Chicago, IL.

Lakoff, R. (1975). *Language and woman's place.* New York: Harper and Row.

Lucaites, J. L., & Condit, C. M. (1985). Reconstructing narrative theory: A functional perspective. *Journal of Communication, 35*(4), 90–108.

Luria, A. R. (1976). *Cognitive development: Its cultural and social foundation.* Cambridge, MA: Harvard University Press.

McGee, M. G., & Nelson, J. S. (1985). Narrative reason in public argument. *Journal of Communication, 35*(4), 144.

MacIntyre, A. (1981). *After virtue: A study in moral theory.* Notre Dame, IN: University of Notré Dame Press.

Meyrowitz, J. (1985). *No sense of place: The impact of electronic media on social behavior.* New York: Oxford University Press.

Olson, D. R. (1977). From utterance to text: The bias of language in speech and writing. *Harvard Educational Review, 47,* 257–281.

Ong, W. J. (1958). *Ramus, method, and the decay of dialogue.* Cambridge, MA.: Harvard University Press.

Ong, W. J. (1982). *Orality and literacy.* New York: Methuen.

Pearson, J. C. (1985). *Gender and communication.* Dubuque, IA: Wm. C. Brown.

Pylyshyn, Z. W. (1984). *Computation and cognition: Toward a foundation for cognitive science.* Cambridge, MA: The MIT Press.

Ricoeur, P. (1976). *Interpretation theory: Discourse and the surplus of meaning.* Fort Worth, TX: The Texas Christian University Press.

Robinson, J. A. (1981). Personal narratives reconsidered. *Journal of American Folklore, 94,* 59–85.

Rosenthal, R., Hall, J. A., Archer, D., DiMatteo, M. R., & Rogers, P. L. (1979). The PONS test: Measuring sensitivity to nonverbal cues. In S. Weitz (Ed.), *Nonverbal communication.* New York: Oxford University Press.

Sacks, H. (1978). Some technical considerations of a dirty joke. In J. Schenkein (Ed.), *Studies in the organization of conversational interactions.* New York: Academic Press.

Scollon, R., & Scollon, S. B. K. (1981). *Narrative literacy, and face in interethnic communication.* Norwood NJ: Ablex.

Sperber, D., & Wilson, D. (1986). *Relevance: Communication and cognition.* Cambridge, MA: Harvard University Press.

Spender, D. (1980). *Man made language.* London: Routledge and Kegan Paul.

Spitzack, C., & Carter, K. (1987). Women in communication studies: A typology for revision. *Quarterly Journal of Speech, 73*(4), 401–423.

Stanley, J. (1979). Gender marking in American English. In A. P. Nilsen, H. Bosmajian, H. L. Gershung, & J. Stanley (Eds.), *Sexism and language* (pp. 44–76). Urbana, IL: National Council of Teachers of English (NCTE).

Tannen, D. (Ed.). *(1982). Spoken and written language.* Norwood, NJ: Ablex.

Thorne, B., & Henley, N. (Eds.). (1975). *Language and sex: Difference and dominance.* Rowley, MA.: Newbury House.

Trotter, R. J. (1983). Baby face. *Psychology Today,* pp. 14–20.

Vetter, H. (1969). *Language, behavior, and psychopathology.* Chicago: Rand McNally and Co.

Warnick, B. (1987). The narrative paradigm: Another story. *Quarterly Journal of Speech, 73,* 172–182.

White, H. (1981). The value of narrativity in the representation of reality. In W. J. T. Mitchell (Ed.), *On narrative* (pp. 1–23). Chicago: The University of Chicago Press.

6

In The Year of Big Sister*: Toward A Rhetorical Theory Accounting for Gender

CATHERINE A. DOBRIS
Department of Communication
La Salle University

Nineteen eighty-four had scarcely ended before scholars and critics descended en masse to dissect the year of "Big Brother." Adding yet another voice to the fray, Bella Abzug observed, "Nineteen eighty-four is not ... the year of Big Brother in our land. It can be the year of Big Sister ... an ordinary woman with a democratic vision and a sense of her own political potential" (1984, p. 6). Extending Abzug's metaphor, the "year of Big Sister" might also refer to both extraordinary and so-called ordinary women exploring their potential in both public and private arenas. The 1980s has certainly seen extraordinary women succeed in the public sector—Sandra Day O'Conner, the first woman appointed to the Supreme Court; Sally Ride, the first woman in space; and Geraldine Ferraro, the first woman nominated as a vice-presidential candidate for a major American party. The so-called ordinary woman is also in the limelight as the much touted "gender gap" is cited increasingly as influencing outcomes of both state and national elections (Abzug & Kelber, 1984, p. 6). Each year the number of women working both full- and part-time outside the home increases, and each year the number of female lawyers, doctors, professors, and other professionals grows also. Gender has become increasingly important as a demographic variable in business, organizational, interpersonal, and public communication, however; increased visibility of women in the public sphere does not necessarily mean that women's communication experiences, whether private or public, are valued within the dominant culture.

Although rhetorical critics have long noted the importance of demographic variables in designing and assessing persuasive messages (e.g., J.

---

* The source of the metaphor, "the Year of Big Sister," as noted by Bella Abzug, is found in Abzug and Kelber (1984, p. 6).

R. Andrews, 1983, pp. 30–34) and have observed and studied gender differences in communication (Baird, 1976; Baird & Bradley, 1979; Berryman & Wilcox, 1980; Borisoff & Merrill, 1985; Pearson, 1985), no rhetorical theory presents a comprehensive treatment of gender as a variable in persuasion. While much communication research treats sex as a variable in research, gender is not construed as a socially organizing force in society. I argue that rhetorical theories which purport to investigate "the nature and role of rhetoric—concerning the use of verbal and nonverbal symbols by man and his institutions to influence human behavior" (Johannesen, 1971a, p. 1) do precisely that—they investigate the nongeneric "man." In other words, historical progress has made women's communication visible, but our theories have assumed a relatively stable picture of humanity which does not include women.

In this chapter, I develop a rhetorical theory that accounts for gender. First, I discuss gender differences in communication and language perception. Second, I discuss perceptions and stereotypes of gender differences in communication. Third, I discuss the ways that rhetorical theory can take real and perceived gender differences into account. Finally, I suggest directions for further research by examining implications of a rhetorical theory that accounts for gender.

GENDER DIFFERENCES IN COMMUNICATION AND LANGUAGE PERCEPTION

Research in the area of gender and communication has generally focused on one of three issues: the treatment of women and men in and by language, the actual communication of women and men, or the stereotypes and perceptions of female and male communication. In what follows I omit a discussion of how language treats women and men, because although the issues raised are certainly compelling, they raise an entirely different set of questions from those dealt with in this essay. Questions such as "Is the language sexist?" and "If we can change the language, will we actually alter sexist attitudes and behaviors?" have been dealt with elsewhere in considerable depth (Adams & Ware, 1975, pp. 487–504; Briere & Lanktree, 1983; Dubois & Crouch, 1975; Key, 1975; Miller & Swift, 1976; Spender, 1980; Thorne, Kramarae, & Henley, 1983). Here I will restrict discussion to issues that bear on persuasion and persuasibility. In other words, I address the gender considerations, if any, that should be taken into account when either a woman or a man seeks to address a mixed-sex audience. Additionally, I examine the gender considerations, if any, that should be acknowledged when either a woman or a man seeks to address either a female or a male population.

The verbal and nonverbal communication of women and men has been studied in interpersonal, small group, and public speaking situations. These studies often yield conflicting results depending on, among other variables, the context. In one of the first attempts to analyze women's speech, Robin Lakoff (1975) outlined six characteristics in women's language (Jerry, 1985): (a) the use of "empty" adjectives such as "divine" and "charming"; (b) question intonation instead of declarative, such as tag questions and rising intonations; (c) the use of hedges including "well," "y'know" and "kinda"; (d) use of the intensive "so"; (e) hypercorrect grammar; and (f) superpolite forms.

Although Lakoff's research has been criticized as "introspection *cum* asystematic, uncontrolled and unverifiable observation," (Dubois & Crouch, 1975, p. 289) and for "generalizing from speculative observations and limited studies" to support "anecdotal claims," (Kramer, Thorne, & Henley, 1978, p. 640) her provocative claims have helped to raise issues that point the way toward more systematic, empirical research. As Spender suggests:

> Her [Lakoff's] study, *Language and Woman's Place*, has been influential; it has also been constrained by some of the sexist assumptions of the linguistic paradigm in which she worked ... For example, Lakoff accepts that men's language is superior and she assumes that this is a feature of their linguistic performance and not of their sex. (p. 8)

Responding to Lakoff's assertions, many scholars have discovered substantive language differences between women and men; however, it is important to recognize that these studies may be influenced by the same sexist assumptions inherent in Lakoff's early work. Reviewing research on language and gender in her text, *Gender and Communication*, Pearson summarizes that women tend to use higher pitch, more expressive language, tag questions in nonprofessional settings, compound requests, verbal fillers and vocal fluencies, intensifiers, hedges, qualifiers and disclaimers, hypercorrections and polite forms (1985, pp. 178–191). Results of research indicate also that women tend to use less hostility, profanity, and expletives, talk less, talk less assertively and for short periods of time, tend to be more supportive conversationalists, and tend to be higher in conformity than are men (Pearson, 1985, pp. 178–191).

In their reexamination of scholarly literature on gender and communication, Maltz and Borker (1982) note that women ask more questions, maintain routine social interaction more frequently, and make greater use of positive minimal responses such as "mm hmm" than do men (pp. 197–198). Women, according to Maltz and Borker's review, are also more likely than are men to adopt a strategy of "silent protest" if interrupted and "show a greater tendency to use the pronouns 'you' and 'we,' which explicitly acknowledge the existence of the other speaker" (p. 198). Men, on the other hand, are said to interrupt, challenge, dispute, and ignore more than do women (p. 198). Research indicates that men control the topic and make more direct declarations of fact or opinion than do women (p. 198).

Although some of these findings may make women's communication appear deficient when contrasted with men's, there are several possible explanations for this. Thorne, Kramarae, and Henley suggest that we have been taught to value men's communicative styles more than women's (1983, pp. 7–24). To the extent that we view male communication as normative or as "ideal," whatever behaviors males tend to exhibit will be seen as establishing the criteria for what is appropriate. When female behaviors differ from male behaviors female communication will immediately be perceived as inadequate. As Spitzack and Carter (1987, p. 410) point out, "When studies take women's speaking to be the problem and fail to question men's speaking with equal rigor, we can expect a storehouse of information that sings the praises of differences, but does little to challenge definitions of competence, influence, and success."

Maltz and Borker (1982) note that other explanations for differences in communication according to gender usually focus on social power of women and men (p. 198). Since men dominate in society, goes the argument, they also dominate in conversations. Further, different sex-role expectations may require women and men to play gender-appropriate roles in communication settings in order to achieve social approval.

While acknowledging that power differences and sex-role conditioning may play some part in the way women and men use language differently, Maltz and Borker (1982) suggest another possibility. They argue that women and men are raised in different "sociolinguistic cultures" and therefore have different "conceptions of friendly conversation . . . [different] rules for engaging in it, and, probably most important . . . [different] rules for interpreting it" (p. 200). Because women and men "have different experiences and operate in different social contexts" (p. 200) they develop particularized communicative needs and therefore develop unique communication styles, values, strengths, and weaknesses.

But whether resulting from biological, social, or cultural disparity, there appear to be some observable gender differences in communication that have been substantiated through empirical research. Although scholars may disagree about the precise nature or cause of gender differences, empirical studies suggest that women's language use may reflect ways of speaking and thinking that are different from men's.

In addition to language use, research in reader-response criticism and feminist literary theory (Bleich, 1985; Fetterley, 1978; Flynn, 1983) indicates possible gender differences in language perception. Some scholars assert that women and men perceive language differently and that these differences may influence language choice and usage. Contrasting reading experience with oral communication, Elizabeth Flynn provides a different perspective on language and gender studies that discount women's speech as less desirable than men's:

> Reading is a silent, private activity and so perhaps affords women a degree of protection not present when they speak. Quite possibly the hedging and tentativeness of women's speech are transformed into useful interpretive strategies—receptivity and yet critical assessment of the text—in the act of reading. A willingness to listen, a sensitivity to emotional nuance, an ability to empathize with and yet judge, may be disadvantages in speech but advantages in reading. We may come to discover that women have interpretive powers which have not been sufficiently appreciated. (1983, p. 252)

Flynn's observation suggests differences in how women and men perceive language. Reading an editorial or a piece of party propaganda, attending a speech or political meeting, and watching a national convention or a television commercial are all "silent, private activit[ies]" and may therefore be subject to women's "useful interpretive strategies" (Flynn, 1983). For example, women who are empathic may be more adept at understanding different perspectives on controversial issues since they may have the ability to "try on" each viewpoint.

Bleich, in his field work in literary criticism, has found additional support for Flynn's theory. Bleich (1985) suggests that, "men read prose fiction differently from the way women [do] ... women *enter* the world of the novel, take it as something 'there' for that purpose; men *see* the novel as a result of someone's action, and construe its meaning or logic in those terms" (p. 7). In one study, Bleich had female and male students retell the same story and concluded that:

> men retold the story as if the purpose was to deliver a clear, simple structure or chain of information ... women presented the narrative as if it were an atmosphere or an experience ... men are ... more literal ... women feel freer to include inferences. (pp. 26–29)

Bleich sees this difference as "a preliminary indication of a possibly deep difference in the *perception* of language according to gender" (p. 26). He suggests that because men find it necessary to "distance" themselves from the text they are "cautious about 'accuracy,' and they thus inhibit themselves from saying things that may not be literally documented" (p. 30). It is Bleich's belief that for men to "understand the language means to repeat the 'facts' ... and to avoid drawing 'extra' inferences," while for women to "understand the language ... *means* to draw such inferences about feelings and motives from the metaphors in the original text" (p. 31).

Similar to Flynn and Bleich—who both suggest that women and men may perceive language differently—P. Andrew's (1985) recent communication study of upward-directed persuasive communication indicates a difference in the perception or interpretation of instructions according to gender. In her empirical study, Andrews asked female and male subjects to read the case histories of five prospective candidates for a life-preserving kidney machine. Each subject was told to choose one of the candidates according to the criteria of age and emotional stability and to present arguments in support of her or his decision to a graduate student who would evaluate the subject's arguments. Subjects were expressly instructed to ignore other criteria such as wealth or income in making their selections. Andrews concludes, "men were far more likely than women to advance arguments that were based on criteria presented in the case as guidelines for decision making ... [and] not only did women make fewer direct references to these criteria, but in several cases the criteria were mentioned only so that the subject might take exception to them" (p. 22). Men tended to treat the criteria as nonnegotiable rules for decision making, whereas women tended either to disregard certain criteria, or to explicitly state that a given criterion was inappropriate in this particular decision-making process.

Andrews suggests that these findings may be interpreted in at least two ways. First, it can be argued that ignoring prescribed guidelines for decision making will likely result in poor decisions. Second, however, Andrews explains "complex decision making often requires one to forsake rules and procedures ... to question them if they seem to be standing in the way of a sound, equitable or humane decision" (pp. 22–23). In this case, Andrews continues, "the decision was one that implicitly called for some consideration of relationships" (pp. 23–24). Therefore, to the extent that women ignore prescribed criteria or even introduce additional criteria, they may make more "sound" or "equitable" decisions than do men.

Whether or not ignoring prescribed guidelines is an asset, it is clear that in Andrew's study—as in Bleich's—men interpret and/or act on instructions more *literally* than do women. Thus, women and men may perceive the same information differently.

Studies of language use and of language perception indicate that women and men may be socialized to both think and speak differently from each other. Unlike some researchers who have suggested that these differences generally work in men's favor, Flynn, Bleich, and Andrews all suggest that women may have an advantage over men in activities as diverse as reading a novel or in making life-threatening decisions. These examples may be used to help rhetorical critics challenge traditional, assumptive bases in communication research. For example, theories which suggest that so-called objective accounts of events are superior to subjective accounts, must be reexamined. As inferences may help a reader gain a fuller understanding of a novelist's intent, so might inferences enable a listener to appreciate fully the talents of an orator. Further research, along the lines of Andrew's study, is needed to explore this implication.

PERCEPTIONS AND STEREOTYPES OF GENDER DIFFERENCES

While studies of actual language use and of language perception may help us to reevaluate paradigms in rhetorical theory and criticism, research on the perception of gender differences in communication offers insight into the rhetorical process itself. Communication principles developed by male theorists for male rhetors addressing male audiences may have different consequences when rhetors or audiences are female.

Although research on the perceptions of gender differences in communication is far from conclusive, several trends do emerge. Cheris Kramer (1974) observes: "Beliefs about sex-related language differences may be as important as the actual sex differences. As long as women play a subordinate role, their speech will be stereotyped as separate and unequal" (p. 85). Kramer (1977) found that women perceive four times the amount of differences as do men. Stereotyped perceptions of gender differences in language include: women talk more and say less (i.e., content is an overabundance of trivia); men are more straightforward and discuss important topics; women's speech is unassertive, passive, and lacking in power while men's speech is aggressive; women are more submissive, susceptible to social pressure, and responsive to other's needs while men are the converse; women use more proper, polite language, avoid harsh language, and talk about "social life, books, food and drinks, caring for their husbands, and social work" (Pearson, 1985, pp. 176–178).

Other studies have explored the perception of gender differences in public speaking settings. The results of these studies (Jerry, 1985; Miller & McReynolds, 1973) indicate that men are perceived as more credible sources than women by both sexes, but especially by other women. In addition, females who use the derogation of opponents as strategy in persuasive settings may be perceived as more extroverted, credible, and generally more effective than males using the same strategy. This effect may be even more pronounced when females derogate other females (Jerry, 1985).

It should be emphasized that findings among studies are not always consistent and that, since communication is fluid and dynamic, what may have been true a few years ago may not be so today. As more women enter the workforce, and even more importantly, as women become commonplace in the business meeting and on the public platform, stereotypes may be proved false in practice, thus altering the perceptions of onlookers and participants, females and males alike.

While there is a danger of constructing a rhetorical theory based on trends and averages or on what may be only slight differences between women and men, it is important to consider the *socialized* differences among people when designing theories of how people supposedly "are." Empirical studies indicate that women and men may be perceived differently even when performing the same task or exhibiting the same behavior (Thorne, Kramarae, & Henley, 1983), but whether differences are real or imagined, they influence the rhetorical process and we need to be cognizant of them.

To ignore differences and to assume that we are all "more or less the same," and that differences of race, ethnic background, and gender are only minor ones is unrealistic. We are necessarily influenced by everything that we are and by everything that we have experienced. Acknowledging those different influences does not necessitate the glorification or condemnation of resulting differences in attitudes and behaviors, nor does it require us to establish so-called norms for women and men. On the contrary, acknowledging differences allows us the freedom to reject rigid behavioral standards since we are forced to examine the full range of human possibility. The "more or less the same" approach may be used as a way to reaffirm the white Protestant male perspective as the "norm," since it denies differences and may result in reifying status-quo notions of humanity. Research on the perceptions of gender differences in communication point out that even imagined differences created through perceptual biases may influence the rhetorical process. Advising "the speaker" to be extroverted or to avoid using profanity, for example, may have different consequences for a female or male speaker addressing a female or male audience.

TOWARD A RHETORICAL THEORY ACCOUNTING FOR GENDER

In the previous sections I observed that research indicates real differences in the way women and men communicate such as higher or lower pitch and lesser or greater conformity. I observed potential differences in language perception such as literal versus inferential interpretation. And I noted differences in stereotypes and perceptions of women and men in communication contexts, such as credible or noncredible, passive or assertive. I argue that the need for developing a rhetorical theory accounting for gender is clear since women and men appear to communicate differently, may perceive language in different ways, and have preconceived notions about the style, credibility, and effectiveness of female and male speakers. Gender research allows us to examine how we speak and listen according to gender, but gender research also enables us to critique the current evaluative criteria and to develop new criteria to challenge the male-centered status quo. As Spitzack and Carter (1987, p. 410) suggest, "the very concept of greatness needs to be reevaluated." A theory which accounts for gender differences will acknowledge these points, creating a better understanding of the persuasion process. What follows is a preliminary guideline for such a theory.

Defining "rhetoric" is a task addressing in countless scholarly articles, and is examined, at least preemptively, in virtually every text on the subject (Brockriede, 1966; Ehninger, 1967; Natanson, 1955; Simons, 1967). Ohmann (1971) sums up the confusion appropriately, observing, "Clearly, the meaning of 'rhetoric' is not clear" (p. 65). Johannesen (1971a) questions, "What are the requisites of any adequate contemporary theory of rhetoric?" and answers "No single answer seems possible" (p. 2).

For the purpose of this discussion, I will define rhetoric as composed of the four meanings identified by Natanson (1955, p. 139), since his description delineates rhetoric's specific functions. Natanson suggests that rhetoric is persuasion on the part of a speaker or writer, the investigation of the devices and modes of argument that are used to persuade, an examination and ordering of the central principles of rhetoric, and the inquiry into the underlying assumptions or philosophical underpinnings of rhetoric. Rhetoric has different meanings for the speaker/writer, critic/teacher, theorist, and philosopher. I will look at the implications for a rhetorical theory that accounts for gender by examining each of Natanson's four meanings of rhetoric. Additionally, I will address two pertinent questions raised by Johannesen (1971a): (a) Should we have plural rhetorics? (b) Must a rhetorical theory be axiological? (p. 6).

The Speaker/Writer

In his introductory public speaking text, *Essentials of Public Communication* (1979), J. R. Andrews addresses the range of issues most of us consider important for a beginning speaker. In considering the implications for the speaker/writer of rhetorical messages, he also considers implications for the audience or receivers of those messages, since the speaker/writer designs messages with the audience in mind. Typical of many introductory texts, Andrews includes a discussion of the speaker's image and style, audience adaptation and involvement, purposeful communication, the structure and form of communicative messages and communication tactics, and argumentation. He notes the importance of acknowledging specific audience characteristics, such as age, sex, subcultures, educational level, occupation, income, principal roles, and membership in groups or organizations. He argues, "a person's sexual identity is crucial to that person's very being. It is inevitable that listeners' understanding of and attitudes toward a speaker and his or her message can be profoundly colored by the listeners' sexual identification" (p. 8).

The interaction between a speaker and same-sex audience members may be different from the interaction between a speaker and opposite-sex audience members to some extent solely because of gender. Likewise, as research indicates, the sex of the speaker may itself help to shape the outcome of the communication situation. For instance, according to some studies cited previously, women who use incorrect grammar or profanity may be judged more harshly than men who do the same. Alternatively, men who use the derogation of opponents' strategy may meet audience disapproval while women may be more successful utilizing the same strategy. Female or male speakers who adopt straightforward, unambiguous language and simple rhetorical strategies may be more or less persuasive depending upon the gender of audience members.

The implications of these studies for women and men as public speakers, as well as in interpersonal, small group, business, and mass media settings, are vast. While the growing body of research on gender is incorporated into special texts on gender and communication (Pearson, 1985; Eakins & Eakins, 1978; Henley, 1977; Kramarae, 1981; Stewart, Cooper, & Friedley, 1986), little is included in mainstream texts to address the differences encountered by female and male speakers and audiences. To some extent, this might be accounted for by the contradictions among research results. While one study might suggest that women can use an aggressive style successfully, another study might indicate the opposite. Textbook authors may be reluctant to include information that may be speculative or misleading.

Clearly, however, sex is often viewed as biologic sex only, rather than as a socially organizing force in society; thus, sex is often accorded no more attention than are other demographic variables such as occupation or income. Authors advise that as speakers we avoid stereotyping our audiences, and one author (Bradley, 1984, p. 94) suggests, "In the future, the speaker will have to look at other factors, such as the group involved, than at the sex of the listeners." In an effort to avoid stereotyping or other forms of overt sexism, text authors may be glossing over the complexities of gender and communication research.

The Teacher/Critic

As more women become active participants in public communication contexts and, as politicians seek to capture "the women's vote," regard for the speaker/writer and the persuasion process becomes a prominent concern. There are, however, equally important matters to consider in constructing a comprehensive theory, not the least of which is the criticism of public discourse. Rhetorical criticism is practiced from almost as many perspectives as there are rhetorical critics (J. R. Andrews, 1973; Black, 1965; Bormann, 1972; Leff, 1980; Thonssen, Baird, & Braden, 1970). James Andrews defines criticism as "the systematic process of illuminating and evaluating products of human activity" (1983, p. 4) "The critic of rhetoric," he continues, "focuses his or her attention on human efforts to be persuasive" (p. 4). A significant implication of the historical Wingspread Conference (Bitzer & Black, 1971) has been to consider human persuasion to reach far beyond conventional speech forms and to include in its scope, among other artifacts, novels, bumper stickers, and diaries, since the "products of human activity" embraces an infinite number of objects of inquiry.

The utilization of alternative critical perspectives, in which certain features are highlighted at the inevitable expense of others, is a current concern of rhetorical critics and theorists seeking either "ultimate truth," or at the least, a greater understanding of human communication behavior. This concern has led to a discussion of rhetorical perspectivism as a method for confronting diversity (Booth, 1979; Brockriede, 1982; Brummet, 1982; Cherwitz & Hikens, 1983; Railsback, 1983). Brockreide envisions the "perspectival approach" as a "useful complement to the traditional approach in such activities as theory, practice, criticism and research" (p. 147). "Emphasizing one dimension," he points out, "does not require a reductionistic elimination of the others, which, characteristically, is the outcome of the traditional mode of analysis into categories or variables that are seen as discrete" (p. 138). Brockriede argues that "pluralists realize the legitimacy of multiple perspectives, of focusing on one dimension at a time, and of doing so in each instance within the landscape of the other dimensions" (p. 138).

Although neither Brockriede, nor the other authors mentioned, explicitly discuss the importance of accounting for gender, certainly a "gender perspective" can be an essential component of a truly pluralist theory. It is not enough, however, to consider women's communication or other gender-related issues in isolation or even "within the landscape of the other dimensions," (Brockriede, p. 138) unless a perspective accounting for gender also helps scholars to fashion new evaluative tools. As Spitzack and Carter (1987) suggest, pluralism has often worked against women since women's communication is still evaluated according to male-defined criteria. A gender perspective provides us with the "other" half of human experience, while allowing us to reexamine the assumptive bases of traditional theory which has previously relied on male experience only. If pluralism is viewed as a way to discover and examine all relevant perspectives, both on their own terms and in conjunction with other perspectives, and not as a method of "discovering" one Absolute Truth, perspectivism may provide the mechanism to integrate a gender perspective in rhetorical theory.

What then would a gender perspective on rhetorical theory and criticism entail? Although there are many possible answers, one feature of such a perspective will likely be the inclusion of a feminist perspective as part of a perspectival approach to analysis. Foss and Foss (see Chapter 3) suggest that from a feminist perspective "gender is not simply one of many variables that a researcher studies; instead, it is understood to be basic to all aspects of human experience." They suggest that the goal of the feminist perspective is to develop "theory that unsettles or challenges common assumptions of the culture, raises fundamental questions about social life, and fosters reconsideration of what has been taken for granted." A feminist perspective in communication research, according to Foss and Foss, "constitutes a deliberate break with past research frameworks" since feminist scholars "seek to change the rules for the construction of knowledge so they reflect women's experiences and incorporate women's values." Beyond the influence of a feminist perspective on research, however, Foss and Foss argue that "the ultimate consequence of research informed by the feminist perspective is social change."

In addition to the description of a feminist perspective in research suggested by the Foss', a feminist perspective can be discussed further by examining the past two decades of evolution in feminist literary theory. An examination of the development of a feminist perspective in literary theory and criticism will be useful as a starting point to suggest implications for the development of a feminist perspective in rhetorical theory and criticism. A comparison between literary theory and rhetorical theory is useful because both focus on the analysis and criticism of human communication. Given that the scope of rhetoric includes oral communication as well as written expression, historical events as well as fictive ones, the implications of feminist criticism for rhetoric may be even more pervasive than for literature.

Literary critic Elaine Showalter (1981) defines the mainstream of criticism as " 'male critical theory' ... a concept of creativity, literary history, or literary interpretation based entirely on male experience and put forward as universal" (p. 183). Mainstream criticism is defined by male values and, to the extent that "the male has ... set himself as the human norm, the subject and referent to which the female is 'other' or alien" (Millet, 1969, p. 65) mainstream criticism has an inherent bias against women.

The patriarchal conception of women is often one associated with suffering, evil, and sin (Millet, 1969; Hays, 1965) and the terms and symbols developed to analyze females are developed almost exclusively by males (Millet, pp. 64–65). Further, the male theorist or critic may not fully identify with women's experiences and thus ridicule, dismiss, or condemn experiences such as childbirth, childrearing, and homemaking. Thus the role of women as second-class citizens in a patriarchal society, is tacitly supported (Showalter, 1981).

Traditional criticism fails women in at least three ways. First, imbued with a male value orientation, traditional criticism fails to align adequately with female value systems. Differences in values between women and men may include an ends-versus-process orientation or differing measurements for success and differing standards for achievement. Since women are viewed as the "inferior sex," male value orientations will nearly always dominate when gender differences conflict. For example, traditional critics may place greatest emphasis on the final impact of a poem, short story, or speech, failing to recognize that the author intended a more conjunctive, less goal-oriented style. If women's literary or rhetorical styles do not meet traditional standards then they may be judged inadequate.

Second, engendered by a patriarchal society, the male bias in mainstream criticism necessarily translates into a bias against women both as creators (e. g., authors, orators) and as subjects. Males establish critical values based on male norms and if women do not conform to those norms their efforts are often labeled as deficient. Thus, women may be criticized for choosing childbirth or women's rights as subject matter, instead of selecting politics or organized sports. Even when women do choose the latter topics, their work is suspect still, since women may be viewed as noncredible sources on "important" topics, or if they are viewed as credible, then their femininity may be at issue. As Spitzack and Carter (1987, pp. 402–403) point out, "Insofar as public career aspirations involving individual advancement and competitive instincts are thought to be secondary and perhaps even incompatible with femininity, the publicly visible woman becomes a contradiction in terms." Finally, since men define what topics are important, often topics that involve women's lives directly, such as childbirth and women's rights, are dismissed as trivial.

Third, male-based criticism may be unable to fully comprehend and analyze female experience since male-based criticism does not take female experience, attitudes, values, and beliefs into account. Feminist criticism not only considers female experience to be valuable and therefore worthy of serious study, but also allows scholars to develop appropriate tools for the task. For example, literary critic Jane Marcus (1987) describes a female aesthetic that deemphasizes competition, is antihierarchical, and antitheoretical. If this aesthetic were used in the formulation of a feminist critical perspective, it would necessitate revision of male-based criticisms that value the foregoing. As literary critic Kolodny (1980) suggests, feminist criticism is an essential critical perspective to combat "the inadequacy of established critical schools and methods" (p. 1).

Kolodny (1980) describes a feminist perspective on criticism as "female consciousness turn[ed] in upon itself, attempting to grasp the deepest conditions of its own unique and multiplicitous realities, in the hope, eventually, of altering the very forms through which the culture perceives, expresses and knows itself" (p. 16). Feminist critic Kaplan (1984) suggests that "feminist criticism is part of a general interest in researching subjects that have been mainly considered from a male point of view" (p. 150). And feminist critic Patterson (1982) explains that feminist criticism "is criticism with a Cause ... ideological and moral ... women's consciousness of being 'the other' in a male-dominated system" (p. 659).

More than two decades of feminist scholarship in literary theory provides a starting point for rhetorical scholars. Similar to strides made in literary theory and criticism (Kolodny, 1980), the development of a feminist perspective in rhetorical theory may facilitate the discovery of lost or forgotten rhetorical works. Although it can be argued that until recently women orators were in scarce supply, it is still important to investigate the neglect of women speakers and speech writers. Even more critically, women have engaged in rhetoric since the development of speech, but because women's discourse often failed to imitate the rhetorical forms developed by males, much of women's communicaiton has been devalued, disregarded, and destroyed. A feminist perspective in rhetoric is critical in this last regard since traditional theoretical models implicitly or explicitly deny us the ability to "see" most female rhetoric. A feminist perspective allows us to value, and therefore to study, communication that is ignored or discounted in traditional rhetorical theory.

The development of a feminist perspective in rhetoric may also inspire and help shape an investigation of unified feminist perspectives in diverse fields. By providing a unique contribution to the emerging body of feminist theory, and, through "discovering and interpreting data about women's interests, attitudes, values and work patterns," we may help construct a "more accurate picture ... of tendencies and directions in the culture as a whole" (Kaplan, 1974, p. 151).

In order to claim the ability to illuminate and evaluate "products of *human* activity," as J. R. Andrews (1973) suggests, we must develop a holistic theory and criticism that encompasses both women and men, and that acknowledges and is accepting of the perspectives of each. Then, if it is appropriate, both a female and a male perspective may coexist, or, if it is not appropriate, each perspective according to gender will inform the other to create new critical perspectives. As literary critic Farwell (1977) argues, we must establish a "wholeness" that can only come from the "interrelationship" of both sexes (p. 194).

The Theory and Philosophy

I have so far discussed the potential impact of a theory accounting for gender on the speaker and the critic without yet discussing theory itself. "A theory of rhetoric," explains Johannesen (1971a), "states the basic facts, central laws, and fundamental components of the rhetorical process. The theory describes how rhetoric operates in human communication transactions" (p. 2). "A philosophy of rhetoric," he continues, "examines the underlying presuppositions and assumptions—the philosophical grounds and starting points—that undergrid any particular theory of rhetoric" (pp. 2–3). Theory and philosophy compose Natanson's (1955) final two meanings of "rhetoric." Since the theory ideally proceeds from the philosophy, and since both are intertwined, I will discuss theory and philosophy together.

Feminists across a myriad of disciplines have argued that there is a male universe of ideas and values put forth as universal that is often contradictory to, or at odds with, a female universe of ideas and values (Spender, 1983, p. 368). Spender (1983) argues, for example, "the knowledge which becomes public and is legitimated in a male dominated society, is the knowledge of men: it is based on their own experience and reflects their own perspective and priorities" (p. 368). In the specific case of communication, since males have practiced rhetoric in public places and have used rhetoric as a tool to persuade, the so-called universal definition of rhetoric usually makes reference to public arenas and to the persuasive process.

Elsewhere, in literature, anthropology, history, and sociology, the male-centered concept of the world has been chronicled and criticized, but in no other discipline is the notion of a male-centered universe more blatant than in speech communication (Gearhart, 1979, p. 195). The entire concept of "rhetoric" has been devised, practiced, and developed in a world where women, like children, were to be seen and *not heard.* Woman, by her male-defined "nature," was automatically excluded from "rhetoric." Thus, for thousands of years rhetoric has been synonymous with persuasion and is usually considered an activity where *men* publicly seek to change the opinions of other *men.* Women's communication contexts, styles, and modes of expression were scarcely noticed until recent years. The " 'personal' as experienced by women in contrast to the 'public' as proclaimed by men" (Spender, 1983, p. 371) was simply not considered relevant to the weighty masculine province of "rhetoric."

Gearhart (1979) observes, "without batting an eye the ancient rhetors, the men of the church, and scholars of argumentation ... have taken as given that it is a proper and even necessary human function to attempt to change others" (p. 195). Gearhart argues that "any intent to persuade is an act of violence" and, given this premise, "of all the human disciplines, it [speech communication] has gone about its task of educating others to violence with the most audacity" (p. 195). She suggests further that while the tools of rhetoric are not themselves inherently evil, it is our use of these tools that is unacceptable.

Clearly because women have been excluded from the defining of rhetoric the traditional conception of rhetoric is a product of male-centered thinking, values, and actions. In response to this situation Gearhart suggests an alternative to persuasion. Whereas traditional rhetoric relies on what Gearhart calls a "conquest/conversion model," (p. 196) based on male experience, her alternative rests on assumptive bases that may be more compatible with feminist ideology. Writes Gearhart:

> Feminism is at the very least the rejection of the conquest/conversion model of interaction and the development of new forms of relationship which allow for wholeness in the individual ... Feminism is an ideology of change which rises out of the experiences of women ... (p. 200)

Whether in a "learning circumstance" or in a "conflict encounter," Gearhart delineates five requirements of her alternative to persuasion (pp. 198–199):

1. Participants contribute to an atmosphere favorable to change.
2. There are differences among participants.
3. Despite differences there is equal power.
4. Participants will acknowledge that communication must be worked at.
5. Participants are willing to yeild positions entirely to others.

She proposes scholars "open the door to alternatives to persuasion" (p. 198) and suggests one:

> Communication can be a deliberate creation or co-creation of an atmosphere in which people or things, if and only if they have the internal basis for change, may change themselves; it can be a milieu in which those who are ready to be persuaded may persuade themselves, may choose to hear or choose to learn ... (p. 198)

While Gearhart's proposal may not be a desirable or plausible replacement for persuasion, hers is a thesis worthy of further investigation precisely because it provides central concerns for a reassessment of the "art" of rhetoric.

For example, Gearhart's proposal may be used to reassess current notions of rhetoric by examining the use of rhetoric as deception. Many of us may accept lying, whether from advertising agencies or political candidates, as a fact of public communication. The use of rhetorical tools to promote lies that are tolerated socially, is integral to the persuasion process. Whether it is Gary Hart proclaiming that he is not having an extramarital affair, or Jim Bakker insisting that he did not have an affair, or Miss America/Universe/World declaring that she will not have an affair, many of us await the inevitable admission of "guilt."

Enterprising companies such as the Isuzu Corporation have capitalized on rhetoric as deception, by marketing commercials that parody the wild claims made by their competitors. "Buy an Isuzu for only six dollars," asserts one spokesperson. Or, "buy an Isuzu and receive a comprehensive dental plan free," claims another television salesperson, as a written disclaimer flashes across the screen.

While the portrayal of persuasion as a necessary evil is certainly not new, the suggestion that persuasion, regardless of its' ends, is simply evil and not at all necessary is an uncommon perspective in twentieth century America. The observation that traditional modes of rhetoric have been developed in public contexts, by men and often for men, must call into question whether or not these modes are necessarily preferable to rhetorical/dialogical modes developed by women in the private sphere. Gearhart requires us to reevaluate our attitudes concerning what is an acceptable use of rhetorical skill. For example, we might ask whether President Reagan has become the "Great Communicator" because his rhetorical abilities highlight his incisive intellect or whether he has earned this distinction for his ability to read snappy one-liners and sound convincing.

When rhetorical theory accounts for gender by acknowledging the validity of female experience, the entire philosophy of rhetoric may be altered profoundly. When we ask, "What does 'rhetoric' mean for women?" we find that 2,000 years of philosophy and theory may not reflect women's experience. There is not sufficient space here to address all of the implications for theory, but a few will be briefly cited, along with suggestions for actual implementation.

First, theories which purport to judge the effectiveness of rhetoric through examining the "effect" or "ends" of rhetoric may need reassessment. If "stasis is impossible" and if "process" replaces "progress," then the language of "goals" and "success" may be inadequate to assess communication. Indeed, even "assess" may be an inappropriate term. A feminist critical approach focuses on the rhetorical process by concentrating on impressions from the speaker/writer and her audience. Such a method may be shaped through individual and group interview, survey, and observation, and could rely primarily on impressionistic recording.

Second, if, as suggested earlier, women and men perceive language differently, theories of persuasion and dialogue will have to account for those differences. Theories might suggest criteria for the effectiveness of persuasive techniques, the conditions under which alternatives to persuasion are preferable, or may specify varying elements of both according to contextual or topical variation.

Analysis of language and linguistic patterns, both in literature and rhetoric, may be useful to examine gender differences in verbal communication. Specifically, scholars may examine pronoun usage, sentence structure, use of questions, tag questions, qualifiers, compound requests, ambiguous language, word endings, forms of address, religious language, hypercorrections, and profanity. Correlations, if any, between language use and theme, may be noted, for example, the choice of pronouns when themes such as cooperation and supportiveness are present. The use of "we," or "us," as opposed to "I," may be a vital strategy to convey these themes. The use of "I," however, may convey inconsistency or contradiction between the stated intention to illustrate cooperation and execution, since "I" may emphasize the individual over the group. Literary trends through genre or historical period may reveal the extent to which cooperation or competitiveness is valued by individuals or groups.

A critic may examine whether dialogue (Arnett, 1981; Clark, 1976; Johannesen, 1971a) is a viable alternative to traditional rhetorical forms and whether dialogue shares similar assumptive bases with feminist perspectives. Examples include those characteristics commonly associated with dialogue: cooperative decision making, unconditional positive regard, mutual equality, empathy, supportiveness, and genuineness. Nondialogic themes may also be examined. Such themes seem incompatible with feminist philosophies of communication. Examples of themes that are contrary to traditional notions of dialogue, include self-centeredness, deception, pretense, display, appearance, artifice, using, profit, unapproachableness, seduction, domination, exploitation, and manipulation (Buber, 1955, 1970). The structure of the analysis should not inhibit the emergence or nonemergence of themes condusive to a dialogic mode.

Finally, a rhetorical theory accounting for gender must necessarily be a flexible barometer of changing sex roles and sex-role stereotypes. A static theory that suggested, for example, that women are more likely to conform to group pressure or that men who use profanity are judged more harshly than are women who do the same, may be outmoded in a decade or even in a year. Further, such theories cannot be applied with cookie-cutter criticisms that attempt to relegate the sexes to their respective corners. Gender-related theories must serve as indicators only of possible outcomes.

A theory accounting for gender will mandate flexibility, vitality, and changeability. The validation of women's communication requires us to question the basic assumptions of rhetorical theory and to learn from new models by continually examining the underpinnings of all theory. A monolithic "rhetoric" will be impossible.

IMPLICATIONS FOR RESEARCH

In this chapter I have examined implications for a rhetorical theory accounting for gender, according to Natanson's four meanings of rhetoric—meanings for the speaker/writer, critic/teacher, theorist, and philosopher. Turning now to implications for additional research, I will return to the two questions raised by Johannesen, suggested earlier: (a) Should we have plural rhetorics?, and (b) Must a rhetorical theory be axiological?

In my discussion of the critic/teacher I address the question of rhetorical perspectivism and suggest that a gender perspective in theory is an essential component of a methodological and philosophical pluralist theory. I quote Kolodney who asserts feminist criticism is an essential critical perspective to combat "the inadequacy of established critical schools and methods." In addition, in the previous section I argue that a theory accounting for gender must be a flexible one considering the changing sex roles and sex-role stereotypes in public and private spheres.

Clearly the arguments presented here favor the existence of plural and multiple rhetorics. Further research needs to expand to include an examination of race, class, and cultural background. Since a majority of research on women has centered on white, heterosexual, middle-class women, we must be careful not to repeat past mistakes of generalizing from one population to another without first establishing whether or not generalizations are justifiable. Research may indicate that the number of potential "rhetorics" are unlimited.

Asking, "must a rhetorical theory be axiological?" is a question that will likely always remain philosophical. In accounting for gender, however, new light is shed on an old issue. To the extent that a female universe of ideas and values differs from, and may actually contradict, a male universe of ideas and values (e.g., means versus ends orientation), an axiological theory would need to discriminate between female and male value systems. In the past, of course, this is precisely what rhetorical theories did; by ignoring female value systems, male values were presented as superior to females'. If, as Gearhart argues, traditional male rhetoric is "violence," then it may be the case that feminine or feminist rhetorics are preferable or even ultimately "superior." Although these questions may be better left to philosophers, there are arenas where the two value systems and communicative styles may be observed, if not actually tested. Scholars may find it useful to look at settings where a woman-centered approach has been substituted for a previously established male-centered approach, where traditionally male-centered and traditionally woman-centered approaches are taken to the same task, or where women and men are required to interact in both traditional and nontraditional rhetorical settings. Suggested for further research are women and men in seminary, social work, and legal practice.

For example, in some ministries both sexes may be taught a stereotypically feminine communication approach that actually enhances credibility for men, but serves to undermine women's authority (Kleinman 1984). Although stereotypical feminine communication is itself valued in this setting, women are *still* at a disadvantage if they display stereotypical feminine communication behaviors.

In psychiatric hospitals, social workers, psychologists, and psychiatrists frequently work in settings where they are part of interdisciplinary teams. Teams may function more efficiently when they consist of all women, due to women's ability to communicate in a manner that offers mutual respect with regard to decision making (A. L. Blum, June 1987). In this setting women using stereotypically feminine communication approaches may have a communication advantage.

Finally a comparison between the dynamics of courtroom litigation and the more informal method of exchange employed in pretrial negotiations, settlement conferences, and chamber discussions may be useful in examining the effectiveness of traditional masculine communicative styles versus traditional feminine styles. Classic litigation exemplifies the stereotypical male rhetorical style where adversaries seek to prevail at the expense of their opponents. In contrast, pretrial communications are conducted with a goal toward compromise and the satisfaction of both parties. An analysis of the effectiveness and efficiency of these divergent approaches may serve as a basis for further research on how women and men employ stereotypical feminine or masculine communication styles in both traditional and nontraditional rhetorical settings (K. C. O'Donnell, July 1987).

In the mid-1980's women are taking their rightful places behind podiums and pulpits, around meeting tables and in rocket ships, but in our eagerness to prove ourselves in the arenas that had previously been denied us, we must not assume that male models are the only models. A rhetorical theory that accounts for gender must recognize the real as well as the perceived differences between the sexes, and must be flexible and sensitive to the constantly shifting landscape of gender relations. Such a change may alter forever how we view philosophy, theory, criticism, and practice of rhetoric. The "year of Big Sister" is yet to be.

REFERENCES

Abzug, B., & Kelber, M. (1984). *Gender gap.* Boston: Houghton Mifflin.

Adams, K., & Ware, N. (1975). The linguistic implications of being a woman. In J. Freeman (Ed.), *Women: A feminist perspective* (pp. 487–504). Palo Alto, CA: Mayfield Publishing Company.

Andrews, J. R. (1973). *A choice of worlds: The practice and criticism of public discourse.* New York: Harper and Row.

Andrews, J. R. (1979). *Essentials of public communication.* New York: John Wiley & Sons.

Andrews, J. R. (1983). *The practice of rhetorical criticism.* New York: Macmillan.

Andrews, P. H. (1985, April). *Upward-directed persuasive communication and attribution of success and failure toward an understanding of the role of gender.* Paper presented at the Central States Speech Association convention, Chicago, IL.

Arnett, R. C. (1981). Toward a phenomenological dialogue. *The Western Journal of Speech Communication, 45,* 201–212.

Baird, J. E. (1976). Sex differences in group communication: A review of relevant research. *The Quarterly Journal of Speech, 62,* 179–192.

Baird, J. E., & Bradley, P. H. (1979). Styles of management and communication: A comparative study of men and women. *Communication Monographs, 46,* 101–111.

Berryman, C., & Wilcox, J. R. (1980). Attitudes toward male and female speech: Experiments on the effects of sex-typical language. *The Western Journal of Speech Communication, 44,* 50–59.

Bitzer, L. F., & Black, E. (Eds.). (1971). *The prospect of rhetoric.* Englewood Cliffs, NJ: Prentice-Hall.

Black, E. (1965). *Rhetorical criticism: A study in method.* Madison, WI: University of Wisconsin Press.

Bleich, D. (1985). *Gender interests in reading and language.* Unpublished manuscript, Indiana University, Department of English, Bloomington, IN.

Blum, A. L. (1987). Interview at Taylor Manor, psychiatric hospital, Ellicot City, MD.

Booth, W. C. (1982). *Critical understanding: The powers and limits of pluralism.* Chicago: University of Chicago Press.

Borisoff, D., & Merrill, L. (1985). *The power to communicate: Gender differences as barriers.* Prospect Heights, IL: Waveland Press Inc.

Bormann, E. G. (1972). Fantasy and rhetorical vision: The rhetorical vision: The rhetorical criticism of reality. *The Quarterly Journal of Speech, 58,* 396–407.

Bradley, B. E. (1984). *Fundamentals of speech communication* (4th ed.). Dubuque, IA: Wm. C. Brown Publishers.

Briere, J., & Lanktree, C. (1983). Sex-role related effects of sex bias in language. *Sex Roles, 9,* 625–632.

Brockriede, W. (1966). Toward a contemporary Aristotelian theory of rhetoric. *The Quarterly Journal of Speech, 52,* 33–40.

Brockriede, W. (1982). Arguing about human understanding. *Communication Monographs, 49,* 137–147.

Brummett, B. (1982). On to rhetorical relativism. *The Quarterly Journal of Speech, 68,* 425–430.

Buber, M. (1955). *Between man and man.* Boston: Beacon Press.

Buber, M. (1970). *I and Thou* (W. Kaufmann, Trans.). New York: Charles Scribner's Sons.

Cherwitz, R., & Hikins, J. W. (1983). Rhetorical perspectivism. *The Quarterly Journal of Speech, 69,* 249–266.

Clark, A. (1976). Martin Buber, dialogue, and the philosophy of rhetoric. In D. G. Douglas (Ed.), *Philosophers on Rhetoric* (pp. 225–242). Skokie, IL: National Textbook Company.

Dubois, B. L., & Crouch, I. (1975). The question of tag questions in women's speech: They don't really use more of them, do they? *Language in Society, 4,* 239–294.

Eakins, B. W., & Eakins, R. G. (1978). *Sex differences in human communication.* Boston: Houghton Mifflin Company.

Ehninger, D. (1967). On rhetoric and rhetorics. *The Western Journal of Speech Communication, 31,* 242–249.

Farwell, M. R. (1977). Adrienne Rich and an organic feminist criticism. *College English, 39,* 191–203.

Fetterley, J. (1978). *The resisting reader: A feminist approach to American fiction.* Bloomington, IN: Indiana University Press.

Flynn, E. A. (1983). Gender and reading. *College English, 45,* 236–253.

Gearhart, S. (1979). The womanization of rhetoric. *Women's Studies International Quarterly, 2,* 195–201.

Hays, H. R. (1965). *The dangerous sex.* New York: Pocket Books.

Henley, N. (1977). *Body politics: Power, sex and nonverbal communication.* Englewood Cliffs, NJ: Prentice-Hall.

Jerry, E. C. (1985, April). *Women's speech and women's persuasiveness.* Paper presented at the Central States Speech Association convention, Indianapolis, IN.

Johannesen, R. (1971a). Editor's introduction: Some trends in contemporary rhetorical theory. In R. Johannesen (Ed.), *Contemporary theories of rhetoric: Selected readings* (pp. 1–6). New York: Harper and Row.

Johannesen, R. (1971b). The emerging concept of communication as dialogue. *The Quarterly Journal of Speech, 57,* 373–382.

Kaplan, A. (1974). Feminist criticism: A survey with analysis of methodological problems. *The University of Michigan Paper's in Women's Studies, 1,* 150–177.

Key, M. R. (1975). *Male/female language.* Metuchen, NJ: Scarecrow Press.

Kleinman, S. (1984). Women in seminary: Dilemmas of professional socialization. *Sociology of Education, 57,* 210–218.

Kolodny, A. (1980). Dancing through the minefield: Some observations of the theory, practice and politics of a feminist literary criticism. *Feminist Studies*, 6, 1–25.

Kramarae C. (1981). *Women and men speaking*. Rowley, MA: Newbury House.

Kramer, C. (1974). Women's speech: Separate but unequal? *The Quarterly Journal of Speech*, 60, 14–24.

Kramer, C. (1977). Perceptions of female and male speech. *Language and Speech*, 20, 151–161.

Lakoff, R. (1975). *Language and woman's place*. New York: Harper Colophon Books.

Leff, M. C. (1980). Rhetorical criticism: The state of the art. *Western Speech*, 44, 337–349.

Maltz, D. N., & Borker, R. A. (1982). A cultural approach to male-female miscommunication. In J. J. Gumperz (Ed.), *Language and social identity* (pp. 197–216). Cambridge, MA: Cambridge University Press.

Marcus, J. (1987). Still practice, a/wrested alphabet: Toward a feminist aesthetic. In S. Benstock (Ed.), *Feminist issues in literary scholarship*. Bloomington, IN: Indiana University Press.

Miller, C., & Swift, K. (1976). *Words and women*. Garden City, NY: Anchor Press/ Doubleday.

Miller, G. R., & McReynolds, M. (1973). Male chauvinism and source competence: A research note. *Speech Monographs*, 40, 154–155.

Millet, K. (1969). *Sexual politics*. New York: Ballantine Books.

Natanson, M. (1955). The limits of rhetoric. *The Qarterly Journal of Speech*, 41, 133–139.

O'Donnell, K. C. (1987). Interview at Office of the Public Defender, Baltimore, MD.

Ohmann, R. (1971). In lieu of a new rhetoric. In R. Johannesen (Ed.), *Contemporary theories of rhetoric: Selected readings* (pp. 63–71). New York: Harper and Row.

Patterson, R. G. (1982). An interchange on feminist criticism: On 'Dancing through the minefield.' *Feminist Studies*, 8, 654–665.

Pearson, J. C. (1985). *Gender and communication*. Dubuque, IA: William C. Brown Publishers.

Railsback, C. C. (1983). Beyond rhetorical relativism: A structural-material model of truth and objective reality. *The Quarterly Journal of Speech*, 69, 351–363.

Showalter, E. (1981). Feminist criticism in the wilderness. *Critical Inquiry*, 8, 179–205.

Simons, H. W. (1967). Toward a new rhetoric. *Pennsylvania Speech Annual*, 24, 7–20. Reprinted in *Contemporary Theories of Rhetoric: Selected Readings*, 50–62.

Spender, D. (1980). *Man made language*. London: Routledge & Kegan Paul.

Spender, D. (1983). Modern feminist theorists: Reinventing rebellion. In D. Spender (Ed.), *Feminist theorists* (pp. 366–380). New York: Pantheon Books

Spitzack, C., & Carter, K. (1987). Women in communication studies: A typology for revision. *The Quarterly Journal of Speech*, 73, 401–423.

Stewart, L. P., Cooper, P. J., & Friedley, S. A. (1986). *Communication between the sexes: Sex differences and sex-role stereotypes.* Scottsdale, AR: Gorsuch Scarisbrick.

Thonssen, L., Baird, A., & Braden, W. (1970). *Speech criticism* (2nd ed.). New York: Ronald Press.

Thorne, B., Kramarae, C., & Henley, N. (Eds.). (1983). *Language, gender and society.* Rowley, MA: Newbury.

7

Soap Opera and Women's Culture: Politics and the Popular

MARY ELLEN BROWN
State University of
New York, Brockport

When I first decided to study the female audiences of soap opera, I went down to the corner shop to buy a copy of *Soap Opera Digest*. I found myself explaining to the clerk that I was not a fan, I was merely studying soaps, a response similar to the one I felt during my research on pornography. In the case of pornography, I was always careful to explain to the person behind the counter that I was not viewing these tapes for my own pleasure but for research purposes. I understood my reaction in the case of pornography but it came as a shock to me with regard to soaps. The point that my experience at the corner supermarket brought home was the extent to which I have internalized the prevailing discourse that deems soaps "trashy". I have linked them in my mind with my reaction to the clerk in the pornography store. Pornography is aimed at a masculine audience and I will probably never understand how men derive pleasure from it, but on the other hand, soaps are a part of my own culture—that of the subcultural group called women. My culture consists of the meanings and pleasures that women can make for themselves within and against a patriarchal society. Culture is finally the sense we make of our experience of everyday life within a particular social system, and texts such as romances or soap operas are some of the most important cultural products that help us find and articulate these meanings. My shock could be called the "shock of the popular"—the contradiction within myself between my enjoyment of a popular form and my adoption of the antithetical value system that devalues popular forms.

What I have described above is an example, on the personal level, of the concept of hegemony. The notion of hegemony is central to the research model used in this study and to cultural studies in general. The concept of hegemony, developed by Gramsci (1971), refers to the exercise of social and cultural leadership by the dominant classes.[1] Dominant classes win support for their ideological positions through cultural and social influences rather than coercion, and in this way they exercise their economic, political, and cultural leadership. As O'Sullivan, Hartley, Saunders, and Fiske put it, "Hegemony naturalises what is historically a class ideology, and renders it into a form of common sense" (1983, pp. 102–104.). Hegemony, however is never static or complete: rather it is always "leaky." Hence the potential for opposition exists since conflicts of interest always exist between the dominant and subordinate classes. Critical and research analyses like mine are the sites where gaps between the dominant symbolic order and the readings and uses of culture by subordinate groups are identified and described as moments of opposition or resistance to dominant hegemony.

I can only feel the need to apologize or excuse my interest in soaps when I am thinking in the naturalized discourse of patriarchy. I have been brought up a woman in a patriarchal society. I was raised in a patriarchal family, schooled in patriarchal educational institutions, and have been subject to all of the cultural and social determinates of patriarchy. Hence I often speak and think patriarchal discourse. Patriarchal discourse is impersonal, objective, scientific, rational, and logical, and it leaves these values unquestioned and thus naturalized. Patriarchal discourse also naturalizes the power of men to dominate society's ways of thinking, communicating, and experiencing; thus it attempts to exclude other modes of experience. Patriarchal discourse is the discourse of power, but disguises the fact through its claims to be based on universal truths rather than truths constructed by itself in the interests of those in power. It claims to be asocial and apolitical. As I have pointed out in relation to the concept of hegemony, in industrialized class- and gender-divided societies, popular culture always contains a collision of discourses because the values that support patriarchy are not always those in which subcultural groups, like women, find pleasure. In gender terms, the dominant ideology which supports both gender and class hierarchy and its attendant values are spoken by patriarchal discourse, while feminine meanings and pleasures speak in an oppositional, feminine one. Without the two complementary discourses, patriarchally-produced mass media cannot become popular with women because popular art always contains traces of the struggle between the dominant and the subjugated. Subjugated social groups must be able to recover traces of their repressed discourse in order to turn the text into their popular culture. For the purposes of this study, I am calling the discourse of the subordinated "feminine discourse." This study looks

---

[1] For a discussion of the role of coersive state apparatuses see Louis Althusser (1971).

at the way soaps' audiences talk about soaps. I maintain that audiences insert the uses and pleasures they derive from participating in fan groups into their communal gossip networks, and that these networks function as a part of women's culture by virtue of their acknowledgement of the subordinate position of women in our culture.

While dominant discourse seeks to construct reality for women in ways that suit the dominant, feminine discourse constructs reality for women in terms of her perceptions of the social order in which she is subordinate. Sometimes feminine discourse is what Barthes (1972) calls "inoculated" or acknowledged in order to be dismissed (p. 150), but often it continues to float freely as what Fiske (1986a) calls "semiotic excess." Semiotic excess functions in the following way according to Fiske:

> The preferred reading of a popular text in mass culture must necessarily, then, attempt a hegemonic function in favor of the culturally dominant. The reader, who statistically is almost certain to be one of the culturally subordinate, is invited to cooperate with the text, to decode it according to codes that fit easily with those of the dominant ideology, and if one accepts the invitation, is rewarded with pleasure. The pleasure is the pleasure of recognition, of privileged knowledge and of dominant specularity, and it produces a subject position that fits into the dominant cultural system with a minimum of strain.... The theory of semiotic excess proposes that once the ideological, hegemonic work has been performed, there is still excess meaning that escapes the control of the dominant and is thus available for the culturally subordinate to use for their own cultural-political interests. The motivation to use the semiotic excess for particular, possibly oppositional subcultural purposes, derives from the differences between the sociocultural experiences of the producers and the readers. (p. 403)

Semiotic excess, then, can be put into use as subordinate groups choose to use it—often to create meanings for themselves. The meanings produced by semiotic excess like those produced in the preferred reading are also rewarded with pleasure. In the case of meaning generation through semiotic excess, however, the pleasure is in the recognition of knowledge gained by the readers' membership in a particular subcultural group, in this case, women. The relationship between subcultural knowledge and patriarchal knowledge is frequently one of contestation or evasion since the two types of knowledge and their appropriate discourses are often in direct opposition to each other. A social system provides the structure of domination which overdetermines social experience, but culture holds the meanings and pleasures (or unpleasures) from which people make sense of experience. Therefore, I use the term "culture" to encompass all that people do say, think, and feel; culture frames human experience in the practice of day-to-day living with all its meanings and pleasures (R. Williams, 1977). Culture includes the shared social and cultural myths that are embodied in both literate and oral practices. Culture also includes myths that are generated through the dialectic between people and popular media forms such as television, magazines, newspapers, and film. The pleasure that subordinate groups derive from popular forms like soap operas has to do with the fact that subordinate groups use popular forms to make sense of their own cultural interests.

Broadcast soap opera, first on radio and then on television, has established itself as a central form of popular culture. Most women who grew up in the post-war period in the United States, even if they had never actually watched a television soap or heard a radio soap, had experiences that are connected to soap operas. Soap watchers, then, are not stratified others separate from one another and me, but are family and friends. My study of soap opera attempts to understand the role of soap opera as and in feminine discourse and to investigate how women use soaps to create meanings within the context of a patriarchal system which reads soap opera quite differently. The political nature of the object of this study has direct methodological implications, the most important of which derives from the explicit recognition of the political dimension of the research methodology and the interpretation of the data. As Stuart Hall and the ethnographic researchers at the University of Birmingham Center for Contemporary Cultural Studies have pointed out, research can proceed from the bottom up (Hall, Hobson, Lowe, & Willis, 1980). Research can allow the people to create their own knowledge rather than have knowledge imposed upon them since any investigation inevitably becomes involved with the knowledge and its creation that is the object of study.

METHODOLOGICAL ISSUES

My discomforting moment in the corner supermarket made me think not only about my topic of research but also about my methodology. The contradictions that made me want to distance myself from my research topic were not only those of a woman in patriarchy, they were also those of a woman academic in patriarchal academia. Patriarchal academia functions to naturalize patriarchal discourse, its values, modes of thought and writing, and therefore its styles of research. In particular patriarchal academia naturalizes the notion that there is an objective, nonsocial, nonpolitical "truth" that is accessible by "objective" research and communicable by "objective" writing. The high value placed on "objectivity" serves to naturalize a definition of the academic that denies a place on the agenda for modes of experience and knowledge that depart from the status quo. During much of my time as a student, as a researcher and as a teacher, I have been involved with the "academic" values of objectivity, critical distance, and depersonalization. Moreover, I have been in danger of taking them as a natural, neutral, and unquestionable given of academic life. By prioritizing as factual knowledge only that which is public, impersonal, and repeatable, patriarchal views devalue personal experiences and knowledges and pretend that women and the challenges they offer to institutionalized knowledges do not really exist. One such challenge is the hierarchical nature of traditional research assumptions, the us/them (researcher/subject) separation made in much positivist research methodology. Oakley (1981) criticizes positivist research methodology in which the interviewer is in control of the knowledge about the study and admits personal empathy only insofar as it can be used to establish "rapport," that is, as it might be used in the service of a higher good, such as the study, the field, or "knowledge." Oakley (1981) makes clear the logic of nondistancing relationships between researchers and researched particularly when both are women:

> Where both share the same gender socialization and critical life-experiences, social distance can be minimal. Where both interviewer and interviewee share membership in the same minority group, the basis for equality may impress itself even more urgently ... (p. 55)

Oakley exposes the masculine fiction of the "proper" interview in much the same way that my analysis seeks to establish control for women over the discourse about soaps. Thus my investigation of soaps involves an approach which seeks to minimize the distance between researcher and researched.

My investigation of the pleasures of soaps for fans involved my becoming a fan within a group of fans. The group consisted of seven women, aged sixteen to eighty and two males aged twelve and eighteen. Their occupations included student, retired nurse, interior decorator, accountant, and college teacher. Those who were students and who also had a job were a lab technician, secretary, and horse groom. They were all friends, relatives, or relatives of friends so that frequently we talked about soaps in the context of other friendly occasions. We watched *Days of Our Lives*, and perused soaps yearbooks and albums published in the popular press. We met in July 1985 to watch an episode of *Days* during which I recorded our conversation. It is the transcript of the conversation that serves as part of the data for this study. The full data also involves our interaction with each other and the material from the soap opera itself. There were three people in the group who could not be at the recording session, they were two women (42 and 16) and a boy (12).

The group was self-selected and was not studied positivistically, that is, as a representative sample of an objective reality. Rather its conversation was studied semiotically, that is, as an instance of how women use the cultural resources offered to them by society to make their meaning and pleasures. This method is closer to that of structuralist linguistics than empirical sociology, for it parallels the linguistic study of the utterance as an example of the way that the socially provided language is used in a concrete situation. I chose to study a group because I was interested in common cultural processes, not in individualistic ones, and these cultural processes would become most apparent and available for study within the interactions of a group.

My research methodology, then, has the following assumptions involving the collection of data:

1. The interviewees are my equals and friends. I am part of their group and our experiences are equally valid, hence I am both interviewee and interviewer. The social relations of the *group* precede that of the researcher-subject.
2. The interviews are conversational rather than bidirectional or linear. The interviewer does not control or chair the discussion.
3. The interviewees are the possessors of knowledge, and I am speaking for them in this research.
4. The audiences involved are active audiences rather than passive receivers of mass cultural messages.

In this article, then, I shall examine the generation of both pleasure and power for women by one of television's most devalued forms—the daytime soap opera. I will maintain that soaps generate a type of feminine discourse which, by articulating feminine desire or pleasure, constitutes a type of resistance to dominant ideology while they function as a part of women's culture.

SOAP OPERA—THE DEVALUED FORM

Viewers vary as to which programs they call soaps. In general, however, I have characterized the daytime soaps by:

1. The centrality of female characters
2. Serial form which resists narrative closure
3. Multiple characters and plots as well as multiple points of view
4. Use of time which parallels actual time and implies that the action continues to take place whether we watch it or not
5. Abrupt segmentation between parts

6. Emphasis on problem solving, and intimate conversation in which dialogue carries the weight of the plot
7. The portrayal of many of the male characters as "sensitive men"
8. The characterization of female characters as powerful, often in the world outside the home
9. The home, or some other place which functions as a home (often a hospital), as the setting for the show
10. Plots which hinge on relationships between people, particularly family and romantic relationships
11. Concerns of nondominant groups being taken seriously

These characteristics vary somewhat from country to country, but it is largely the programed time slot, and therefore the soap's intended audience, which determines its production conventions and content. My research focuses on *Days of Our Lives* as a typical example of American soaps aimed at women, usually broadcast between 10 a.m. and 3 p.m. on weekdays.

A list like the one above does little to show why soap operas have been consistently denigrated as the lowest form of the lowest medium (television), yet that has been their fate in patriarchy. Such a fate has to do in part with the fact that soaps do not resemble the classical realist tradition favored by dominant aesthetic systems. Like romance novels and the woman's films of the 1930s and 1940s, soaps have been characterized in patriarchal discourse by their excesses. However, despite (or because of) the universal disdain heaped upon them in dominant cultural practices and discourse, each of these genres was, or is, immensely popular with many women. The soap opera however, differs from the other two genres because it breaks with the classical narrative form. The soap opera refuses closure, contains nonhierarchical and multiple plots and characters, and features a point of view balanced between unproblematic perspectives on female cultural existence—competent women, "sensitive" men—and the traditional problems of women living within patriarchy such as the social rules that govern sexual conduct.

SOAPS AND THEIR AUDIENCES

The history of soaps shows how soap operas developed to serve dominant gender and economic interests. Thus an analysis of soaps history traces the formation of the ideological frame within and against which feminine culture struggles to exist. Many of the daytime soaps in the United States are still produced by soap conglomerates such as Procter and Gamble and Colgate-Palmolive. Soaps as a genre grew out of radio, in response to the isolation of women in the home in the 1930s and the subsequent colonization of these women as consumers of domestic products. By 1940 there were 64 soaps broadcast in the United States each day (Cantor & Pingree, 1983). Radio soaps were usually 15 minutes long and often featured a matriarch *(Ma Perkins)* who gave advice about problems to other characters on the show. Additional favorite anchoring characters were the woman alone *(Helen Trent)* or the woman who married into a strange environment *(Our Gal Sunday)*. The first character type, the matriarch acting as surrogate mother (or grandmother), often gave advice on the best laundry detergent to use while she was counseling other characters on personal problems. The early radio soaps, then, combined the confessional form with the giving of advice, a device which fits well into the commercial sponsor's needs because both "problem" and "solution" are articulated.

As soaps evolved into television productions in the 1950s, the need to maintain an audience for the advertisement of household products was strengthened and, by 1973, most television soaps in the United States had adopted an hour-long format to extend their hold over audiences for a longer period. With the hour format, multiple plots and large numbers of characters (around 40 per show) became the norm. In addition, the female characters on the soaps began to hold high-status jobs—for example, surgeon, psychiatrist, or research scientist. In 1977, when *General Hospital* added younger characters and more adventurous plot variations, thereby attracting a teenage audience of both sexes, the other daytime soaps followed suit in response to perceived new audiences and therefore new consumers and higher ratings.

The daytime soaps are extremely profitable for broadcasters since broadcast advertising income is determined by audience size. The soaps are inexpensive to produce because they are, for the most part, shot in broadcast studios in the sequence in which they are to be shown, thereby avoiding costly location shooting and extensive editing. At the same time, soaps attract large audiences—20 million in 1981 among the three commercial broadcast networks—and 70 percent of the audience consists of women over 18 years of age (Cantor & Pingree, 1983). Audiences *do* write to let the producers know what they want to happen on particular soaps. Since soaps are often produced only two weeks in advance of their air date, it is possible that producers and sponsors take their suggestions under consideration when writing the show.

Not surprisingly soaps are shot through with patriarchal capitalism, but this does not mean that their only cultural function for viewers is hegemonic, or to sway audiences to a dominant point of view. Women also use soaps as part of their feminine friendship and gossip networks. Through these networks and within feminine culture they are discriminatory and begin to forge links of solidarity. Even though the watching of soaps can be a solitary experience, most often the experience is discussed with others who form a community of soap viewers of particular soaps.

Although daytime soaps are similarly constructed and similar in appearance, viewers usually choose a particular soap to watch which is referred to as "my soap." Such nomination gives a soap a privileged position in that woman's cultural experience. The time slots in which particular soaps are programmed are important in the choice of which soap to watch. They are often associated with breaks in the day's activities and form part of the structuring devices of a woman's day if she is working in the house. A quotation from the *Days of Our Lives* group illustrates this point:

> *O:* Well I watched them during lunch time. That's how I got to watching *Loving. Loving* comes on at 11.30 and by that time I'm just fooling around.
>
> And I started watching it and I got interested in it. It's about a very wealthy family and how they are dressed to the peak, to the 9's. It's real interesting. And then I have lunch and watch *Days of Our Lives*.

However once a soap is chosen, fans usually remain loyal until there is a substantial change in their soap. Changes may cause them to switch loyalties. Friends of a viewer often switch to the same soap which suggests that viewers are not just loyal to a particular soap, but are also loyal to the community of viewers with whom they are affiliated.

Women also carry their interest in soaps outside of the home and into the public sphere of the workplace. Women working outside the home sometimes tape their soap while they are at work and watch it when they return home in the evenings. A missed episode is often the topic of conversation among working women: an office video monitor may be the lunch time site of soap watching for working fans during the working day.

The process of being a soap fan, however, is not always just the process of watching. For long periods at a time, some fans miss watching their soap but "keep up" with it through conversations with other fans. A person who has been a fan of a particular show over a long period of time does not simply stop watching and erase the show from her memory. Sometimes fans report having not seen a show for years, only to catch up for the missed years by watching an episode or two. Fans can catch up on a soap's plot by what Timberg (1987) calls "backstory" which is the recounting of past events and relationships so that a new viewer or a returning former viewer can catch up quickly. As one member of our group recounts:

> *K:* How many years have you been watching? (to L.)
> *L:* Seven or eight years, but only off and on, I've never had a television set. I just sort of keep up off and on.

The pleasure for this viewer is in the kinship with other fans, not in the text itself. The *use* of the text is the real politics for her, in that it enables her to participate in the feminine cultural community of fans: it is a way of collectivizing individual experience.

Daughters are often raised with a particular soap and continue to watch it after they leave home. The progress of the soap is then a topic of conversation when mothers and daughters converse over the years. A particular soap becomes a part of a family's shared history handed down in the same way that mothers and daughters share recipes and, with both recipes and soaps, the memories of shared hours in the kitchen or near the television set. Close women friends often watch the same soap and share information about the soap. The community of fans provides an aspect of women's oral culture that bridges geographical distance, a bridge that is vital for oral culture in a mass, mobile culture like ours. For example, a mother and daughter in the soaps' group discuss the mothers introduction to the soaps' network in a new town and the daughter's first memories of watching soaps:

S: In 1976, I moved to Knoxville and I went to bridge and they were talking about people just like this. Back then it was 1:30. No, it was the 2 o'clock soap opera back then. They stopped lunch, bridge. Anything. If I was going to be their friend, I had to watch it if I was going to carry on a conversation, and then Kim was born I would make her sleep during that time.

K: (S's daughter) No, I would sit next to you.

S: Oh yes later on. Not early.

Sons less often share in feminine cultural practice I have described. The twelve-year-old boy who was part of our group told me that after the summer he planned to stop watching *Days of Our Lives* because he had now outgrown the soap, an act which seems to parallel the male child's need to reject that which is female in pulling away from his mother. While the girl child may feel comfortable in the culture of women of which soaps are a part, the boy child has to reject it. Chodorow (1978) points out that female gender identity is learned in everyday life and is "exemplified by the person (or kind of people—women) with whom she has been most involved" (p. 51). Soaps are a part of the culture within which girls are socialized, and women construct pleasures and meanings for themselves sometimes through their association with soaps. Hobson (1982), in analyzing the results of hours spent watching the program and talking with fans of the British soap *Crossroads*, concludes that: "The message is not solely in the 'text' but can be changed or 'worked on' by the audience as they make their own interpretation of a programme" (p. 106). The reworking to which Hobson refers involves, among other things, the recasting of sexually defined and limited social relations not as restraints but as communal practices among that community of women. In other words, soaps designed to reinforce existing social practices, isolating women and casting them as mere consumers, instead can be used to promote a woman's community which gets pleasure from itself. Women (and on occasion, men) create their own discourse and their own pleasure from the text. Such talk, or gossip (see below) is an example of the way the mass media can be mobilized and inserted into oral culture, and thus serve as a means of building and maintaining a sense of community among women. The pleasure is not just the pleasure of seeing women's interests and concerns represented on the screen: rather it lies in the active and selective use of these representations in women's everyday lives and shared social experiences. The representations are only pleasurable insofar as they can be activated in this way.

FEMININE DISCOURSE

Pleasure for women exists structually outside of, or marginal to, the patriarchal discourse of desire. Feminine pleasures are often silenced or muted by patriarchal discourse, social constraints, or historical methodology. Showalter (in Williams, L., 1985) describes feminine discourse as "double voiced." She implies that women are capable of participating in both dominant discourse and feminine discourse.

The narrative enactment of such discourse can be found in the Dutch film *A Question of Silence* (Marleen Gorris, 1982). In the film, a dress shop owner is killed by three women when he accuses one of shoplifting. The deed is done in response to the frustration of having one's discourse silenced by patriarchal social norms. The norms have defined the women's existence despite their wish to articulate their own norms. The women chose to make their silencing obvious by refusing to speak. Thus the three women and the female witnesses refuse to "talk." They, in effect, use their silenced discourse as a weapon. A female psychologist likewise refuses to declare the group of women insane since she also understands the silenced feminine discourse and therefore does not consider the women crazy. In court, all simply laugh. From their position of strategic silence, they gain power over the discourses that maintain the patriarchal social system. The strategy in the narrative reveals a conscious awareness of the way things are (patriarchal consciousness) and the possibility of feminine excess (feminine consciousness, which goes beyond the boundaries of dominant discourse). The excess here is an excess of silence. The women's excessive enactment of one way in which patriarchy silences women as a class reverses patriarchal meaning and politics. Instead of being a sign of women's submissiveness to patriarchy, silence becomes a weapon in the struggle with dominant discourse. Silence then becomes a *positive* element in women's culture because it evades masculine control. In a similar way, women's continual loyalty to soap opera, even though it is considered bad taste, is a defiance of masculine control. Feminine discourse, however, must be distinguished from political feminism which presupposes an involvement with the politics of the women's movement. Feminine discourse evidences an awareness of the subordination of women but does not necessarily transform the awareness into political action. Although the film, *A Question of Silence*, is an example of feminist discourse, it speaks to the issues of feminine discourse.

The work of Foucault (1980) delineates the power of discourse to shape what is considered truth in a given discursive tradition. He defines discourse by its parameters of containment, by which he refers to those discursive practices that surround a social practice (sexuality, for example) and ultimately construct a dominant "reality" for the practice under consideration. Foucault relates the power to make meaning within discourse to a will to power which is combined with a will to knowledge. He sees all power relationships as containing within their structure the possibility of resistance:

> Every power relationship implies, at least in potential, a strategy of struggle, in which the two forces are not superimposed, do not lose their specific nature, do not finally become confused. Each constitutes for the other a kind of permanent limit, a point of possible reversal. (1982, p. 225)

Thus Foucault speaks to the potentially resistive power within specific discourses. In *The History of Sexuality* (1980) he points out that since the Renaissance, sexuality has become the major if not the sole indicator of selfhood. According to Foucault, the age of psychiatry marked by the "surveillance" of the body has led to a sensualization of power. In psychoanalytic criticism, sensualized power and narrative discourse are brought together in the term "desire." Desire is used in psychoanalytic theory and psychoanalytic film criticism to delineate the structure by which pleasure is produced either in lived or narrative experience. Much feminist film criticism has used the psychoanalytical notion of pleasure.

According to the psychoanalytic model in film criticism, pleasure in cinematic terms has to do with the tension created between the possibility of sexual excess and the taming of that excess to effect narrative closure. The classic Hollywood narrative starts with equilibrium, introduces a conflict or problem, and the resolution of the conflict provides the climax after which there is a return to equilibrium. Since desire itself is based on the absence of, or inability to attain something, this is a satisfactory way to resolve a narrative, the end of the story being the absence of (more) story. Mulvey (1975) argues that visual pleasure in classical Hollywood cinema is structured on male desire mediated by a collective unconscious. Her article offers an analysis which, because it excludes female spectatorial positions, reflects female frustrations in dealing with the Lacanian "unconscious structured like a language" (p. 9). She argues that the built-in "pattern of pleasure and identification seemed to impose masculinity as 'point of view'" (p. 8–9) in classical Hollywood cinema. Mulvey and others (1981; Heath, 1978; Bergstrom, 1979; Doane, 1983) have sought to address the issue of how a female spectator places herself in relation to psychoanalytical constructs in film form. In this work I would like to conceptualize pleasure more in social than in psychoanalytical terms. Pleasure here is not based on absence, but on satisfaction; and pleasure is active rather than passive.

It is necessary then, in order to theorize pleasure, to substitute for and add to traditional, patriarchially constructed psychoanalytical theory which functions, in part, to naturalize patriarchal structures. The social-psychological account of male and female personality differences delineated by Chodorow (1974) theorizes a construction of feminine personality based on patriarchal child-rearing practices.

> In any given society, feminine personality comes to define itself in relation to a connection with other people more than masculine personality does. (In psychoanalytic terms, women are less individuated than men; they have more flexible ego boundaries.) Moreover, issues of dependency are handled and experienced differently by men and women. For boys and men, both individuation and dependency issues become tied up with the sense of masculinity, or masculine identity. For girls and women, by contrast, issues of femininity or feminine identity, are not problematic in the same way. The structural situation of child rearing, reinforced by female and male role training, produces those differences, which are replicated and reproduced in the sexual sociology of adult life. (1974, p. 44)

Chodorow's recasting of the Oedipal drama into social terms goes far in releasing psychoanalysis from the prison of dominant discourse. And it is this discourse which has constructed narrative formations in line with patriarchal concepts of desire. For women to conceptualize and experience pleasure in these psychoanalytic terms has involved a complex realignment with masculine perspective. The conceptualizing of pleasure which I would like to put forth has two aspects. First, that pleasure is not threatening as Mulvey conceptualizes it, but involves a feminine appropriation of the power to give and receive pleasure. Secondly, because of this appropriation feminine pleasure is active, not passive: it does not involve the search for the lost "other" implied in a psychoanalytic perspective but a finding of oneself, or an unproblematic relationship with the "other" which is, in fact, other women and herself.

Feminine discourse is often classified as "trash"[2] in patriarchal discourse and "excessive" in critical discourse (Feuer, 1984)—that which is "left over," more than a moderate amount. The word "trash" has a number of connotations that are relevant in our cultural analysis of feminine discourse. First, trash connotes that which ought to be discarded, a sort of instant garbage; second, it connotes cheapness, shoddiness, the overflow of the capitalist commodity system. Third, it connotes a superficial glitter designed to appeal to those whose tastes are ill-formed according to the dominant perspective, or at the very least whose tastes are different from those whose use of the dominant value system allows them to dismiss popular art forms as trash. Fourth, trash is excessive: it has more vulgarity, more tastelessness, more offensiveness than is necessary for its function as a cheap commodity. All of these connotations point to its uncomfortably contradictory nature: in the dominant value system which supports patriarchal discourse, trash is the disparaged way of exploiting the subordinate, of appealing cynically to their vulgar tastes. In the discourse of the subordinate, however, "trash" is used defiantly, the devalued commodity is detached from its devaluation, and used positively in the subordinated culture as a source of meanings and pleasure that are formed partly in the knowledge that they are devalued by the dominant value system. For Hobson's (1982, pp. 109–110) soap opera fans, as for Radway's (1984, pp. 90–91) fans of romance, part of the viewer's/reader's pleasure lies in the knowledge that men disapprove of their taste and their defiant assertion of their right to pleasure in the face of masculine disapproval. The insistance on their right to their own pleasure is not only an act of cultural resistance within the politics of the family in that it defies masculine power within the patriarchal family, but such insistance is also a recognition that the differences between masculine and feminine tastes can only be understood in terms of a power relationship of domination and resistance since, in fact, the reading or viewing practices are viewed as an act of defiance. The term "trash" is so rich because it contains within it the social struggle for power articulated in terms of cultural taste and preference.

---

[2] The following is an example:

Trash is an art. A great trashy movie will dazzle you with costumes, flesh and sets: it will make you hoot at catty, nasty lines; it will make you laugh at a preposterous plot; but still, it will make you watch. It has fun with itself. In its first night *Lace II* is just that, TV junk food served on silver trays, delicious. But in its second night *Lace II* turns stale, for trash that's left too long can start to smell. (*People Weekly*, May 6, 1985, p. 9)

The word "excess" has been much more widely used to describe women's genres within patriarchy (Feuer, 1984). The word "excess" also contains traces of the same sociocultural struggle as the term "trash," but its emphasis is sightly different. An excessive representation is one that exaggerates the more conventional representation of an ideological value, and through exaggeration it critiques both the conventional representation and the ideological system of which it is a practical example. Thus the frequency with which presently "respectable" women have past experience as prostitutes in soaps' narratives is an example of excess. Because the plot takes the patriarchal conventions of representing woman as either the virgin-mother or the whore and pushes the dichotomy to excess, the program implies that the only way for a woman to experience her sexuality outside the confines of a monogamous marriage is by becoming a whore. The soap thus uses prostitution as a critique of patriarchy's control of feminine sexuality. The program performs the patriarchal function of saying that the nonmonogamous woman must be a whore, but its excessiveness allows for an overspill of meaning that is beyond that required by its patriarchal function. Thus semiotic excess, which I have described earlier in this paper, is then available for both feminine meanings of feminine sexuality and for a feminine critique of the patriarchal meaning. The meanings of prostitution in soaps are not confined to the patriarchal meaning, but overspill into a range of feminine, resistive meanings. It is quite logical, then, that the dominant culture should characterize soaps, films designed to make women cry or women's "weepies," and romance novels as trash because these media forms are full of such possibilities for questioning patriarchal and other forms of dominant ideology. It is through the common understanding among women of feminine discourse that feminine cultural practices are given meaning by women. Within women's cultural practices talk to other women about the individual or particular groups in relation to cultural norms is called gossip. Gossip is denigrated in much the same way that soaps and other cultural forms practiced by women are denigrated, and gossip among women offers resistance to patriarchal dominance in an even more direct way than soaps since, because it is a spoken form, it involves the collaboration of two or more people.

WOMEN'S GOSSIP

Central to feminine culture is "women's talk" or gossip, "a form of unarticulated female power" (Oakley, 1972, p. 15). Deborah Jones (1980) defines gossip in the context of women's oral culture as:

a way of talking between women in their roles as women, intimate in style, personal and domestic in topic and setting, a female cultural event which springs from and perpetuates the restrictions of the female role, but also gives the comfort of validation. (p. 194)

The soaps generate gossip both inside and outside of the programs themselves. The characters gossip about each other, and the fans gossip about the characters in a way that weakens the boundary between text and social experience. Gossip is a form of feminine discourse and a source of feminine pleasure in that it articulates and shares women's interests in the existing cultural system.

According to Gluckman (1963) what is important about gossip is that it signifies membership in a group:

> The right to gossip about certain people is a privilege which is only extended to a person when he or she is accepted as a member of a group or set. It is a hallmark of membership. Hence rights to gossip serve to mark off a particular group. (p. 313)

Gossiping about a soap with other fans gives women the shared privileged position as members of a group who, in fact, know a soap family well enough to gossip about it (Hobson, 1982, p. 125). Gossip also has other features salient to the soaps. According to Jones (1980) gossip in the home is necessarily serial, taken up and put down between work and children. Gossip, like soaps, is trivialized in dominant discourse and like any form of female solidarity gossip poses a threat to established codes. Women's gossip, which Jones (p. 195) characterizes as a language of female secrets, is one of women's strengths and, like all our strengths, it is both discounted and attacked.

The way that women's gossip functions lies partly in its form, its reciprocity, and paralinguistic responses (Jones, 1980)—the raised eyebrow, the sigh, the silence—forms that are typical of repressed discourses, and that assume and articulate the shared experience of repression. The implications of such conversations, according to Jones (1980), are contemplated, not argued, and each participant contributes her own experience to the pattern of discourse. Chesler (1972) describes women's conversations similarly: "Their theme, method and goal are non-verbal and/or non-verbalized. Facial expressions, pauses, sighs and seemingly unrelated (or "non-abstract") responses to statements are crucial to such dialogue" (p. 268). These non-verbal conventions are also codified in soap opera, where what is not said is often of crucial importance, and the audience understands its significance because of their familiarity with the show's history. This familiarity is a form of solidarity among soaps fans.

Jones (1980) lists as the four functions of gossip house-talk, scandal, bitching, and chatting. House-talk is basically women's talk about housework, husband and children—training in the female role. Scandal involves judgment about domestic morality over which women, according to Jones, have been appointed guardians. Ideologically, then, scandal reinforces sexist moral codes which women enforce but have not created. Scandal, however, also serves a second function: it caters to women's interest in each other's lives. It provides a "cultural medium which reflects female reality, and a connection between the lives of women who have otherwise been isolated from each other" (p. 197). Likewise, Jones maintains, it has an entertainment value "perhaps a kind of vicarious enjoyment of a range of experience beyond the small sphere to which the individual woman is restricted" (p. 197). Bitching, the third function of gossip, is an overt expression of women's anger at their restricted role and inferior social status. Consciousness raising in the women's movement is a political form of bitching. Chatting, the fourth function, is mutual self-disclosure. It implies a trusting relationship between the participants and serves the purpose of nurturing other women. Gossip then has specific discursive functions in women's culture. It validates their area of expertise (the home); it points out contradictions in institutionally expected social behavior as opposed to actual social behavior; it provides entertainment in the form of storytelling; and it provokes a sense of intimacy. Thus by modeling soaps' narrative form on this oral tradition among women, soaps' producers are able to tap into an intimate level of involvement with their audiences.

I would suggest that one prevailing pleasure that women find in soaps is validation for their own kind of talk. Such talk produces, circulates, and validates feminine meanings and pleasures within and against patriarchy. Some of this feminine culture may, by some women, be translated into direct political action, but all of it forms a grass-roots consciousness that the political activists need, whether they recognize it or not, for their power base. The political effectivity of such grass-roots consciousness should not be underestimated on account of the lack of direct political consequences, for the first step toward political action is an awareness of oppression by subordinate groups. But the gossip networks surrounding soaps are not their only claim to resistance. The form of the soap's text also sets up resistive relationships when looked at in relation to the classic narrative structure, as described by Mulvey (1975), mentioned earlier in this chapter.

THE TEXT, THE SUBJECT, AND RESISTANCE

I am suggesting that the form of the soap opera is progressive and is oppositional to the conventional "realism" in television narratives (e.g. action dramas) which feature a single hero or heroine, one major plot, and final closure. Some authors (Davies, 1984; Fiske, 1987) would argue that the serial form of soaps parallels the process of seduction. Others argue that the form of soaps typifies housework (Modleski, 1982) while the action drama typifies work outside of the home thought to be more goal-oriented. Both Modleski (1982) and Allen (1985) suggest that the soap evolved out of the literary form of the domestic novel. Although all of these ideas are semiotically valid, I would suggest, in addition, that the material conditions of the development of the soaps' form on radio also be looked at. Viewed and listened to in this way soaps can also be seen as closely connected with orality. Although primary oral cultures with no knowledge of writing are not prevalent today, "secondary orality" still exists. According to Ong (1982) in *Orality and Literacy.*

> It [primary orality] is primary by contrast with the "secondary orality" of present day high-technology culture, in which a new orality is sustained by telephone, radio, television, and other electronic devices that depend for their existence and functioning on writing and print. Today primary oral culture in the strict sense hardly exists since every culture knows of writing and has some experience of its effects. Still, to varying degrees many cultures and subcultures, even in a high-technology ambiance, preserve much of the mind-set of primary orality. (p. 11)

Thus to say that soap opera on television is like an oral form is not to say that it is a throwback to a previous historical moment, but that it possesses the characteristics of orality which can determine not just modes of expression but thought processes as well. Written forms of expression are derived from a literate cultural set and possess a narrative form which embodies a literate thought process. The narrative form and conventions of the soap opera embody the characteristics of orally-based thought and expession listed by Ong (1982). They can be characterized as follows:

1. Additive rather than subordinate.
2. Aggregative rather than analytic.
3. Redundant or "copious".
4. Conservative or traditionalist.
5. Close to the human lifeworld.
6. Agnostically toned.
7. Emphatic and participatory rather than objectively distanced.
8. Homeostatic.
9. Situational rather than abstract. (pp. 37–49)

Ong's list of characteristics accounts for many of the ways that soaps are criticized in dominant culture. Since the feminine culture and feminine discourse that I am describing are primarily oral, I would contend that part of the soaps' power to generate alternative meanings has to do with their structuring of a type of realism that is more characteristic of oral than literate narrative conventions.

For example, the characterization of particular characters sometimes changes when a new actor is assigned the part as in the following:

K: Remember Mary Anderson? She really changed. They had the blond Mary Anderson who was sweet and then they had the red head for a while who turned into a real witch.

ME: You mean they don't keep the same characteristics when a new actress or actor comes in?

S: The first Laura would never have done anything evil, but the third Laura, you were ready for her to go.

It is not that the viewers of soaps do not know that literate conventions of presentation are being broken, but that they accept the conventions of soaps in the light of the constraints imposed by practical considerations like the show's budget and oral traditions in which the characters may vary with each telling of the story.

Entering into the world of soap viewing thus involves the knowledge of the constraints imposed on soap operas by dominant culture. Here is an example from the conversation among the *Days of Our Lives* fans:

S: There's a new bad person on the scene.

L: What if he's Stefano? (laughter)

S: Stefano's dead!

O: We don't know Stefano's dead. We just think he is.

C: No one ever found his body.

K: Some people think that Roman is still alive?

ME: Why do you think that Roman is still alive?

S: Because they didn't find his body, and, I'd swear, on one soap opera they said Stefano's dead, but they put his body on ice.

O: Roman left the program. He wasn't pleased with something - his money or his part. Before he was killed, there was an article in *TV Guide* or one of the books that he was going to leave, that he wasn't pleased. I don't know whether it was ... I think it was over his part, the way it was developed.

The above conversation illustrates an aspect of audience reading practices (or play) which involves a suspension of the world of dominant culture and the playful crossing over of the boundary between fiction and reality. "Real life" is, of course, that contained and articulated by dominant discursive practices, and viewers talking about the characters *as though* they were real defies the dominant conception of what constitutes reality.[3]

---

[3] For a more elaborate discussion of the carnivalesque and soap opera as utterance see Brown and Barwick (1987).

There is, among soaps' viewers, amusement at the absurdities of soaps' plots and the complex interrelations among their characters. Take the following conversation about *Days of Our Lives* for example:

S: Oh, Alex and Marie. They weren't married. Marie was a nun. Before she was a nun, she lived in New York. Even before that there was Tom Horton, Jr., who had amnesia and who somehow or another had plastic surgery and somehow or another he wandered back to Salem with plastic surgery and nobody knew him and he didn't know anybody.

ME: You mean Tom has a son?

S: Yeh. He fell in love with his sister, Marie. And they did their thing and they were going to get married and all of a sudden Tom Horton, Jr., remembered. So Marie got sick and she fled and nobody knew where she was for a while and then later on she went in a convent and became a nun. But meanwhile, when nobody knew where she was, she went to New York and had an affair with Alex and had a baby.

ME: Who's Alex?

S: Alex is the really bad one.

K: The consummate evil one.

S: He did Stefano's dirty work.

ME: So he and Marie had a daughter?

S: I'd forgotten about her. She got married. Who did she get married to?

K: She married Joshua. She was engaged to Jake, the Salem Strangler.

O: Oh yeh.

In the group discussion noted above, everyone laughed when it was mentioned that Jessica, Marie's daughter, was once engaged to the Salem Strangler. The humor takes in not only the absurdity of the specific situation but also the character's history. If one has followed Marie's story over the years, one knows that she has been subjected to the most absurdly terrible (and, because of the excess, humorous) series of tragedies that one can imagine. These events may or may not be different in kind and degree from those which might beset another character—Marlena, for example. Marlena's litany of problems, however, would also elicit laughter. It is the cumulative effect emerging when one is talking about them that makes them funny. The same viewers who at the moment of viewing enter wholeheartedly into the pathos of a particular situation, at the level of metadiscourse are quite capable of laughing at the same event.

Setting offers another level of interest and speculation among soaps' viewers in relation to soap opera realism. The following quote from the soaps discussion transcript discusses setting:

ME: Does anyone know where Salem is?

K: We've been trying to figure that out for years. They mention Chicago a lot and they mention New York a lot.

S: I think it's closer to New York City.
L: I think it's closer to Chicago.
C: I think it's in Ohio....
ME: So we can't figure out where that is.
K.   Some of the soaps like *General Hospital.* You know where that is.
ME: Where is it?
S.   Port Charles, New York.
ME: And where is Port Charles?
L: It's upstate New York, isn't it?
S: It's a real place.
K: They make allusions to places that you know.
C: Like it's only a couple of hours to New York.

Salem (like Port Charles) is not a real place, but it seems real. The above speculation stimulates gossip because it values the pleasure of direct comparison to women's different experiences of America—it can be, and is, close to New York, Chicago, and Ohio—and its factual indeterminancy makes it a recurrent source of pleasure: "We've been trying to figure it out for years;" so different from *Kojak's* New York, *The Streets of San Francisco*, or *Miami Vice's* Miami. Classic (masculine) realism depends on reference to external reality (closed): soap opera realism is internal (open). Since we do not know where Salem is, it can become ours. Salem can be anywhere we want it to be. The same type of speculation about place exists in relation to *Hill Street Blues*, a program that, in its early days, evidenced many of the characteristics of daytime soaps.

Incongruities of time are also tolerated (or enjoyed) by soaps' viewers. Time is not necessarily altered in order to make cause and effect relationships clearer or more logical but in order to emphasize those moments of heightened emotional intensity.

ME: Time goes faster?
K: They can warp it however they want. Time can go really slowly or it can go fast, you know. It just depends on what they want. They can make one evening last for three days and then a year can go by like that (snaps fingers). But it's funny the way they slip it in. Like just the other day Marlena was saying Roman's been dead all this time. They're making it sound like Roman's been dead for years when in real time it's only been about six months.

Soaps allow the audience to speed through story details which are without much emotional appeal; and like memories or gossip, they sometimes allow us to linger over moments of pleasure.

Because of the longevity of the viewers' association with the characters and content of soaps, there is also the pleasure involved in familiarity and regularity. Brunsdon (1984) refers to this as "ritual pleasure." Over a long period of time the viewer goes through the day-to-day issues with soap characters as well as the celebration of holidays and special events like weddings, births, and other gatherings of the soap "family." As the women in the *Days of our Lives* group put it:

S: I'll tell you what I like is Christmas. When they put those ornaments on the tree.
O: Each one has their own name on it. Each one that comes in the family has a Christmas ball with their own name on it. And each one puts their own name on the tree.

There is also ritual pleasure involved in returning to a continuous soap very much like returning to a childhood home or neighborhood after a long period of absence.

When dealing with the problems presented on the soaps the viewer is aware of both the content of the show and the problem as it relates to the social experience of the viewer. As Brunsdon (1984) notes:

> For the soap fan, one of the moments of pleasure is when you can say 'Oh, I *knew* that was going to happen.' But this is not the same feeling as the attendant fascination of *how* it is going to happen. At the moment, I really don't think that Sheila Grant is going to have the baby she is pregnant with. My reasons are partly generic—I know that a very high proportion of soap opera pregnancies come to little more than a few months' story. They (her reasons) are partly what I experience as 'intuitive'—she is in her forties, she has already got three children, the house isn't big enough. (p. 83)

Rather than experiencing as frustrations the constant postponement of the resolution to problems in soaps, Brunsdon and the viewers with whom I spoke experience them in the nature of story problems as suggested in the dialogue quoted below.

S: And you always know, if something doesn't work out, it will with somebody else later on. You always know that. Except for Mickey. Why hasn't Mickey had a relationship lately?
O: I don't know.
K: He's too old.
S: It doesn't have anything to do with his being old. Old people have relationships. I will have Mickey have a relationship to prove you wrong.
O: I think he should have one. He's lonely right now.
S: Yes, he is and he's mellowed out.
O: Ah huh.

The ongoing puzzles, then, offer little tests of our ability to outguess the writing and production considerations inherent in the genre as well as the social implications of possible choices if made by the characters or if made by us.

Dominant notions of character usually stress the idea of identification whereby audiences identify, or put themselves in the place of a main character, whose feelings and insights the audience shares. Fiske (1986b) suggests two ways of reading character, a discursive strategy and a psychologistic reading. The discursive strategy is:

> structuralist in inflection and understands character as a textual construct that performs definable functions in the text. Character is a textual device for mobilizing and enacting social and personal discourses within a metaphoric representation of the individual. (pp. 3–4)

The psychologistic construct sees character as an analogue of a real person and the viewer "identifies with that character in the process of self projection" (p. 17). According to Fiske:

> Reading character as a psychologistic construct rather than a textual one is a reading practice of the ideology of individualism. Such a reading is naturalised into the only possible way of understanding character in a society for whom the individual is the prime source and definer of experience. (p. 17)

The idea of the well-rounded character is a product of individualistic or dominant discourse or a discourse which minimizes class, gender, race, or age distinctions. If the psychologistic concept of character centers on the individual for whom the reading described by Fiske is culturally rewarded, then the soaps, with their multiple characters and lack of specific heroine or hero, can be seen as standing in opposition to that view. Since the ideology of the individual considers each person responsible (or to blame) for her or his own position in society, it denies gender politics. It does not consider social and class organization as definers of meaning but rather considers the individual's unique, personal characteristics as the elements responsible for defining experience. By generating multiple characters for which the relationship of the audience to character is more ambiguous than identification with a specific character, television daytime soaps are resistive to this dominant narrative construct, which for most television realism is a dominant stylistic device. Multiple characters, then, foster for women what Fiske describes as a discursive reading strategy involving the enactment by many characters of some of the social and personal discourses available to women. For example, the fact that there are many characters enables an issue to be discussed and/or settled by several characters in different ways which leaves the text open to several meaning possibilities.

Even though the concept of identification with specific characters may be a construct associated with dominant thinking, this is not to say that audiences are not intensely involved with soaps. As Davies (1984) aptly points out: "Soap opera audiences are not passive consumers of light entertainment, but active participants in negotiating complex role models and contradictory ideologies with definite, if unconscious motivation." (p. 33) Davies (1984, p. 33) suggests that once "hooked," people vacillate between their need to know, or the pleasure of anticipation, and an *implication* with characters which is more complicated than identification. An implicatory reading would imply that the audience chooses a reading position that recognizes discursive possibilities in character types—the villianess, the ingenue, the good mother—but at the same time, a position that is intensely involved with the characters. Implication as a reading strategy is audience-controlled and is therefore active pleasure. I would suggest that a reader does not just view a soap, but that she adopts it along with all of its characters, good and bad, and then treats that soap and its characters with a familial loyalty. The use of multiple characters refuses a single- or fixed-subject identification. At the same time it prevents the hierarchy of discourse present when there is a privileged well-rounded main character. Likewise since issues are seen from each character's perspective sequentially, there is no preferred point of view. Kaplan (1983) points out that the radical text or the text that addresses subcultural readings refuses to construct a fixed spectator but instead seeks to position the viewer as one involved in the processes of the narrative instead of being captured by it. The type of characterization on the soaps and the way that fans interact with the characters suggests that the literary idea of identification and of the well-rounded character are not applicable to soaps. One way that soaps may be considered radical is by their refusal of hierarchical character construction. In addition to issues around characterization, audience positioning in terms of relationships and control are crucial to an understanding of audience pleasure in relation to soaps texts.

Some critics contend that soap audiences "are positioned as relatively powerless low-income masses" (Davies, 1984). Such a reading presents problems in relation to readers' viewing practices. Davies describes the target soap opera audience: "As in classic Marxist theory, they have nothing to sell but their bodies. Hence your body is your prime possession" (p. 32). He points out that as well as being the instrument of the economy of patriarchal capitalist success (for women, getting a man and keeping him; and, for men, succeeding in becoming rich and famous with women being one of the rewards) the body is also the site of primal pleasures in soaps. It is the unspoken discourse of sexuality which the audience, however constructed, thoroughly understands.

There is no need to reiterate here the number of pregnancies, the importance attached to paternity and to maternity, or the large number of sexual liaisons between characters in soap operas. Contrary to the discourse that places the pregnant woman as powerless over natural events, however, often women in soaps use pregnancy as power over the father of the unborn child (Modleski, 1982, p. 95). The father will often marry the mother of his child, whether or not he loves her (or whether or not the pregnancy is real), thereby achieving the female character's constructed need to be taken care of in the only way that is available to her in the dominant system, somewhat of a contradiction in this case because most women on the soaps do a good job of taking care of themselves. Women characters in the soaps, then, often use their bodies to achieve their own ends. As Rubin (1975) points out, kinship systems based on the exchange of women are systems in which women do not have full rights to themselves. According to Rubin the social organization of sex, in order to maintain this system, rests upon gender, heterosexuality, the incest taboo, and the constraint of female sexuality. Soaps pay elaborate attention to these social organizations of sex. On the other hand, the power that female characters in soaps assert over the relationships in which they participate does not support the dominant idea of the exchange of women as passive commodities. However, control over kinship relations is the heart of women's gossip and is very important in the soaps.

S: Do you know that Tom and Alice are something like great, great grandparents?
K: I think they've got something like great, great grandchildren.
S: Let's see. Hope is a great, great grandchild.
O: No, she isn't. Mickey is their son and Hope is the daughter.
    So she is the granddaughter and Melissa is the granddaughter.
K: No, Julie was the granddaughter.
S: Julie was the granddaughter. Julie is Doug and Addie's daughter.
O: Oh, that's right.

Such "endless genealogies" are a potent source of gossip because women in many societies are the traditional keepers of family records, thus knowledge of the intricacies of kinship relations is a form of power over those relationships.

The soaps operate with a concept of the body quite different from the bourgeois ego or the individual biological body. In the soaps, bodies are not "revealed" as in many other forms of representation, as individualized bodies or as objectified female bodies, the usual objects of the male gaze in the classic Hollywood narrative (Mulvey, 1975). Instead, the body in its more carnivalesque sense is present. Close-ups of people at the peak of emotional conflict expose this agnostic body to scrutiny in much the same way that a grotesque image reveals too much, defying dominant rules of propriety about how much emotion is acceptable to show. The emotional constraints and the resolved emotional conflicts of the dominant literary tradition tell us that it is possible to live "happily ever after," but the soaps tell us otherwise. They codify life in some humorous and grotesque ways. Soaps help us to laugh at ourselves and the absurdities of subordinate cultural positioning. As consumers of soap operas, women do participate in existing dominant systems, but the extent to which women can be said to be the passive objects or victims of dominant discursive practices by watching and enjoying soap operas is limited by the women's use of these same cultural forms to affirm their own positions of subjectivity in a women's discursive tradition. Soap companies may profit financially from the soaps, but from the perspective of women viewers the transaction is not one-sided. Soaps may exist for one set of cultural practices but are often used for another. The set of pleasures afforded some women by the soaps is perhaps much less perverse than we have been led to believe by patriarchal discourse. The other side of the discursive coin resists the control of dominant discursive practices in favor of reading practices which defy established rules in narrative, discursive, and social contexts. The breaking of the rules can be a source of pleasure in feminine discursive traditions. The taking of cultural pleasure into one's own hands is both an act of pleasure and a defiance of dominant order.

CONCLUSION

That a woman's culture exists alongside dominant culture is amply evidenced by the study of communication theory (Foucault, 1980; Showalter, 1985; L. Williams, 1985); history (Smith-Rosenberg, 1975); and folklore (Jordan & de Caro, 1986). The issue is problematized, as in all feminist theory, by the fact that feminine subjects exist in a relationship to dominant patriarchal systems that is uniquely related to and constructed within and by masculine culture and discourses. Women's culture, like folk culture, is transmitted informally outside of established institutions, and is recognized, though differently characterized, by both insiders (women themselves) and outsiders (men, dominant institutions). In the present age of "secondary orality," that is orality sustained "by telephone, radio, television, and other electronic devices that depend for their existence and functioning on writing and print" (Ong, 1982, p. 11), oral culture exists on the borderlines between life and art, between talk and language, between folk and official, between subculture and dominant culture. It is shaped by the power play between dominant and nondominant discourses.

Women's talk in general is seen from a dominant perspective as excessive, and is characterized in dominant terms by such descriptions as "running off at the mouth." In dominant discourse, talking for a purpose is acceptable, but talking for pleasure is not. Men's public purposeful talk (preaching, politics) is revered, but women's private talk is denigrated as purposeless and malicious. Dominant discourse thus construes personal talk as a potential draining of the power of masculine discursive positions and institutions; the latter privilege order, rules, and rational progressions over the affective pleasures of the uncontrolled utterances of talk that does not play by the rules. Gossip among women, for example, has the potential to evoke weakness, disorder, and emotional excess (crying or laughing), all of which potentially escape the order necessary for the perpetuation of the power of dominant cultural traditions. Gossip is feared, along with other feminine excesses, as dangerous to dominant culture; but for women gossip may be a source of power. It is empowering in that, through talk, women may understand the system and workings of official culture (and sometimes laugh at it).

Gossip, soap operas, and the like are a constant irritant to masculine dominant culture because the valuing of talk as activity and performance is a definance of goal-oriented definitions of dominant cultural practices. Both gossip and soap operas are perpetually in process, and their apparent aimlessness marks them as "unfaithful" and as incapable of serving a "useful" message-bearing function. Soap operas claim for women a space and time in which there is freedom to play with dialogue—dialogue that does not "advance the plot," but is simply there for pleasure.

Women, in the relationship established through gossip *about* the soaps, and in the affective pleasure of communal watching practices, establish a solidarity among themselves which operates as a threat to dominant representational systems because such gossip is evidence of a solidarity among women established through feminine discourse. Gossip, as well as the soaps themselves, establishes an openness that defies established boundaries instigated within patriarchal representational systems. Gossip is open-ended, as are the soaps, and such openness challenges the cultural dominance of other representational systems which close off, limit, and contain meaning for women. Within the serial and open structure of the soaps lies the possibility of feminine resistance and even subversion of the dominant classical narrative form, a form which by its construction and ability to define masculine ego boundaries by voicing dominant and patriarchal rules and values, almost always subverts women's expression. Linda Barwick (1985), in her work on women's oral song in performance, describes a song in which the women's voice is narratively silenced:

> In fact it does not matter in narrative terms whether the woman is a willing or unwilling partner in the seducer's plans. Because of the woman's inability to express herself in straightforward terms, the plot develops the same way regardless of her intentions. Although Donna Lombarda is the central figure of the narrative, her actions are redundant, her speeches expendable, and her intentions are immaterial. (p. 247)

In this quotation we see dominant discourse through its preferred narrative conventions effectively silencing the feminine discourse by its willful closure of the narrative. In the soaps as well as in women's gossip about the soaps, there lies the openness to possibility which, in relation to the closed system of the classical narrative, becomes subversive.

In my research, gossip has been central to both my subject and my method. It is the "social cement" that binds me to my soap and to my family and friends who are my fellow fans. But gossip also connects me, my research, and soap opera to culture at large by allowing me to operate from the inside, from inside me, from inside the culture. But, like women's culture in general, feminine academic work, too, has to make space for itself within a patriarchal frame. The public form of this essay has been developed by an academic history that, like that of the soaps, is patriarchal to the core. Yet I hope my readers will, like soap opera fans, be able to hear the gossipy, scandalous, resisting voice of the feminine within the form of academic essay. The soap opera has progressed further than the academic essay: for, in soaps, by using a patriarchal form for their own purposes women have "stolen the language of the patriarchy" (Ostriker, 1985) and used it to question patriarchal myths in a way that we are only beginning to do in academia. The form of the soap opera, while using patriarchal myths, structures these myths in such a way that audiences can use them for their own purposes. By activating the potential for gossip in soaps, women can use them to validate the value of a feminine culture which patriarchy may have invalidated but has been unable to suppress. The relegation of the soaps to the marginal world of trash in masculine discourse has not contained them, nor the women's voices they both contain and provoke. Women continue to understand and validate feminine culture while at the same time understanding the masculine conception as well which gives us a source of power. All that remains is for us to use it.

APPENDIX 1

Recorded conversation cited in the chapter:

Brown, M. E. Interview with American fans of *Days of Our Lives* (six women aged 18 to 80, one man aged 18). Audiotape. Recorded July, 1985. Private collection.

REFERENCES

Allen, R. (1985). *Speaking of soap operas*. Chapel Hill: University of North Carolina Press.

Althusser, L. (1971). Ideology and the ideological state apparatuses. In B. Brewster (trans.), *Lenin and philosophy and other essays.* (pp. 127–186). London: New Left Books.

Barthes, R. (1972). *Mythologies.* New York: Hill and Wang.

Barwick, L. (1985). *Critical perspectives on oral song in performance: The case of Donna Lombarda.* Unpublished Ph.D dissertation, South Australia: Flinders. University.

Bergstrom, J. (1979). Enunciation and sexual difference (Part 1), *Camera Obscura,* (3–4), 33–70.

Brown, M. E. (1986). The politics of soaps: Pleasure and feminine empowerment. *The Australian Journal of Cultural Studies, 4*(2), 1–25.

Brown, M. E., & Barwick, L. (1987, May). Motley moments, soap operas and the power of the utterance. Paper presented at the Annual Conference of the Society for Cinema Studies, Montreal, Canada.

Brunsdon, C. (1984). Writing about soap opera. In L. Masterman (Ed.), *Television mythologies.* (pp. 82–87). London: Comedia.

Cantor, M., & Pingree, S. (1983). *The soap opera.* London: Sage.

Chesler, P. (1972). *Women and madness.* New York: Avon.

Chodorow, N. (1974). Family structure and feminine personality. In M. Z. Rosaldo & L. Lamphere (Eds.), *Women, culture and society.* Stanford: Stanford University Press.

Chodorow, N. (1978). *The reproduction of mothering: Psychoanalysis and the sociology of gender.* Berkeley, CA: University of California Press.

Davies, J. (1984). Soap and other operas. *Metro, 65,* 31–3.

Doane, M. A. (1983). Film and the masquerade: Theorizing the female spectator, *Screen Education, 23* (3–4), 74–84.

Fiske, J. (1986a). Television: Polysemy and popularity. *Critical Studies In Mass Communication, 3* (4), 391–408.

Fiske, J. (1986b). Cagney and Lacy: Reading character structurally and politically. *Communication, 13* (4), 399–426.

Fiske, J. (1987). *Television culture.* London: Methuen.

Foucault, M. (1980). *The history of sexuality: Volume I: An introduction.* New York: Random House.

Foucault, M. (1982). The subject and power. In H. L. Dreyfus & P. Rabinow (Eds.), *Michael Foucault: Beyond structuralism and hermeneutics* (pp. 208–226). Brighton: Harvester Press.

Feuer, J. (1984). Melodrama, social form and television today. *Screen, 25*(1), 4–17.

Gluckman, M. (1963). Gossip and scandal. *Current Anthropology, 3,* 307–16.

Gramsci, A. (1971). *Selections from the prison notebooks.* Q. Hoare & G. Nowell-Smith (Ed. and Trans.). New York: International Publishers.

Hall, S., Hobson, D., Lowe, A., & Willis, P. (1980). *Culture, media, language.* London: Hutchinson.

Heath, S. (1978). Difference. *Screen, 19* (3), 51–112.

Hobson, D. (1982). *"Crossroads," the drama of a soap opera.* London: Methuen.

Jones, D. (1980). Gossip: Notes on women's oral culture. *Women's Studies International Quarterly, 3,* 193–8.

Jordan, R. A., & De Caro, F. (1986). Women and the study of folklore. *Signs, 11*(3), 500–18.

Kaplan, A. (1983). The realist debate in the feminist film: A historical overview of theories and strategies in realism and the avant garde theory film (1971–81). *Women and film: Both sides of the camera.* New York: Methuen.

Modleski, T. (1982). *Loving with a vengeance: Mass-produced fantasies for women.* London: Methuen.

Mulvey, L. (1975). Visual pleasure and narrative cinema. *Screen, 16* (3), 6–18.

Mulvey, L. (1981). On "Duel in the Sun": Afterthoughts on "Visual Pleasure and Narrative Cinema." *Framework, 15–17,* 12–15.

Oakley, A. (1972). *Sex, gender, and society.* Melbourne: Sun Books.

Oakley, A. (1981). Interviewing women: A contradiction in terms. In H. Roberts (Ed.), *Doing feminist research.* (pp. 30–61). London: Routledge and Kegan Paul.

Ong, W. (1982). *Orality and literacy.* London: Methuen.

Ostriker, A. (1985). The thieves of language: Women poets and revisionist myth making. In E. Showalter (Ed.), *The new feminist criticism: Essays on women's literature and theory.* (pp. 314–338). New York: Pantheon.

O'Sullivan, T., Hartley, J., Saunders, D., and Fiske, J. (Eds.) (1983). *Key concepts in communication.* London: Methuen.

Radway, J. (1984). *Reading the romance: Women, patriarchy and popular literature.* Chapel Hill: University of North Carolina Press.

Rubin, G. (1975). The traffic in women: Notes on the political economy of sex. In R. R. Reiter (Ed.), *Toward an anthropology of women.* (pp. 157–210). New York: Monthly Review Press.

Showalter, E. (1985). Feminist criticism in the wilderness. In E. Showalter (Ed.), *The new feminist criticism: Essays on women, literature and theory.* (pp. 243–270). New York: Pantheon.

Smith-Rosenberg, C. (1975). The female world of love and ritual. *Signs, 1*(1), 1–29.

Timberg, B. (1987). The rhetoric of the camera in television soap opera. In H. Newcomb (Ed.), *Television: The critical view: Fourth edition.* (pp. 164–178). Oxford: Oxford University Press.

Williams, L. (1985, June). A jury of their peers: Questions of silence, speech and judgment in films by women. Paper presented at the Society for Cinema Studies Annual Conference, New York.

Williams, R. (1977). *Marxism and literature.* London: Fontanna.

FILMOGRAPHY/VIDEOGRAPHY

A Question of Silence. Sigma Films 1982; *p:* Matthijs van Heijningen; *d/sc:* Marleen Gorris; *ph:* Frans Bromet; *ed:* Hans van Dongen. *l.p:* Edda Barends *(Christine),* Nelly Frijda *(Annie),* Henriette Tol *(Andrea),* Cox Habbema *(Dr Janine van den Bos),* Eddy Brugman *(Janine's husband).* 96 mins.

Days of Our Lives. Corday (with Columbia). Began 1965. Shown on NBC, 1–2 pm in the United States, Monday–Friday. 60 mins.

III

Methods for Studying Women's Communication

8

Interviewing Women: A Phenomenological Approach to Feminist Communication Research*

KRISTIN M. LANGELLIER
Department of Speech Communication
University of Maine

DEANNA L. HALL
Department of Speech Communication
University of Maine

The interview is a standard and ubiquitous research instrument in the human sciences, including communication studies. Sociologist Ann Oakley (1981, p. 31) compares interviewing to marriage: "Everybody knows what it is, an awful lot of people do it, and yet behind each closed front door there is a world of secrets." The "secrets of interviewing" especially concern interpretive research (e.g., phenomenology, hermeneutics, ethnomethodology, ethnography) which takes the relation of the researcher and the researched as the historical, social, and interpersonal conditions under which knowledge is generated and understood (Polkinghorne, 1983). Feminist researchers (Oakley, 1981; Acker, Barry, & Essenveld, 1983; Gluck, 1979; Armitage, 1983) are also concerned with the "secrets of interviewing women." In accordance with the conventions of research reporting, the interview process is routinely underreported and thereby mystified (Briggs, 1986) in both traditional and feminist research. The orderly, coherent, and logically organized descriptions reported in research are far removed from the often chaotic, confusing, and contradictory experience of doing interviews.

Doing an interview constitutes a communicative event with particular

---

* An earlier version of this paper was presented at the Eastern Communication Association Convention, Atlantic City, NJ, May 1 1986.

norms and rules. When the interview is itself understood as a communicative event, the process of interviewing women to study their communication requires investigation: how does the interview access women's communication? In this essay we explore the process of interviewing women from an approach that combines phenomenology and feminism. As an empirical illustration of our argument, we analyze the interview process in a phenomenological study of mother–daughter storytelling conducted by one of us (Hall, 1985).

Our investigation of interviewing women proceeds in three phases. In a first section, we consider methodological issues in combining phenomenology with the demands of feminist communication research as an approach to interviewing women. Second, we examine the interview as a research method for accessing one form of women's communication—personal narratives, or the stories people tell about their experiences. Third, we present concrete exemplars from our studies of mother–daughter storytelling, paying particular attention to the relational dynamics of the interview process.

PHENOMENOLOGY AND FEMINIST COMMUNICATION RESEARCH

Like most other speech communication scholars, we learned a research methodology in graduate school—in our case, phenomenology—without special reference to studying women's communication, and only later and on our own studied feminist scholarship. To what extent is phenomenological research compatible with feminist research? On the basis of our research experience studying women's communication, we argue, with other feminists (Bartky, 1977; Reinharz, 1983; Stanley & Wise, 1983a, 1983b; Bowles, 1984), that phenomenology is an appropriate methodology for studying women's communication. In broad methodological terms, phenomenology and feminism share two assumptions. First, both perspectives sharply criticize positivism's separation between the knower (researcher) and the known (researched) "out there" to be researched *on*. What is known and what is understood is accessible only through the researcher's consciousness and in her relationship to the researched. There are no theoretically neutral or objective methodological positions from which to conduct research (Kuhn, 1970); there are no methods or techniques of doing research other than through the researcher (Polkinghorne, 1983). Feminist criticism of the human sciences shows that knowledge previously considered to be objective is, in fact, androcentric, or male-centered. Androcentric research ignores and devalues women, stereotypes and distorts their experiences, and judges them to be deviant or deficient by comparison to male models (Westkott, 1979; Spender, 1985). Second, both phenomenology and feminism take as foundational the primacy of lived experience. Lived experience, our being-in-the-world, is the data of the human realm. As such, lived experience cannot be taken for granted, but requires rigorous and sensitive interpretation. Phenomenology and feminism converge in a concern to "be true to the phenomenon"—the phenomenon of women's experience.

But to be sure, feminism is also something more than phenomenology. In feminist research the researcher is pointedly a feminist and the re-searched are women.[1] Before examining the congruencies of phenomenology and feminism, it is necessary to establish a framework for feminist research. Feminism extends phenomenology through a specific hermeneutic—interpretation in the interest of women. Westkott (1979) and Duelli Klein (1983) distinguish research *on* women from research *for* women. Research *on* women is like putting new wine in old bottles (Mies, 1983). Research *on* women "adds-on" knowledge about women to existing knowledge, uses concepts and techniques that strip women from the complex contexts of their lives, and asks research questions and evaluates research findings against male-as-norm standards. Speech communication research *on* women includes, for example, adding a few great women speakers to the public address canon; studying sex differences in verbosity, management style, and speech organization; and studying women's speech for such "deficiencies" as tag questions and disclaimers (Foss & Foss, 1983). When women are viewed as new objects of research, substitutable for male subjects, the androcentric frame of research is left undisturbed; indeed, such business-as-usual legitimates and perpetuates androcentrism. Women in the particularity of their lives remain invisible, silent, and unchanged.[2]

Research *for* women, by contrast, does not simply generate new knowledge about women for the sake of knowledge, but conducts research with the purpose of empowering women. Research *for* women "tries to take women's needs, interests, and experiences into account and aims at being instrumental in improving women's lives in one way or another" (Duelli

---

[1] Our discussion assumes a feminist who is female. For discussions of male feminists, see Jardine and Smith (1987).

[2] Westkott (1979) warns that research *on* women could result in the academic exploitation of women. Viewed as the latest academic fad, women are data-generating objects and marketable commodities that further individual researchers' careers, increase publishers' profits, and swell class enrollments. Westkott (1979) further suggests that research *on* women can be compared to research on blacks in the 1960s which resulted in new knowledge about blacks, but little or no change in the black ghettos. She also asks if—like black studies—women's studies will soon be academically *passé* without having changed women's lives. See also Currie & Kazi (1987).

Klein, 1983, p. 90). The different needs and interests of women are valued in their own right rather than against male-as-norm. Moreover, such a human science is not content to resign itself to the present it discovers, but also suggests a vision for the future that opposes the very facts of oppression it discovers (Westkott, 1979). Research *for* women assumes that women can be self-emancipating, and that the researcher can assist in women's liberation by analyzing how personal experiences in women's lives are constrained by social and historical structures (Acker, et al., 1983).

In the next paragraphs, we develop the intersection of phenomenology and feminist research as an approach for studying women's communication. Because communication scholars have already introduced the philosophical foundations of a phenomenology of communication (Lanigan, 1979; Stewart, 1978; Hawes, 1977; Deetz, 1973; Hyde, 1980), our focus here is on the themes in phenomenology that converge with feminism, and on the ways in which feminism extends phenomenology.

Phenomenology can be understood as a philosophy of the person and a research methodology in the human sciences.[3] Persons have as their defining characteristic *conscious experience* (Lanigan, 1979). Conscious experience is the meaningful relation of a person and the lived world she or he inhabits, including thoughts, emotions, and values. The "personalistic ontology" of phenomenology focuses on human experience as it is lived, and on how lived experience is organized and made meaningful. As a research methodology, phenomenology can be used to study the range of human experience, for example, anger, imagination, sexuality, listening, and storytelling. A phenomenology of human communication investigates *being* as it manifests itself in and through speaking (Hawes, 1977; Lanigan, 1979).

Phenomenology means "to the things themselves." For a phenomenologist, reality is not outside of, behind, beneath, or beyond lived experience, but is constructed daily in routine and mundane interactions with others. The task of a phenomenological method is to *move toward* a phenomenon through a "thick description" (Geertz, 1973) and interpretation (hermeneutic) of experience. For example, Hyde (1980) distinguishes *moving toward* the phenomenon of communication anxiety through a phenomenological analysis from the scientific tendency to *move away* from a phenomenon by assuming the experience as already created, defined, fixed, and measurable by a research instrument. In the scientific orientation of variable analysis, anxiety is presumed to be a cause which explains

---

[3] Phenomenlogy as it is used in this essay entails its modifications by existential philosophy. Our discussion of phenomenology is in the tradition of Heidegger's and Merleau-Ponty's revisions of Husserl's pure, or transcendental, phenomenology.

measurable communicative effects. The effort to measure the communicative effects of anxiety leaves the experience of anxiety behind—implicit, clouded, concealed. By moving away from a phenomenon, the scientist also assumes and *explains away* the experience. In contrast, phenomenology *explicates* a phenomenon by describing the structures of experience that give meaning and form to consciousness. To explicate a structure means to make clear that which is implied, obscured, and concealed within an experience taken as a concrete whole.

Like phenomenology, feminism ascribes to a personalistic ontology in its commitment to women's experiences. Feminism focuses on what women experience in their everyday lives: "The analytic use of feeling and experience in an examination of 'the personal' should be the main principle on which feminist research is based" (Stanley & Wise, 1983a, p. 177–178).[4] The feminist anthem "the personal is the political" raises particular ontological questions about what it means to be a woman and to be treated as a woman. As consciousness-raising groups recover women's experience as real and important, feminist research makes the personal a part of human science methodology. The personal contrasts with the impersonal which moves away from women's experience and removes women from the context of their lives. The social structure of women's oppression is experienced in everyday living. "The personal is the political" because society is not "out there," but constituted daily in language, talk, and interaction. Feminist research not only values the personal, but elucidates its embeddedness in the larger social structure. Communication studies would do well to consider this insight of feminism; interpersonal communication, for example, is socially and politically constrained, although little of our research and few textbooks reflect these constraints on women's communication (Rakow, 1986).[5]

Phenomenology seeks to situate the personal in the research process by defining the nature of consciousness. "Consciousness, to the phenomenologist, is not a mental, psychological construct but rather the very direction, intention, or mode of doing in the world" (Deetz, 1973, p. 42). The hallmark of phenomenology asserts the intentionality of consciousness. By intentionality, phenomenologists mean that all consciousness is consciousness *of something;* all acts of consciousness refer to an object of some kind. To describe the contents of consciousness is to describe what is felt, believed, desired, or feared. "And, when linguistically expressed, such descriptions [of consciousness] are phenomenon of the 'outer' world-

---

[4] For a critique of the personal in feminism, see Currie and Kazi (1987).

[5] For an introductory-level approach to interpersonal communication which does consider social constraints on women's speech, see Peterson (1987). For an upper-level text, see Thorne, Kramarae, and Henley (1983).

in-common, as much as they are expressions of inner-private life" (Roche, 1973, p. 36).

The construct of intentionality provides an alternative way to understand the world which is not dependent on a subject-object dichotomy because the intentionality of consciousness is prior to the subjectivity and objectivity assumed by positivism (Polkinghorne, 1983). As Lanigan (1979) states, "we discover that the conscious experience that each of us knows as subjectivity is linked to the intersubjectivity of the social world, i.e., interpersonal relationships define the person" (p. 8). Communication scholars have understood intentionality to ground a social phenomenological approach to language as an alternative to subjectivism (Deetz, 1973), a hemeneutic approach to communication that is dialectically opposed to positivism (Hawes, 1977), and a dialogic approach to communication (Stewart, 1978).[6]

For several reasons many feminist theories share with phenomenology a forceful critique of the subject-object dichotomy as a foundation for the research process and a characterization of consciousness. First, the criterion of objectivity disallows and discounts women's experiences as "facts" because women's experiences are considered to be rooted in the personal, the emotional, and the "merely subjective." Until the advent of academic feminism in the 1970s, such "objectivity" allowed researchers to virtually ignore the particular experiences, emotions, and understandings of women. Studies such as Gilligan's (1982) landmark analysis of women's moral development reveal and address the androcentrism of objectivity. Second, the objectivity of conventional social science tends to replicate the objectification of women and other minorities in society. The intent of objectivity is to transform research subjects into objects of scrutiny and manipulation (Acker et al., 1983). Such objective methods for gaining knowledge can become another mode for oppressing women. Third, consciousness for a feminist researcher refers to *feminist* consciousness that specifies phenomenology's understanding of intentionality.

Feminist consciousness can take a variety of forms and ideologies (e.g., Jagger & Rothenberg, 1984). In analyzing feminist consciousness from a phenomenological perspective, Bartky (1977) argues that "to be a feminist, one has first to become one. For many feminists, this takes the form of a personal transformation, an experience that goes far beyond that sphere of human activity ordinarily regarded as 'political' " (pp. 22–23). Feminist consciousness involves a new way of seeing self, others, and social reality.

---

[6] The nature of subjectivity, objectivity, and experience continue to be debated in phenomenology. See Schrag (1986) and Polkinghorne (1983). For discussions in a phenomenology of communication, see Grossberg (1982); Arnett (1981, 1982); and Anderson (1982). Feminist theorists also debate these questions. See, for example, Acker et al. (1983); de Lauretis (1982); and Marks and de Courtivron (1981).

New conceptions of self and society may come directly in conflict with older ideas about women's roles, women's communication, and women's nature. "This 'new way' of seeing the *same* reality, whilst also seeing a new reality, involves a situation in which women come to understand the (seemingly endless) contradictions within life" (Stanley & Wise, 1983a, p. 54).

In communication studies, Wood and Conrad (1983) analyze paradox in the experiences of professional women by arguing that there is a basic contradiction between the abstract social definitions of being a woman and the normative behavioral definitions of being a professional. Appointed as the sole female member of a university committee, for example, the woman professor and her colleagues continuously question who she is: does she speak as a *colleague* who is a female or a *female* who is a colleague? As Wood and Conrad conclude, the contradictions in her experiences often result in a double bind which the professional woman cannot win: "If she defines herself as a colleague and adopts appropriate actions, she risks castigation for acting masculine. If she defines herself as a woman, perhaps to represent women's concerns at large, she may be accused of not being professional or—worse yet—of acting like a woman!" (p. 310). Feminist scholars bring this consciousness of "women's reality" to the research process, paying particular attention to contradictions and using contradictions to understand more deeply the communication of women.

Understanding the particular realities of women requires an examination of language. From a social phenomenological perspective, Deetz (1973) shows that language does not simply represent reality but constitutes reality. Rather than a tool for sharing experience, language makes present the possibilities of experience. Spender (1985) describes the multidimensional reality that women inhabit and especially alerts speech communication scholars to the role of language in constituting reality. Spender argues that language constitutes a man-made reality, and as such, it distorts or renders invisible the experiences of women.[7] From the perspective of man-made language, the communication phenomenon most in need of explanation is women's silence. The importance of naming ("the problem with no name"), of renaming from women's perspectives, and of giving voice to silence reflect feminist concerns. Feminist communication researchers are called to investigate the expressions of women as they simultaneously speak out of and resist man-made language. Women need to describe their own experiences in their own terms.

For example, early researchers studying personal narratives gathered data almost exclusively on male storytellers in public places (street cor-

---

[7] For a critique of Spender's view of language, see Cameron (1985).

ners, country stores, parking lots), thus legitimating the types of stories and performance modes preferred by men. Judged from the perspective of male-as-norm, women's storytelling is either invisible or judged to be deficient or deviant. Women do not tell stories "right" or "well"—just as women cannot tell jokes—or what women tell are not "real" or "good" stories, but "old wives tales," "just gossip," or "chit chat." Examination of women's personal narratives, however, reveals that women effectively tell stories in more conversational and private settings, that is, at home or in small social gatherings (Yokum, 1985). Women's storytelling speaks out of a multidimensional reality which embraces women's experiences. Thus, a phenomenological analysis of women's personal narratives reveals that public performance to an audience is a nonessential structure of personal narratives and a product of man-made language and androcentrism (Langellier & Peterson, 1984).

Feminism adds to phenomenology a concern with the place of women in theory construction. Many feminists have been suspicious, even hostile, to theory, and with good reason. Theories have been used against women, and theorizing is associated with elite knowledge which is not accessible to most women. In developing theories for women, feminist concerns are twofold: to ground theory in women's experiences, and to put women-centered theories into practice. Feminism shares phenomenology's aim for grounded theory (Reinharz, 1983) and also its rejection of generalizations characteristic of social science theorizing. The generalization, categorization, and abstraction of theorizing removes women from the context and concreteness of their personal and social histories. Feminist critiques of theory have been aimed not only at social science, but at feminist theories as well. When Stanley and Wise (1983b, p. 111) say that "we object to our lived experiences being turned into generalized mush," they refer not just to androcentric theories that distort and deny women's experiences, but also to general theories of women's oppression that lose the particularities of women's lives.

But rather than rejecting theory altogether, feminism insists that theory, research, and practice cannot be divorced from one another. Research *for* women should self-critically examine presuppositions and contradictions in its own process. Acker et al. (1983) provide an excellent critique of their own research process, emphasizing connections among research, theory, and practice. They explore, for example, the contradiction between doing social analyses of women's experiences—which unavoidably must generalize—and differences among women. Perhaps the best evidence of feminist self-critique are recent developments in "theories of differences" among women (e.g., Eisenstein & Jardine, 1985). Although they have not always done so, feminists have a special commitment and obligation to be sensitive to differences among women—differences in class, race, ethnicity, age, and sexual preference. Feminist communication studies require a similar self-critique, for example, in the area of organizational communication where concern focuses on managerial women (white and middle class) rather than the experience of the large majority of women as workers in factory, clerical, and service sectors.

Phenomenology as a research methodology recognizes that all research involves an interaction, a relationship between the researcher and the researched. Phenomenology approaches the researched not as objects to do research *on*, but as participants in dialogue. Although most experience is lived-through rather than reflected on, "every person is *capable* of being self-consciously aware of their mental acts and what they are doing" (Roche, 1973, p. 8). Phenomenology aims to understand the participant's world in the participant's own terms. Polkinghorne (1983) argues that the exemplar of data collection in human science is the face-to-face interview because it provides the richest access to human experience. Furthermore, the dialogic relationship between the researcher and researched may extend beyond the interview when researchers present their descriptive analyses to the participants. Participants judge the accuracy of the descriptions in terms of their own experience, and on the basis of such critique, the analysis may be reworked.

Because feminists desire to do research *for* women in distinction from research *on* women, the relationship between the researcher and the researched receives special emphasis. Westkott (1979) writes that "women studying women reveals the complex way in which women as objects of knowledge reflect back upon women as subjects of knowledge. Knowledge of the self and knowledge of the other are mutually informing, because the self and other share a common condition of being women" (p. 426). A dialogic interview facilitates access to women's experience, and it facilitates women's constitution of their world. But this dialogue must take into account the *unavoidable* power relationship between researcher and researched, and, moreover, to reduce that power relationship wherever possible (Acker et al., 1983). This reduction takes the form of both empowering the researched (e.g., by using a nonhierarchical interview technique) and making the researcher more vulnerable, for example, by reporting and discussing omissions and contradictions in the research process. While traditional research methodologies have been concerned with how the researcher affects the researched, seldom have they considered how the researched affect the researcher. For feminist communication researchers, it is especially critical to examine their relationship with the researched as it is *mutually* developed and constrained. Notably, constraints both *facilitate* and *restrict* communication (Wilden, 1987).

We are now in a position to answer why we chose phenomenology and feminism to study women's communication. The preceding themes clarify the intersection of phenomoenological and feminist research in the place of the personal, the role of feminist consciousness, the theory-practice-research connection, and the dialogic relationship between the researcher and the researched. In each theme we show how feminism is consonant with and how it extends phenomenology on behalf of research *for* women. As extended by feminist theory, phenomenology offers a rigorous methodology for studying women's communication experience through interviews. Our discussion also suggests certain caveats for feminist communication researchers to bear in mind: the social-political nature of interpersonal communication, the power of language to construct reality, the need to address differences among women's communication experience and behavior, and the unavoidable communication constraints in the researcher-researched relationship. The communicational constraints of the interviewing situation are the specific focus of the remainder of this essay. We turn next to examine our choice of the interview as a method of data collection for studying mother–daughter storytelling.

INTERVIEWING WOMEN

Phenomenology and feminism converge to focus on *women's experience as lived* rather than on sex as a variable measured against male-as-norm or on gender as a social condition based on theoretical generalizations. Lived-experience is available through the communication that persons have with each other, for example, personal narratives, or everyday storytelling. Our phenomenological studies of mother-daughter storytelling (Hall, 1985; Hall & Langellier, 1988) examine personal narratives about food—preparing food, eating, and dieting. We wanted to understand how personal narratives construct meanings for their lived experiences of food and how storytelling constitutes the mother-daughter relationship. And we wanted to consider mother-daughter storytelling in its own right, in their own words, and in the context of their own relationships and families.

Based on our methodological considerations, we chose the qualitative interview (Patton, 1980) for data collection. The interview is itself a communicative event with particular norms and rules. Therefore, researchers must critically examine the compatibility of the interview with the communicative norms of the interviewees (Briggs, 1986). We considered the compatibility of the interview with women's communication in the following ways.

Gluck (1979) and Armitage (1983) assert that the interview is especially successful in accessing women's experience because it allows women to speak for and about themselves. Interviewing women is a research strategy that documents women's own accounts of their lives. But Oakley

(1981) argues that *interviewing women* is a contradiction in terms because women ask questions back. Oakley critiques four aspects of the traditional interview: (a) the interviewer defines the role of the interviewee as subordinate; (b) extracting information is more highly valued than yielding it; (c) the interview convention of interviewer-interviewee hierarchy is a rationalization for inequality; and (d) what is good for the interviewer is not necessarily good for the interviewee.

To move beyond the limitations of the traditional interview technique, Oakley stresses the need to establish a nonhierarchical relationship when interviewing women. A hierarchical, superior–subordinate relationship mitigates against rapport and trust between interviewer and interviewee. The interviewer needs to convey to the interviewee that all information they share is valuable and will be held in confidence. To encourage the interviewee's sharing of experiences, the interviewer must be prepared to invest her own personality in the relationship through answering questions and validating women's personal experiences. Oakley's analysis emphasizes the *mutual* and *reciprocal* communication between interviewer and interviewee. It also suggests the important sense in which the interviewee influences the interviewer as well as vice versa.

Fowler, Hodge, Gunther, and Trew (1979) describe the interview as an asymmetrical relationship characterized by an unequal distribution of power. Formal rules of status differences are expressed in language use, especially control through interviewer questioning. They hypothesize that the interview is a "peculiar conversation" that shares in and institutionally validates power differences (e.g., gender, class, age) inherent in all social communication. Fowler et al. contribute an important modification to Oakley's analysis because they specify multiple dimensions along which control and power may be distributed simultaneously. In the mother–daughter interviews, for example, we found it necessary to consider how hierarchy within the family (i.e., that mothers have a higher status than daughters) and age (whether the interviewer is older or younger than the interviewee) constrained the interview relationship. Indeed, these other dimensions can reduce or even reverse the traditional superior–subordinate interview relationship. Moreover, the analysis of power differences inherent in all social communication suggests how difficult it is to maintain Oakley's ideal of a nonhierarchical relationship even when women interview women because social and cultural differences among women remain (Riessman, 1987).

Other researchers focus more specifically on interviewing as a way to access personal narratives. Robinson (1981) suggests that the structural characteristics of personal narratives identified by researchers reflect the interview genre: "The form and content of a narrative is heavily influenced by the fact that it is primarily an answer to the interviewer's question" (p.

69). The asymmetry and control in the interview genre obscure the nature and function of personal narratives as they occur in conversation (Wolfson, 1976). Robinson focuses on how, in conversation, a personal narrative's tellability and point are jointly determined by storyteller and listener(s) according to norms of conversational etiquette, discourse structures of narrative, and pragmatic features of the situation.

The conversational mode of storytelling is particularly characteristic of women. Hence, interviewing women for personal narratives also requires attention to the communicative norms of women's storytelling, especially its conversational features. Langellier and Peterson's (1984) theoretical analysis of women's storytelling articulates women's use of "kernel stories" (Kalčik, 1975; Jenkins, 1982) developed progressively and collaboratively within the conversational context and in the course of the participants' shared history. According to Kalčik (1975), "a kernel story is a brief reference to the subject, the central action, or a piece of dialogue from a longer story" (p. 7). This reference, or kernel, may develop in a variety of ways depending upon group participation. Women's collaborative storytelling strategies include linking remarks, filling in, clarifying questions, and serializing stories over time. Collaborative strategies structure horizontal relationships among the participants characterized by, for example, the use of personal and inclusive pronouns, positive minimal responses, supportive comments, and sharing similar experiences. Thus, the interview should consider how personal narratives emerge in women's conversation and reflect their interactional patterns.

Mies (1983) also addresses the relationship between the communicative norms of the interview and the norms of women's speech. She argues that "the emphasis on interviews of individuals at a given time need to be shifted toward group discussions, if possible at repeated intervals" (p. 128). Group interviews over time resemble women's talk and especially the consciousness-raising groups exemplary of activist feminism. Repeated interviews with groups allow both for kernel stories and the conversational storytelling characteristic of women. For these reasons, we used both repeated interviews and joint mother–daughter interviews. Mothers and daughters were interviewed individually first and then in mother–daughter pairs. In this way, we aimed to take advantage of their shared family history and of their collaborative storytelling strategies.

Based on these theoretical critiques of interviewing, we modified the traditional interview paradigm in three ways in order to study mothers' and daughters' storytelling about their food experiences. First, to facilitate women's telling their own experiences in their own words, a guided interview technique (Patton, 1980; Lanigan, 1983) was employed to maximize the interviewee's language and to minimize the interviewer's categories. The guided interview outlines topics to be explored, but does not list standardized questions in advance of the interview. The interviewer adapts language and sequence of questions in the conversational context of the actual interview. Second, following Oakley's suggestion, the interviewer encouraged a nonhierarchical relationship with the interviewee by answering her questions and validating her experience. Third, in addition to individual interviews with mothers and daughters, mother–daughter pairs were jointly interviewed in order to access their interaction in a conversational mode. Taken together, these modifications made the communicative norms of the interview more compatible with the norms of women's speech and storytelling.

THE INTERVIEWS

Five mother-daughter pairs of a variety of ages, religious, ethnic, economic, and family backgrounds participated in the interviews. Participants were not selected randomly for the purposes of generalizability, but were selected for variation (Polkinghorne, 1983). For example, daughters ranged in age from 11 to 33 years old, and mothers from 37 to 55 years old. There were Jewish, Roman Catholic, and Protestant women. Three of the five pairs were from Maine. One mother grew up in Georgia, and she and her daughter now live in Connecticut. Another pair are originally from New York and now live in Maine.

There was an economic range within the participants' backgrounds. Some reflect on growing up in "hard times" while others reflect on frequent trips to nice restaurants. Some participants are full-time students on restricted incomes. One woman has recently suffered a drastic cut in pay. All mothers said that they have a higher economic status now than when they were growing up. The participants come from different family sizes: some grew up in large families of nine or 10 children, others in families of three to five children, and some in small families of one or two children. One daughter is also a mother. One mother divorced when her daughter was two years old and has raised her daughter alone. One daughter is diabetic.

Two individuals approached for interviews responded that they were unwilling to participate in the study because their food experiences in relation to their mothers were "too fraught with conflict." In the next two sections, we divulge some "secrets of interviewing" that occurred in the individual and joint interviews with mothers and daughters.

The Individual Interviews

The individual interviews were semistructured. Ten open-ended questions were constructed to guide women's reflections on their childhood, teenage, and recent memorable experiences with food. Although the questions were prestructured, the interviewer did not adhere to them strictly; rather the interviewer followed the interviewee's lead as the interview unfolded.[8] If the interviewee did not understand a question or was having trouble recalling an experience, the interviewer would ask the interviewee to consider specific relationships or occasions (such as best friends or birthdays), thus providing a more concrete context in which to think.

During the interviews, mothers and daughters communicated a variety of stories. They also directed questions and comments to the interviewer. Oakley (1981) identifies four types of questions which occurred in her interviews with women on the transition to motherhood: requests for information, personal questions, requests for advice, and questions about the research. Of these types, fully three-quarters were requests for information from Oakley, who was herself a mother. By contrast, requests for information were not present in our interviews, nor were requests for advice. In fact, the mothers in the study gave the interviewer information and advice, for example, about recipes and when coupons came out in the local paper. The differences in these questions suggest that age and knowledge of topic (mothers-to-be discussing childbirth and baby care in Oakley's study vs. mothers and daughters talking about eating, dieting, and preparing food in our interviews) affects interaction in the interview.

While Oakley (1981) found questions about the research to be of a general nature (who was paying for the research? was she writing a book?), our studies found interviewee remarks to be directed more to the specific interview topic and situation. Especially early in the interviews, mothers and daughters frequently asked, "did I answer your question?", "is this what you want to know?", "am I telling you the right things?" The interviewer became aware of how the participants questioned the value of their experiences. After such questions the interviewer would respond confirmingly, "yes, you answered my question" or "everything you tell me is important." Perhaps most importantly, the interviewer simply listened with engagement and enthusiasm. Mothers and daughters also expressed concern that they were not helping the interviewer: "I'm afraid I'm not helping you," "Maybe Pat [daughter] will be able to help you out more than I can," and "I don't know how you are going to get anything out of this." Again the interviewer responded confirmingly, "you are helping me out; these are good stories." The woman seemed to need reassurance that they were giving the interviewer the "right" stories, prefacing and following stories with qualifications such as, "well, I can think of an experience, but it's not about food, it's about a candy bar." In reflecting on their mundane, lived experiences, some women seemed to doubt their experiences as a worthwhile focus of research.

---

[8] In all cases the interviewer is Deanna Hall.

Interviewee questions and concerns about the research project reveal two dynamics in the interview process when women interview women. First, the interviewee's were anxious to be "good interviewees," to produce the appropriate behavior and responses. In this way, they signaled their understanding and acceptance of the subordinate interviewee role characteristic of a hierarchical interview. Moreover, they were genuinely concerned to "help" the interviewer. Second, interviewees questioned the worth of their stories and by implication, the significance of the research. The interviewee question "Is this what you want to know?" points to the contradiction between the perceived insignificance of women's everyday experiences and data considered to be significant enough for research. In response to this concern, the interviewer tried to validate the interviewees' experiences by telling them that their stories were important and worth telling. As the interviewer listened to the stories with obvious attention and interest, the participants responded with more comfort and confidence. In fact, they became enthusiastic storytellers.

A second type of interviewee question focused on the interviewer's attitudes and experiences. Some questions were requests for personal information ("what do you eat?" "how many are in your family?"), but more were seeking confirmation for their experiences, for example, "do you think that's typical for families?" The following example shows the combination of seeking personal information from the interviewer and confirmation of the interviewee's experience: "I'm sure you grew up in the same way" spoken with a rising intonation. The interviewee simultaneously puts forward an assumption about the interviewer's experience in her family and seeks its confirmation. Questions directed to the interviewer were present throughout the interview, but more likely to occur as the interview came to a close and the tape recorder was turned off. Some of the mothers wanted to know how the interviewer knew their daughters and if they were friends. Others asked why the interviewer was interested in the topic of food experiences. These interviewee questions are requests for reciprocity from the interviewer. They ask the interviewer to invest some of herself in the research relationship within and outside the interview frame. Encouraging interviewees to question and comment on the interview itself also extends to them some of the privilege usually reserved only for the interviewer.

When the interviewer was asked why she was interested in food experiences, she shared some of her own experiences with food and diet. She explained that food and diet were very important issues in her childhood, adolescent, and adult family experiences because her father is a food nutritionist; yet it is her mother with whom she talks about food. In the course of the interviews, the interviewer made many statements of comparison between her family and the interviewees' families. The interviewer also confided some of her experiences sharing an apartment with a woman who had an eating disorder. At the close of one interview, the interviewer and interviewee discussed women's problems with dieting and weight. The interviewer recommended reading Kim Chernin's *The Obsession*, explaining how it helped her to change the way she thought about eating and her body. The interviewer's sharing of self helped to establish trust in the individual interviews and to establish a history which was brought to the mother–daughter joint interviews.

Stories told in the individual interview were often dependent on interviewer-interviewee trust. Some stories were confided to the interviewer and required her trustworthiness. Daughters told stories and asked the interviewer not to tell their mothers. ("that's when I started smoking, don't tell my mother" or "she's [mother] tired, she's going through the change of life. Don't tell her I told you; she may anyway"). Mothers confided anxiety about their daughters' eating behaviors. Although they did not state "don't tell my daughter," that message was implied. Thus, both mothers and daughters contributed private information about the mother–daughter relationship to the interviewer. Each also expressed curiosity about what stories the other would tell in the individual interview. Learning privileged information sometimes placed the interviewer in an awkward and contradictory position. The interviewer wanted to protect the confidentiality of the interviewees who had already told their stories while at the same time responding to present questions. The answers to some questions asked by mothers would have violated their daughter's trust and confidence in the interviewer.

For example, one interview with a daughter took place over lunch. The daughter ate an orange and some prepackaged cheese crackers with peanut butter. In the course of the interview, the daughter confided that she didn't eat as well as she should and, furthermore, that she was keeping her poor eating habits from her mother. Later that same day while interviewing the mother, the mother asked, "what did she [daughter] have for lunch today?" In an effort to be responsive to the mother's question and simultaneously to honor the daughter's confidence, the interviewer responded hesitantly that the daughter ate an "orange and some cheese and crackers." The interviewer did respond to the mother's question, but with a partial truth. She did not volunteer the information that the mother really wanted and that the daughter had supplied—how the daughter really eats.[9]

Other stories involved risk for the interviewee and required a more personal response from the interviewer. One mother, for example, discusses the problem of "running a restaurant" to meet the different desires of her

---

[9] The topic of the daughter's diet surfaces again in the mother-daughter interview. For an in-depth analysis of the storytelling related to this topic, see Hall and Langellier (1987).

son, daughter, husband, and herself. She does not question the demands of the mother role, but rather betrays her anxiety about being a "good mother." Throughout the storytelling, the interviewer supports the mother's telling through the use of head nods, appropriate laughter, positive minimal responses, and the expressions "sure," "OK," and "right." The interviewer compares the mother's story of her son's "picky" eating behaviors to the interviewer's own brother: "Oh, that sounds like my brother." The interviewer also comments on the meaning of the story as if she has experienced what the mother expresses: "And it gets frustrating, too?" This statement not only confirms the mother's feelings, but also encourages her to continue to explore her experience, which she does.

Interviewing may also involve the interviewer in self-exploration. A mother discussing the perceptions her children have about their parents' weight gain and loss concludes that her children notice their father's weight changes but not her own. The interviewer responds, "When you're talking, I'm thinking of my own family and I'm wondering if it's OK for moms to be overweight but not for dads because. . . ." The interviewer continues to describe her experience and then offers her explanation for the interviewee's original observation. This example shows how the interviewer and interviewee explore an issue together. Thus, the interview process may involve not only the risk of self-disclosure, but also may involve all the participants in self-discovery and self-evaluation. Interviewees narrated experiences they did not intend to tell or whose meanings they did not yet understand. The risk to the interviewees calls for a reciprocal responsibility in the interviewer to provide personal information and emotional support.

Joint Interviews

The joint interviews with the mother–daughter pairs were less structured than the individual interviews. To begin, the mothers and daughters were asked to reflect on some of the stories they had shared during the individual interview and any other food-related experiences they had thought about since the first interview. Then they were asked to share one of the stories with each other, feeling free to comment or add to each other's story. From there the conversation spiraled. The joint interviews altered the roles between the interviewer and interviewees. The interviewer did considerably less talking in the joint interviews. She participated more as an observer and listener than as a questioner because the mothers and daughters themselves conducted the interview by asking questions of each other, for example, "what do you remember?" and "what else can we tell her?" If there was a long pause, the interviewer would facilitate discussion by mentioning a story that one of the women told during the individual interview and then the pair would take over.

Because the mother–daughter joint interview occurred after the individual interviews, all participants now shared some history. This shared history affected the interview process and the developing relationship between the interviewer and the mother–daughter pair. Now each interviewee was familiar with the interviewer and more comfortable with the interview situation. The interviewees were assured of the interviewer's interest in their stories about food. They had also had time to reflect on their individual interviews and to prepare for the mother–daughter joint interview. Some of the stories told individually were retold together. Some stories were new to either the mother or the daughter but not to the interviewer. Other stories were completely new to the joint interview. The storytelling in these interviews constituted a variety of mother–daughter–interviewer relationships.

The mothers and daughters told stories collaboratively about similar experiences in the joint interviews. In so doing they demonstrated their support for each other's experience and for the common experience of being women. For example, one daughter states, "we've tried diets . . . but it's a never-ending theme that we've lived with." The daughter continues to describe the problem of losing enthusiasm and "getting lax" with dieting. Her mother supports her by providing an explanation for the experience of "getting lax." The daughter then supports her mother's explanation by providing an example from her own experience. The mother-daughter pair is engaged in "talking to learn," or heuristic storytelling (Robinson, 1981) as together they articulate and discover problems with dieting. Although the interviewer did not talk in this interaction, she had discussed dieting in the individual interviews. Throughout the telling, she contributes positive minimal responses and supportive laughter. As the experience of "women dieting" is shared, distinct family roles (mother and daughter) and distinct genre roles (interviewer and interviewee) blur. At this point, the interviewer holds a position "inside" women's culture despite her "outside" status as a nonfamily member and interviewer.

During the joint interviews, some of the stories told created tension or conflict in the mother-daughter relationship. Mother–daughter conflict places the interviewer in a complex communication situation. One problem concerns the presentation of the family to the interviewer, who is an "outsider." Another problem concerns whether the interviewer takes sides, or appears to take sides, in a disagreement and thus creates a coalition against the third person.

In one story a diabetic daughter begins to tell her experience of a bad insulin reaction. The story soon becomes tense in the telling as the mother learns that her daughter is presently not as careful about her diet as the mother thought she was. The daughter states, "Let's not start getting on that," indicating the issue is always present in their relationship. The mother does not push the issue, perhaps because of the interviewer's presence and her concern to present the family in a positive way, or because this mother strives for harmony in her family interactions. Although mother-daughter conflict is clearly indicated in the story, the mother and daughter agree not to pursue it, and at this point, ally to define the interviewer as an "outsider" to the family.

In a second example, conflict is present in the telling of the story as well as the meaning for the experience. The story concerns tension and hostility that disrupts family mealtime. The daughter introduces the story she had previously told the interviewer in the individual interview. The mother says twice that the daughter should not be telling the story and adds, "this is only a few occasions now, she's telling you the worse times we've had. We really shouldn't be telling this. . . ." But the daughter persists and talks over her mother, successfully finishing the story. It is important to note that this mother-daughter pair have known the interviewer and her mother for eight years. Their personal relationship most likely explains why a story the mother considers a private, family affair may be tellable to family friends.

The mother, daughter, and interviewer each have a different meaning for this story. The daughter reflects on mealtime scenes in a humorous, even flippant, way. She sees this tension as a typical and silly ritual. The mother, however, considers this story embarrassing. She wants to keep this family "problem" hidden. She seems to view this mealtime tension as a more serious issue than does her daughter, perhaps indicative of problems in her mothering. During the telling, the interviewer states, "Now, Ann, that happened in my family, too." The interviewer empathized with the mother's embarrassment, and her intent was to make Ann feel better by showing how their families were similar. But the interviewer's statement served to disconfirm the mother's feelings and to confirm the daughter's meaning for the story. The daughter-interviewer alignment which emerged had the effect of alienating the mother: the original experience of mealtime tension for the mother is trivialized and her present emotions are devalued. This example of the interview process shows the complex and changing relations among the participants—mothers, daughters, and interviewer—that affect the stories, their telling, and their meanings.

In other instances, the interviewer functioned as a family "insider," especially to experiences between mothers and daughters. One story involves the birth of a younger sister. The mother and daughter collaboratively tell this story, developing the plot and point of view together. In fact, they narrate each other's experience of the childbirth. For example, the mother tells about how excited the daughter was at school the day of the birth and marvels that the daughter could concentrate on her exams at all. The daughter says, "... she [mother] was thinking of getting through the meal and probably would go to the hospital after supper, and, uh, I said, 'I don't think you ought to wait,' so she called a friend and her friend came down and took her to the hospital." This story is obviously a special one to the mother–daughter pair, and they take great delight in its excited telling. There is a sense of their doing a "command performance" of the story for the interviewer, a performance that is both spontaneous and well-rehearsed. Their familiarity with the story details and dialogue and with their roles in telling suggests that the story has been told many times before to other family members. During the telling, they present no special exposition for the interviewer. For her part, the interviewer contributes looks and laughs of anticipation, recognition, and appreciation. The story-telling is so inclusive of the interviewer that it is almost as if the story is about her, as if for the duration of the telling, she plays the role of the younger sister in the family. In fact, by age the interviewer could be the younger sister to the daughter, and the daughter to the mother.

Another story told collaboratively by a mother and daughter also concerns women's experience within the family system, but it has a very different tone than the childbirth story. The story is introduced by the daughter, who also told it in her individual interview, and describes her mother's feelings about "cooking for Dad." Throughout the storytelling, the mother shows agreement with her daughter's description through positive minimal responses and eye contact, but she does not elaborate on the experience. For example, the daughter says, "I was telling Deanna [the interviewer] that although you have an eight-hour job yourself, you're still expected to have dinner ready for Dad when he gets home." The mother responds, "Yeh." The daughter continues, "And on holidays it's.... just expected and therefore carried out." Again, the mother does not elaborate how she feels, but explains why the father expects to be waited on: "They grew up in a house where the mother never worked and she always waited on the men.... and it's hard to break those old expectations." The daughter responds, "At times I know it bothers you because it's a demand that in all reality Dad would perform just as well." The mother responds with the single word, "Definitely."

Because it is told so cautiously, this story contrasts sharply with the animated childbirth story. The daughter makes clear that she has already told this story to the interviewer, so that the primary listener in this telling is the mother. Throughout the telling the mother assents to the narrative, but with restraint and without further development of the details. The daughter is speaking for her mother, which allows the mother to see her position in the family from her daughter's perspective in addition to her own. The daughter leads her mother to a critical voice the mother did not otherwise assume during the interviews. Although the mother is self-critical throughout the interviews in relation to her own behavior (her cooking skills, a lack of self-control in her diet, the cleanliness of her home, her mothering skills), she is not critical of women's roles within the traditional family system.

When the daughter encourages her mother to take a stand against her husband's behavior—perhaps against her will—the act assumes many levels of risk for the mother. The mother risks seeing a contradiction in her experience that could lead to a change in consciousness. Moreover, the mother risks changing family alliances by identifying with her daughter against her husband. For the mother to agree with her daughter and condemn her husband's behavior involves not only personal risk, but a political act which criticizes men's roles within the family. The emergence of this new (for the mother) and shared (with the daughter) voice depends upon the relationship with the interviewer—mother and daughter entrust the story to her. Mother, daughter, and interviewer identify as women in an act of feminist consciousness. Even though the story may lack the trauma and drama of a "dark family secret," its personal and political implications, especially for the mother, are considerable.

Interviewing for Women

We have argued that feminist research is *for* women. What the participants gain from the interview experience is a question usually ignored by traditional research. We believe the interview experience benefited the interviewees in the following ways.

First, the interviewees were implicitly and explicitly told that their mundane, daily experiences were significant, a message usually absent in social and familial cultures that devalue women's work and experience. When interviewees asked, "Is this what you want to know?" or "I don't know how you are going to get anything out of this," the interviewer confirmed the importance of their experiences. Recall that research *for* women values the personal and analyzes women's experience in its own right rather than against androcentric criteria of significance. Upon receiving confirmation that their experiences were important and worthy of study, all interviewees shared their stories enthusiastically. Many of the participants are still in contact with the interviewer and frequently volunteer new stories, stories they forgot to tell, or stories they had no opportunity to tell during the interview. Some women have asked to read the analysis, which has been made available to them.

Second, the joint interviews gave the mothers and daughters a reason to get together and an opportunity to reflect on their experiences and focus on their relationship. For example, one daughter told the interviewer how the joint interview provided her with an excuse to visit with her mother; the daughter is busy and making time to go home is an infrequent occurrence. Another daughter, who is herself a mother, commented on the time and opportunity to discuss new ideas with her mother. A mother commented that, since the interviews, she has had more discussions with her daughter about women's experiences in the family. On the whole, the interviews functioned to bring the mothers and daughters closer together and to confirm the value of their relationship.

But mother–daughter conflict also occurred during the joint interviews, for example, the diabetic daughter's story about a bad insulin reaction and the "don't tell" story involving mealtime tension. When women discuss and reflect on their experiences and relationships, they discover their differences as well as their similarities. Both collaboration and conflict are part of dialogue. At this point, we might do well to recall that two mother–daughter pairs declined to participate in the study because it would be "too fraught with conflict." While the joint interviews do give access to mother-daughter dialogue, it is likely that when participants anticipate telling stories together, mother-daughter pairs who are comfortable and willing at the outset to talk about their food experiences together will self-select for participation in the study.

Third, the storytelling served a consciousness-raising function during both the individual and joint interviews. In the individual interviews, women often commented about their stories that "I never thought about that before," or "It's funny the things you might choose to forget." The individual interviews were an opportunity for self-exploration—to see the self in a new way—and to have these experiences confirmed. Such confirmation implies that their experiences are shared by other women. Many women explored contradictions in their lives in the individual interviews. In the joint interviews heuristic storytelling occurred when together mothers and daughters discovered different and new meanings for their experiences. For example, one mother-daughter pair discovered problems women experience with dieting. In the "cooking for Dad" story, the daughter led her mother to reflect on her position in the family. This collaborative telling allowed the mother to critique her role, however cautiously, and intimates the discovery that "the personal is the political." The interviews functioned as research *for* women not because the interviewer imposed feminist interpretations as a partner in dialogue, but because she facilitated the interviewee's constitution of reality. Research *for* women assumes that women can be self-empowering; interviewing *for* women supports their dialogue with self and society.

We have also argued that interviewing women is a dialogue that benefits the interviewer as a woman. The process of interviewing women strengthened the interviewer's relationship to her own mother and grand-mother, to women, and to feminism. Interviewing mothers and daughters increased the interviewer's participation in her own family storytelling. She especially asks for and shares family stories with her mother. In fact, they rarely talk of anything but women these days. In reflecting on her own family experiences, the interviewer has also discovered how similar her experiences are to the mothers and daughters interviewed. But at the same time, she is becoming increasingly aware of the many social differences between women, for example, the effects of different economic conditions, different religious backgrounds, different regional environments, and different family structures, generations, and relationships. Finally, interviewing women has contributed to the interviewer's developing feminism, in particular the importance of valuing and understanding women's everyday experiences both as a women and a researcher.

CONCLUSION

Our purpose in this essay has been to divulge some "secrets of interviewing" in order to interrogate the relationship of the researcher and the researched doing feminist communication research. We first developed a rationale for how and why we combine phenomenology and feminism in order to do communication research *for* women. A closer look at interviewing women focused on making the norms of the interview compatible with the norms of women's speech in order to ground our research method for collecting personal narratives from mothers and daughters. We then presented concrete exemplars from a phenomenological study of mother–daughter storytelling and analyzed relational dynamics in the interviews.

The interview (individual and joint) is shown to be a communicative event that constrains all participants and the emerging data. The mother–daughter storytelling data constitutes a strategic response to the constraints of the interviewing situation as mothers and daughters define their relationship to the interviewer and to each other. In the mother–daughter interviews, both hierarchical and nonhierarchical relationships occur. Nonhierarchial relationships are characterized by, for example, reciprocal questions between the interviewer and interviewees, by interviewees' taking the lead in the interview, and by interviewees' taking the interviewer into their confidence and risking self-disclosure. Heuristic storytelling allows meanings to be explored, discovered, even changed in the dialogue rather than assumed, sedimented, and reified. Previous relationship history and the developing relationships among the mother–daughter–interviewer constrained the data in particular ways.

Collaborative strategies that result in shared storytelling exemplify horizontal relationships among participants that are consistent with the characteristics of women's talk (Langellier & Peterson, 1984).

Hierarchical relationships were also present among the interactants. Especially in the initial stages of interviewing, interviewees expected and accepted a subordinate role in the interview, and, indeed, seemed to want the interviewer to be more controlling and directive in the interview. The individual interviews became more dialogic as the interview progressed. In the joint interviews, the simple interviewer-interviewee hierarchy was altered, sometimes for horizontal relationships among all participants and sometimes for changing coalitions within the triad. The joint interviewers were especially revealing of mother-daughter interactions as they dynamically define their relationship to each other and to the interviewer.

It is important to note that even when interviewer–interviewee relationships are less hierarchical, other power dimensions mark differences in status. Although many dimensions are possible, especially class and race, we note the following three in our research. First, age and experience mark differences. The interviewer was younger than all of the mothers and one of the daughters; and she is not herself a mother. To this extent, her status was ambiguous as a combination of researcher/superior and young nonmother/subordinate. This ambiguity may account for interviewees' concern to "help" her out and to give her advice as well as to comply with her requests for stories.

Second, position in the family culture marks differences. The interviewer's position is again ambiguous: as a person unrelated to the mother and daughter, she is an "outsider" to the family, but as a woman she is an "insider" to their roles within the family. Her double position as an outsider–insider may suggest that stories mothers and daughters considered to be private, family matters were not told, while stories mothers and daughters considered unworthy or insignificant were told. Furthermore, it suggests why interviewees so openly reflected on the details of their family experiences, but so rarely and reluctantly critiqued family roles.

Third, and perhaps most subtly, mother-daughter roles mark differences. Acker et al. (1983) argue that feminist research must locate the researcher in a social relationship with the researched. What family role does the interviewer play in research on mother–daughter storytelling? Chodorow and Contratto (1981) examine recent writing on motherhood and identify a recurrent theme in which mothers are conceived as totally responsible for the outcome of their mothering, even if their behavior is shaped by androcentric society. "Belief in the all-powerful mother spawns a recurrent tendency to blame the mother on the one hand, and a fantasy of maternal perfectability on the other" (p. 55). They argue that feminists and nonfeminists alike consider the mother–daughter relationship from a daughter's perspective. Daughters participate in "the fantasy of the perfect mother," whether the mother is idealized as perfectly good or blamed as perfectly evil.

In the case of mother–daughter storytelling, we suggest that the interviewer tended to take the daughter's perspective that idealizes the mother. For example, when asked questions about her own family, the interviewer answered from the perspective of being a daughter. The interviewer was also given advice about food preparation and recipes, especially, although not exclusively, by the mothers in the study. The stories about mealtime tension and "running a restaurant" show the interviewer's efforts to allay the mothers' anxiety and confirm them as "good mothers." Furthermore, the daughters were less cautious as storytellers and more inclined to critique family roles than were mothers. Recall how the daughter carefully leads her mother to a critical voice in the "cooking for Dad" story. Thus, both the mothers and the daughters seemed to gain support from the interviewer's role as daughter who idealizes the mother in the interview situation.

In interrogating our relationship as researchers to the researched, our intent is to situate ourselves within the constraints of interviewing women rather than to assume a position outside it. We cannot completely transcend the "fantasy of the perfect mother," nor can researchers avoid a social relationship with the researched and taking a position in the communication system they study. We present a description of our research process and show mothers, daughters, and the interviewer talking in particular situations. Our analysis illustrates how interviewing women is a communication situation characterized by constraints. Our research report shows all participants responding strategically to the constraints of the interview situation as well as to the demands of storytelling and the dynamics of their relationships. By making public some "secrets of interviewing women," we contribute to a phenomenological research methodology that is also feminist because it empowers women as subjects and objects of communication research.

REFERENCES

Acker, J., Barry, K., & Essenveld, J. (1983). Objectivity and truth: Problems in doing feminist research. *Women's Studies International Forum, 6*, 423–435.

Anderson, R. (1982). Phenomenological dialogue, humanistic psychology and pseudo-walls: A response and extension. *Western Journal of Speech Communication, 46*, 344–357.

Armitage, S. H. (1983). The next step. *Frontiers, 7*, 3–8.

Arnett, R. (1981). Toward a phenomenological dialogue. *Western Journal of Speech Communication, 45*, 201–212.

Arnett, R. (1982). Rogers and Buber: Similarities, yet fundamental differences. *Western Journal of Speech Communication, 46,* 358–372.

Bartky, S. L. (1977). Toward a phenomenology of feminist consciousness. In M. Vetterling-Braggin, F. A. Elliston, & J. English (Eds.), *Feminism and philosophy* (pp. 22–34). Totowa, NJ: Littlefield, Adams, and Co.

Bowles, G. (1984). The uses of hermeneutics for feminist scholarship. *Women's Studies International Forum, 7,* 185–188.

Briggs, C. L. (1986). *Learning how to ask: A sociological appraisal of the role of the interview in social science research.* Cambridge: Cambridge University.

Cameron, D. (1985). *Feminism and linguistic theory.* New York: St. Martin's Press.

Chodorow, N., & Contratto, S. (1981). The fantasy of the perfect mother. In B. Thorne & M. Yalom (Eds.), *Rethinking the family: Some feminist questions* (pp. 54–75). New York: Longman.

Currie, D., & Kazi, H. (1987). Academic feminism and the process of de-radicalization: Re-examining the issues. *Feminist Review, 25,* 77–98.

Deetz, S. (1973). Words without things: Toward a social phenomenology of language. *The Quarterly Journal of Speech, 59,* 40–51.

de Lauretis, T. (1982). *Alice doesn't: Feminism, semiotics, cinema.* Bloomington, IN: Indiana University Press.

Duelli Klein, R. (1983). How to do what we want to do: Thoughts about feminist methodology. In G. Bowles & R. Duelli Klein (Eds.), *Theories of women's studies* (pp. 88–104). London: Routledge & Kegan Paul.

Eisenstein, H., & Jardine, A. (Eds.). (1985). *The future of difference.* New Brunswick, NJ: Rutgers University Press.

Foss, K. A., & Foss, S. K. (1983). The status of research on women and communication. *Communication Quarterly, 31,* 195–204.

Fowler, R., Hodge, B., Gunther, K., & Trew, T. (1979). *Language and control.* London: Routledge & Kegan Paul.

Geertz, C. (1973). *The interpretation of cultures.* New York: Basic Books.

Gilligan, C. (1982). *In a different voice: Psychological theory and women's development.* Cambridge, MA: Harvard University Press.

Gluck, S. (1979). What's so special about women? Women's oral history. *Frontiers, 2,* 3–11.

Grossberg, L. (1982). The ideology of communication: Post-structuralism and the limits of communication. *Man and World, 15,* 83–101.

Hawes, L. C. (1977). Toward a hermeneutic phenomenology of communication. *Communication Quarterly, 25,* 30–41.

Hall, D. (1985). *Mothers' and daughters' lived experiences of food: An analysis of women's storytelling.* Unpublished master's thesis, University of Maine, Orono, ME.

Hall, D. L., & Langellier, K. M. (1987, May). *Narrating the 'same' experience: Mother-daughter storytelling.* Paper presented at the International Communication Association Convention, Montreal, Canada.

Hall, D. L., & Langellier, K. M. (1988). Strategies in mother-daughter storytelling. In A. Taylor & B. Bate (Eds.), *Women communicating (pp. 107–126).* New York: Ablex.

Hyde, M. J. (1980). The experience of anxiety: A phenomenological investigation. *The Quarterly Journal of Speech, 66,* 140–154.

Jagger, A. M., & Rothenberg, P. S. (1984). *Feminist frameworks: Alternative theoretical accounts of the relations between women and men.* New York: McGraw-Hill.

Jardine, A., & Smith, P. (1987). *Men in feminism.* New York: Methuen.

Jenkins, M. M. (1982). The story is in the telling: A cooperative style of conversation among women. In S. Trömel-Plötz (Ed.), *Gewalt durch sprache: Die vergewaltingung von frauen in gesprächen.* Frankfurt am Main: Fischer Taschenbuch Verlag (ERIC Document Reproduction Service No. ED 238 083).

Kalčik, S. (1975). "... like Ann's gynecologist or the time I was almost raped": Personal narratives in women's rap groups." *Journal of American Folklore, 88,* 3–11. Austin: University of Texas.

Kuhn, T. S. (1970). *The structure of scientific revolutions* (2nd ed.). Chicago: University of Chicago Press.

Langellier, K. M., & Peterson, E. E. (1984, November). *Spinstorying: A communication analysis of women storytelling.* Paper presented at the Speech Communication Association Convention, Chicago, IL.

Lanigan, R. L. (1979). The phenomenology of human communication. *Philosophy Today, 23,* 3–15.

Lanigan, R. L. (1983, October). *Life-histories: A research and teaching model for semiotic phenomenology.* Paper presented at the annual meeting of Semiotic Society of America, Snowbird, UT.

Marks, E., & de Courtivron, I. (Eds.). (1981). *New French feminisms.* New York: Schocken.

Mies, M. (1983). Towards a methodology for feminist research. In G. Bowles & R. Duelli Klein (Eds.), *Theories of women's studies* (pp. 117–139). London: Routledge & Kegan Paul.

Oakley, A. (1981). Interviewing women: A contradiction in terms. In J. Roberts (Ed.), *Doing feminst research* (pp. 30–61). London: Routledge & Kegan Paul.

Patton, M. Q. (1980). *Qualitative evaluation methods.* Beverly Hills, CA: Sage.

Peterson, E. E. (Ed.) with Pickering, M., Langellier K. M., & Endress, V. (1987). *Contemporary issues in interpersonal communication* (2nd ed.). Lexington, MA: Ginn.

Polkinghorne, D. (1983). *Methodology for the human sciences: Systems of inquiry.* Albany: State University of New York Press.

Rakow, L. F. (1986). Rethinking gender research in communication. *Journal of Communication, 36,* 11–26.

Reinharz, S. (1983). Experiential analysis: A contribution to feminist research. In G. Bowles & R. Duelli Klein (Eds.), *Theories of women's studies* (pp. 162–191). London: Routledge & Kegan Paul.

Riessman, C. K. (1987). When gender is not enough: Women interviewing women. *Gender & Society, 1,* 172–207.

Robinson, J. (1981). Personal narratives reconsidered. *Journal of American Folklore, 94,* 59–85.

Roche, M. (1973). *Phenomenology, language, and the social sciences.* London: Routledge & Kegan Paul.

Schrag, C. D. (1986). *Communicative praxis and the space of subjectivity.* Bloomington: Indiana University Press.

Spender, D. (1985). *Man made language* (2nd ed.). London: Routledge & Kegan Paul.

Stanley, L., & Wise, S. (1983a). *Breaking out: Feminist consciousness and feminist research.* London: Routledge & Kegan Paul.

Stanley, L., & Wise, S. (1983b). 'Back into the personal' or: Our attempt to construct 'feminist research.' In G. Bowles & R. Duelli Klein (Eds.), *Theories of women's studies* (pp. 192–209). London: Routledge & Kegan Paul.

Stewart, J. (1978). Foundations of dialogic communication. *The Quarterly Journal of Speech, 64,* 183–201.

Thorne, B., Kramarae, C., & Henley, N. M. (1983). *Language, gender, and society.* Rowley, MA: Newbury House.

Westkott, M. (1979). Feminist criticism of the social sciences. *Harvard Educational Review, 49,* 422–430.

Wilden, A. (1987). *The rules are no game: The strategy of communication.* London: Routledge & Kegan Paul.

Wolfson, N. (1976). Speech events and natural speech: Some implications for sociolinguistic methodology. *Language in Society, 5,* 189–209.

Wood, J., & Conrad, C. (1983). Paradox in the experience of professional women. *Western Journal of Speech Communication, 47,* 305–322.

Yokum, M. R. (1985). Woman to woman: Fieldwork and the private sphere. In R. A. Jordan & S. J. Kalčik (Eds.), *Women's folklore, women's culture* (pp. 45–53). Philadelphia: University of Pennsylvania Press.

9

Phenomenology as Feminist Methodology: Explicating Interviews

JENNY L. NELSON
School of Telecommunications
Ohio University

My purpose here is to contribute to the insights offered by those feminist scholars who have designated interviewing as an appropriate method for gathering data on women's communication styles. My purpose is to go beyond methods for gathering experiential data (interviewing as technique) to the next step in the research process: what to do with what you've got. Although a great deal of feminist research has explicated the interviewing process, relatively little work has been done in offering methods for interpreting interviews. For instance, most ethnographic studies of women's experience include excerpts from actual interviews, and these excerpts do clarify and illustrate whatever point, or theme, is being made by the researcher (Campbell, 1984). What is not explicated, however, are the procedures by which these researchers choose, organize, and make sense of these excerpts from an often bewildering abundance of recorded speech. The issues that I address, then, are those that every qualitative researcher must deal with when confronted with the data she has gathered. How do I make interpretive choices? What methodological principles ground that choice?

These methodological issues are particularly important in the development of a body of work on women's communication research. The variety of theoretical perspectives currently in circulation can perhaps be clarified further by an explication of methodological issues in the context of actual research practice and performance. Or, as Meese (1986, p. x) describes it, the task is "to enact theorizing as a process (a way of understanding informed by certain values) that inhabits certain readings and to display aspects of theory (ways of reading that reflect those understandings and values)." Communication researchers must explicate procedural processes so that they are no longer muted, implicit, and taken-for-granted, but rather are rendered public, problematic, and available to others. When we talk to each other on the pages of feminist anthologies such as this one, it seems important to be clear and frank about the stakes of our work, the ways in which we have reached a practical understanding of the ways in which we work. This seems to be an especially critical enterprise when it is women interviewing women, given that much of the research on feminist criticism/interpretation deals with a feminist reinterpretation of masculine texts or the status of female authorship (Modleski, 1986). As Gilligan's (1982) critique of Kolberg's all-male studies of morality development suggests, women eschew abstract principles, a feature that Kolberg ignored. Their choices tend to be grounded in situational and contextual features rather than in an abstract theory of what does or does not necessarily constitute "moral choice." Gilligan's insights into female experience as connective are helpful in that they give women validation for their ways of moving through the world. But we also need to make a specific material move that reveals the political working mechanisms which reinsert women into the very realm opened up by Gilligan, but in a marginalizing fashion. The shift from Gilligan to interpretive techniques attempts that critical move.

In the following sections, I explicate the phenomenological procedures of description, reduction (bracketing and free variation), and interpretation. In the first section, I consider philosophical and methodological principles that feminism and phenomenology share. Second, I examine ways of interpreting interview transcripts, using concrete exemplars from my own phenomenological study of televisual experience (Nelson, 1986). My procedures have much in common with Mary Daly's procedural reflections in *Gyn/Ecology* (1978) and *Pure Lust* (1985). In addition, they offer concrete and systematic guidelines for the qualitative researcher. Such a systematization should not be looked upon as an unnecessary constraint, nor as an imposed structure. Rather, the phenomenological method corroborates what is often called "intuition." Phenomenology demonstrates that "intuitive reasoning" is neither haphazard nor illogical, but that it instantiates an abductive, situational logic, one that moves from the particular to the abstract and back again. The phenomenological procedures performed in one study cannot be exactly replicated in another, precisely because the phenomenological method is grounded in, and dependent upon, adhering to the specificity of the experience/phenomenon under investigation. In addition, the method is dependent on its very performance, because how the re-searcher "lives" with the data becomes a central feature of the research itself. For instance, this essay may exhibit certain "interpretive leaps" that the reader may not be able to follow. Due to revisions and the capability of word processors to insert revisions easily and invisibly, this essay was not written in linear fashion. Most research isn't. I try to make explicit how changes in authorial voice and focus occur to me, which is often a difficult enterprise. I expanded certain sections on the basis of rereadings and, after awhile, it became difficult to distinguish the methodology of the research project I conducted/lived a year ago from the methodology of the *writing-about* the research project as I am living it now. Both feminism and phenomenology call for a recognition of the ways in which I as a person (in this case, as female feminist researcher) am positioned within the discourse I am seeking to understand. So in the process of doing research, I am "displaced" and simultaneously repositioned. Research becomes an ongoing construction of procedures and constantly shifting perspectives which are enabled by the situation in which the researcher finds herself. This forces her to reanchor herself repeatedly in each of the positions from which she speaks.

One of the questions facing women's communication research is, how does such tacit, unformulated, and nonthematized human speech enter into and transform the research experience? The appropriate model of speech, and the most difficult area of sense-making representations to trace, is the almost irrecoverable talk and conversation which women/researchers use to place and render meaningful their own immediate experience. Here we are dealing with a veritable development of meaning, rather than a meaning that is already in place "out there," a pure realm existing prior to the researcher's engagement with it. Daly (1978, p. 172) indicates the political significance of the care that must be taken in studying the specifics of power relationships as they are lived and expressed within a particular discursive structure:

> It is truly *racist* to keep silent in the face of these atrocities, merely "studying" them, speaking and writing deceptively about them, applying different (male-created) standards to them, failing to see and name the connections among them. Beyond racism is sisterhood, *naming* the crimes against women without paying mindless respect to the 'social fabric' of the various androcratic societies, including the one in which we find our Selves imprisoned.

Foucault also encourages an examination of the specifics of power relationships when he develops the idea of human speech as counter-discourse: "When the prisoners began to speak, they possesed an individual theory of prisons, the penal system, and justice. It is this form of discourse which ultimately matters, a discourse against power, the counter-discourse of prisoners and those we call delinquents—and not a theory about delinquency" (Bouchard, 1977, p. 209). In other words, we must relate to the situation of women outside the established theoretical framework, instead of imposing a false order of meaning on women's speaking, dismembering women's personal histories, and recomposing them to match the procedure. And, as Merleau-Ponty (1962, p. 10) says about phenomenology, "The primary emphasis is on the phenomenon itself exactly as it reveals itself to the experiencing subject in all its concreteness and particularly." This means that the phenomenological approach is grounded in and begins with the lived-experience as told and described by the person concentrating upon the experience. Many experiences are common sociocultural phenomena; therefore, they must also have shared meanings for persons as an aspect of their situatedness in the world. As persons express their experiences, as they tell their stories, we perceive a discursive process of consciousness that explicates that interconnections among personal, social, and cultural realities (Kamler, 1983). In short, the narration of experience instantiates the existential value and meaning of society. Phemomenology can reveal the movement of experience within discursive mechanisms. Insofar as experience and meaning are constructions, then a blending of deconstruction and phenomenology as a methodology can work well because phenomenology allows us to comprehend that which is violated by discourse, and deconstruction can reveal the discursive mechanisms.

PHENOMENOLOGY AND FEMINISM

Phenomenology is, by definition, a philosophy of human beings in the life-world *(Lebenswelt)* and a qualitative methodology for describing, thematizing, and interpreting the meanings of this largely taken-for-granted world in a rigorous manner. As a philosophy of conscious experience, phenomenology systematically grounds the attempt to make explicit the phenomenon under investigation as it is lived through and embodied in an enworlded subject, rather than against us, isolated from our engagement with it and from the world in which it occurs. As a research procedure, phenomenology calls us to a series of systematic reflections within which we describe, thematize, and interpret that which we intimately live but which has been "forgotten" through sedimentation of our awareness of ourselves in everyday life. The radical reflections of phenomenology attempt to dis-cover and re-animate the sedimented, taken-for-granted phenomena of existence. Phenomenologists subscribe to Husserl's famous phrase, "to the things themselves" *(Zu den Sachen)*, meaning by it a fresh approach to concretely experienced phenomena, as free as possible from conceptual presuppositions and an attempt to describe them as faithfully as possible. Through careful study of experiential description and by systematic variation of these examples, it is possible for the researcher to gain insight into the essential structures and relationships that hold these descriptions together (Spiegelberg, 1982, pp. 10–11).

The phenomenologist's emphasis on the lived experience of the person as the basis for study has as its counterpart the feminist theme of "the personal is political." Since the lived experiences of women take place within a larger social and political structure, feminist scholars stress the need to "bracket" the presuppositions of patriarchal structures in order to fully describe and define women's experience as it is lived and communicated by women, rather than in terms prescribed by dominant (masculine) structures of discourse. Women's personal and existential choices, both conscious and preconscious, necessarily carry political implications that more or less confirm or disconfirm existing structures of experience. In the same vein, political (conscious) choice carries personal (existential) implications. As such, the exploration of the everyday lives of women is a crucial area of scholarly pursuit for feminists, phenomenologists, and deconstructionists alike (Spivak, 1983). Both the personal and political are explored. The personal is reinserted back into the political in order to build a common background for political action.

In returning to the things themselves, phenomenology focuses on the lived experiences of the person. The body plays a central role in phenomenological research in that it is the experience of one's own body that elicits precise descriptions. Rather than relying on theories about experience—the notion of "free will," for example, which many women have internalized to a greater or lesser degree, phenomenology attempts to elicit experiential descriptions of everyday life. In this way, women have the potential to express themselves as speaking subjects rather than to remain silent as objects already spoken for. Bodies are made sensible (literally and metaphorically) within sociopolitical boundaries, such as the boundaries on gender and sexuality (Daly, 1978; Spender, 1985). Women's bodies have been controlled by and described by men, for purposes prescribed by and perpetuated by men, just as the bodies/selves of prisoners and delinquents are inscribed and constrained by institutional structures of power. Due to their marginal status within dominant culture, women understand (at various levels) the games of domination and discourse because their bodies and words are mediated by, and mediators within, dominant paradigms (Spender, 1985). The subjection to objectification has been the point of resistance for feminists and deconstructionists alike. Women's subsequent dis-covery and re-covery of their bodies is directly linked to the re-covery of womens' speaking. A woman must remember her body (experience) because it is here that her speaking originates and where she has most often been repressed and denied (Cixous, 1976; Irigaray, 1980). For Merleau-Ponty, too, speech is a power that the lived-body has of reflecting on and expressing itself. In a chapter entitled "The Body as Expression, And Speech" (1962, pp. 174ff.), he shows how speech is founded on and extends the expressive function of the body. He recognizes that bodily existence is neither merely biological nor neutered, but is already full of, and transformed by, personal and social attitudes, and conversely, personal existence always carries engendered meaning. For feminists and phenomenologists alike, then, women's communication cannot be the same as men's. Women experience and express the world differently, and thus, perhaps, experience/express a *different* world.

Like phenomenology, feminist researchers recognize the necessity to give both experience (events) and consciousness (issues) a fuller and fairer hearing. Cahill (1984, p. 19) points out that "the grasping of women's experience is contingent on a methodological structure which is feminine . . . fluid, dynamic, contextual and relational in nature, i.e., qualitative." As such, the methodological structure that seeks to dis-cover feminine experience must also be qualitative. On a superficial level, Cahill's statement seems somewhat reductive in that it appears to equate an essential "feminine" experience (singular) to an essential "qualitative" method. There is no singular feminine experience and no singular method for dis/covering it. Cahill does, however, address the need for a methodology that can take into account contextual and relational (processual) features of communication. In addition, her approach recognizes the inherent connections among theories and methods.

Just as phenomenology entails both a theory and a method, so does feminist research. Feminism has been described as the *theory* of women's point of view (MacKinnon, 1982). Its *method* is consciousness raising, or the collective critical reconstitution of the meaning of women's social experience, as women live through it. Consciousness raising groups establish, at a grass-roots level, a personal/political praxis that informs feminist theory and methodology today. Here, women gather to talk about their everyday experiences and discover a common ground of experience that enables them to become conscious of a political inscription shared by others. The structure of consciousness-raising groups emphasize the sharing of personal stories without an imposed hierarchy of authority and turn-taking. The commitment to an intersubjective, horizontal structure was particularly and painfully evident in the women's movement's relation to the mass media, where "coverage" of the movement was impeded by media reporters' traditional empiricist methods of gathering information, their reliance on a single spokesman, and their inability/refusal to recognize and accommodate the informal structure and after-hours meetings of women already constrained by the temporal demands of domestic and wage labor (Eddings, 1980). Reporters focused on "events" (brute, visible data) rather than on "issues," and, as such, the movement was trivialized and sensationalized, "spoken for" in terms of bra burnings and the like.

Traditional empiricists consider the description of realities beyond those things that are directly given and observable to be merely "speculative," thus they are eliminated from so-called "scientific" statements. Such systematic eliminations are mirrored by what Bartky (1977, p. 29) calls the "double ontological shock" experienced by feminists: "First, the realization that what is really happening is quite different from what appears to be happening; and second, the frequent inability to tell what is really happening at all." For the traditional empiricist, the social and political world exists independently of a person's conscious experience of it. As such, this scientific method can never articulate the full richness of communication as a process which entails both the personal and the social (Cahill, 1984).

Phenomenology, on the other hand, is a *radical empiricism* in that its common concern is to give phenomena "a fuller and fairer hearing than traditional empiricism has accorded them" (Spiegelberg, 1982, p. 656). Phenomenology can lead qualitative researchers back to concrete experience in which sociopolitical meanings and values are experienced *as* lived-through phenomena, rather than as mere subjective additions to experience or, conversely, as political structures removed from experience. Phenomenology seeks to understand the essential intersubjectivity inherent in all modes of being-in-the world. The ultimate task of phenomenology is to describe, define, and interpret both the personal and political, not as different kinds of experience, but as the experience of different levels of consciousness (Lanigan, 1979, p. 13).

The inherent and essential intersubjectivity of being-in-the-world is reflected in feminist research on a number of different levels. On a methodological level, intersubjectivity is perhaps most clearly exemplified in the relationship created between interview partners. Oakley (1981) discusses this relationship at length. Rather than assuming a strict and hierarchical dichotomy between interviewer/respondent as a condition for objectivity, Oakley demonstrates a necessary condition of establishing rapport with the person being interviewed, and why this stance is particularly relevant when interviewing women. In traditional empiricism, it is the interviewer, in a masculine position of authority, who speaks. The woman (interviewee) is only represented; she is spoken for by the interviewer. In feminist and phenomenological research alike, the interviewer/interviewee structure is replaced by the *practices of coresearchers*. This involves a willingness on the part of the interviewer to disclose information (about the study, about the interview process, about herself as a person) that, in empiricist approaches, would be considered an instance of manipulating the data by unduly influencing the respondent. In my own research, I have discovered that disclosure on my part can open the entire interview situation to more explicit descriptions on the part of my coresearchers. When I tell a story, this can help to elicit a story from the other person. The stories may not be similar (in fact, they often express variations), and my input provides the respondent with a comfortable format by which she can relate her story. In short, "sharing of stories," or "spinstorying" (Langellier & Peterson, 1984), minimizes the perceived authority of the interviewer, and promotes an intersubjective, conversational style to the situation.

Before I discuss the spiraling, interdependent procedures of *description, reduction,* and *interpretation,* and how they may be used in interpreting interviews, I shall discuss one of the first dilemmas the phenomenologist faces with interviews: to transcribe or not to transcribe? or how and how much to transcribe? Transcription is probably the least discussed, most marginal of procedural issues in qualitative research. Transcription is considered a personal choice or preference, a technical means to an important end product (a transcript). The kind of transcription I refer to should not be confused with that of speech act theorists, who are interested in the structuring of utterances, and who have constructed an elaborate coding system designed to draw attention to structure. At first glance, the written transcription of the oral interview appears to be a violation of the conditions or orality because it can be viewed as transferring the immediacy of personal expression into a static, linear mode of anonymous discourse. It should be noted, however, that oral and literate modes of discourse can be found in both speech and writing. Cahill (1984), for instance, points out the orality of Jane Gallop's writings. And just as the recorded interview reduces the entire interview situation to speech (auditory data), so the transcription reduces speech to words (visual data). The actual experience can never be completely contained by any one of these symbolic descriptions, just as description is not contained solely in recorded speech, but is manifest in vocal inflection and bodily gestures as well.

It is useful to view the process of transcribing as an illustration of the phenomenological reduction (epochè and free variation). The reduction brackets the two basic poles of the communicative exchange (sender/receiver) in order to re-turn us to a kind of prepersonal embodiment (neither speaker nor listener) out of which an intersubjective subject might then emerge. The entire research situation is transformed in the act of transcription, from speech to writing, from proximity to distance, from the visible (body)/invisible (speech) to the invisible (body)/visible (speech), and the subsequent reading implies a perceptual change from an emphasis on listening to an emphasis on seeing. According to Lowe (1982), hearing is intensive and enwombing, whereas seeing is distancing and extensive. Seeing, as a centrifugal, abstract movement, is more discriminating, enabling us to locate a coherent entity against a broad background. In each case, however, "sensation is intentional because I find that in the sensible a certain rhythm of existence is put forward—abduction or adduction—and that, following up this hint, ... I am brought into relation with an external being, whether it be in order to open myself to it or shut myself off from it" (Merleau-Ponty, 1962, pp. 213–14).

Transcription, then, is not opposed to, but is a variation of the intentional, human relationship experienced in the interview situation. It is *during* the labor of transcribing that the researcher performs the actual transformation from the listening to speech to the writing of speech, of making visible the invisible. This labor requires a process of concretization rather than one of distancing. The researcher hears the same phrases over and over again, rewinds the audiotape an inch at a time and listens again, until the words seem to be emptied of meaning (meaning is bracketed) and s/he listens only for the words (form). The researcher also brackets attention to vocal style by creating a distance from the voice (transcribing), just as s/he bracketed attention to gesture by creating a distance from the body (audio recording). The researcher is left only with patterns of graphic signs. The methodology entailed in Merleau-Ponty's phenomenology requires that no hierarchy of value be established between writing and speech. One is not inherently more significant than the other, but rather, each expresses different ways of being-in-relation. In this manner of free variation, phenomenology restores to both speech and writing their truths. What is bereft of meaning in one perspective may find it in another. Variation of perspective is a concern in feminist research as well (Moraga, 1986; O'Neale, 1986), especially in terms of race and class, where the experiences of racial and cultural difference are essential to the working out of a cohesive, inclusive feminist perspective. The dominant white middle-class context is bracketed in order to ensure maximum variation in female perceptions and expressions that might otherwise be lost.

At this point, let me tell a story that represents, for me, the logical culmination of what can happen with the exchanges between coresearchers, not only in the interviewing phase of the procedure, but also in the listening/transcribing process afterwards. One of my interview partner's speaking style was (unbeknownst to me at the time) very similar to my own, so much so that when I first listened to the interview tape, I had some difficulty distinguishing her voice from my own. The unintended and disconcerting result was that I listened to the beginnings of my own stories as if they were someone else's! This literal and metaphorical exchange of voices induced in me a momentary panic at not being able to assign difference, otherness, boundaries. Despite my stated committment to the partic-

ularity of individual experiences, I had somehow expected that the particularity of my respondents would be gradually erased during the course of
analysis. Listening to the audiotapes, I surmised, would function as a first
step toward that erasure, an erasure of the other's body and of the interviewing situation so that I might become more "objective" and disinterested in my coresearchers as persons. I did not expect that it would be
my body in its particularity and author-ity, that would be erased/displaced.
In trying to establish an identity for that anonymous voice, my response
went something like this: "It's her (not me)—no, it's *not* her (still not
me)—who? me?" But by this point, establishing an identity for that voice
provided little comfort or stability. First of all, this episode illustrates my
own propensity for adhering to the established role of "objective analyst."
Because I had taken great care to facilitate intersubjectivity in the interview situation itself, I mistakenly assumed that similar care would not be
necessary once the event was over. Having established intersubjectivity in
the interview situation, and having captured it on audiotape, I thought I
could withdraw to the proverbial armchair and bask in an ensured and
stable authenticity. However, I discovered that those bipolar categories of
interview/analysis, speech/writing, and objectivity/subjectivity simply do
not apply to this research situation, because it is impossible to erase the
contextual features of the research process, that is, one's own experiences
in several phases. The experience challenged my intended objectivity. As
de Beauvoir observes, no one volunteers to serve as the Other (Meese,
1986, p. 75). I fall short of an ultimate identity that would place me outside
time; rather, I am always in and of a situation and it is this condition that
best illustrates intersubjectivity. Even though I may be reading the words
I had heard previously, thus repeating the initial structure, the situation is
qualitatively different.

Transcribed speech, too, is an instance of repetition—not the return of
the same through the reiteration of the identical, but rather the production
(to bring into existence) of difference. As such, transcriptions, as phenomena of repetition, can "furnish a privileged approach to the most authentic
understanding of difference" (Descombes, 1980, p. 154). But in order for
there to be authenticity in this difference, "the restructuring which yields
a new meaning [difference] must truly repeat the initial structure, even
though it has gaps and opacities" (Merleau-Ponty, 1973, p. 127). This condition suggests that transcription involves more than just the literal transcribing of speech, or the "effacing" of speech. Pauses should be transcribed, as should laughter, imitative noises, and so on. The attention to
paralinguistic features functions to discover the invisible—that which was
vocalized but not verbalized by the speaker, and that which was heard but
not foregrounded by the hearer. For example, the pause (belonging to a
temporal order) is transferred to a spatial order in the form of a textual

gap. The visual order can often enable one to see spontaneous patterns of organization emerging. For example, while listening to the audiotapes for my project on televisual experience, I failed to "hear" a number of variations in speech that proved to be central to later interpretations. For instance, when a respondent said, "I was watching Dynasty and then I saw that it was a rerun," I first heard/categorized this utterance as a "Dynasty story" or "a rerun story." The verbs used to describe the experience were, at that time, interchangeable and invisible to me. They functioned as mere synonyms pointing to the "real" subject (reruns). Only on paper could I see that, if "see," "watch," and "look" are used in a single utterance, they are expressive of different degrees of perception, attention, and intention. Even though the precise words were often interchangeable between respondents, within each utterance itself, each word expressed a particular bodily experience. Thus, I began to pay less attention to the words per se and more attention to the experiences signified by the words. In this way, the words function as existential signifiers. They do not refer automatically to a predetermined dictionary meaning, but rather, are expressive of perceptual variation in a complex web of signification embodied by that person.

PHENOMENOLOGICAL DESCRIPTION

Here, the re-searcher approaches the interviews by placing herself as nearly as possible in the concrete situation and assuming personal responsibility for the choices to be made. Such a position activates a complex structure of memories, feelings, and capacities and requires a process of concretization rather than one of abstraction. Yet, how can concretization occur in a situation which, by its very nature, involves a spatial and temporal distance not found in the immediacy of the interview situation? First of all, in each listening, reading, rereading, and reduction, there remains, as a re-active and subdued force, the researcher's memories of previous readings and insights gleaned therein. This occurs within each interview as well as among several interviews. By arranging the revelatory phrases according to themes, the experience is explicated in terms of relations (differentiations as related for one respondent) and in terms of correlations (differentiations as related among respondents). In order to abstract valid themes of relation, for instance, the re-searcher has as a context the interview situation, and the respondent's inflections in the audiotape. The verbal inflections, in turn, recall certain bodily gestures. In effect, that which the researcher somehow perceives as relevant and important is most often the dynamic result of a preconscious and simultaneous process of retention and protention. When you become familiar with the structure of the interview, for instance, when you "know what comes next," you are, in a sense, free from that structure. In phenomenological terms, the formal structure is bracketed, and a new perceptual variation becomes possible. You "know" from familiarity that this person's talk about "Dynasty" leads to stories about others' responses to it, and these stories lead to stories about the person's responses to those responses.

By the time the interviews have been transcribed, the three-part interdependent procedure of description, reduction, and interpretation has already been accomplished once. The respondents' stories serve as the fundamental descriptions, which the researcher then reduces to auditory data (tape recordings) and visual data (transcripts). The description phase of the analysis proper is inextricably linked to the Interpretation phase involved in transcribing the interviews. That is to say, the listening and writing/reading already serves as a preliminary interpretation. By this time, the researcher is already familiar with the general structure of the interview. For instance, I listened to all of the recorded interviews twice before transcribing each one (a listening that involves a different degree and focus of attention). Then I read through each transcript several times before I began to get a sense of emerging themes. My initial description of content followed a consistent, though not always explicit, pattern. After highlighting relevant phrases from each interview, I arranged a tentative list of eight to ten thematic topics as disclosed by each respondent. For example, interspersed throughout one interview were various depictions and stories: one about how an "unconscious alarm goes off" every Sunday at 4 p.m., reminding her of a particular program to watch, another about how her evening meals always coincide with a particular program, how she "lacks the time to be an ideal viewer," and how her present experience of a rerun differs from the way she used to experience it. I clustered these stories together under the thematic topic, "Televisual Temporality" because each story expressed some bodily organization of experiences of time in relation to television.

Some of the thematic topics entail subtopics, or include descriptive illustrations so that I would not forget details and subtle nuances of meaning. For instance, one of the thematic topics that emerges from one person is: "TV provides an escape from a compulsive mind set, but not a release." Below that topic, I note two thematic descriptions that offer clarification: (a) "TV numbing, like a drug," and (b) "TV enables you not to work through issues you feel unprepared to deal with." The first thematic description is a vivid metaphor. The second thematic description clarifies the topic by specifying the meaning of "escape" as an enabling function for the person. "A compulsive mind set" entails "issues one feels unprepared to deal with, and "release" implies the "working through" that is not accomplished. Since the thematic topic and the second thematic description are essentially redundant, that is, reflexive of each other, they could conceivably be interchanged, or one might be completely omitted since its essential meaning is entailed in the other. However, the phrase I chose as a thematic topic seems more conducive to my purposes in that it more readily evokes, for me, other respondent expressions pertaining to that topic. The chosen thematic topic serves as a reminder of similar expressions across interviews (correlations), while the thematic descriptions are reminders of complexity within that particular interview (relations).

After determining the thematic topics for each respondent, I began the second step, which involves the explicit cross-checking of descriptive meanings in thematic topics among interviews (correlations). For instance, I noted that each respondent invokes other experiences when describing TV—the two most noticeable general categories being other mass media experiences and other immediate experiences (i.e., "real" and interpersonal, of the human realm). Other correlative thematic topics emerge, like "Presence of Others" and "Judgments About Self" but, at this point in my analysis, these appear to be more complex and more diffused structures of experience in that a greater variety of thematic descriptions are involved. I felt that these more complex thematic topics might better be understood in the context of the first two "simpler" topics. In a sense, the first two topics consist in more "objective," overt, and explicit descriptions by the respondents, for example., "TV is like a verbose person" and "TV serves the same purpose as music." By explicating what it is that renders televisual experience unique, that is, different from other forms of experience, I felt that I could become more sensitive to the complexities of televisual experience in itself. This is another form of the phenomenological epoche. The free variation among the descriptions of other mediated experiences provides insight into the specificity of televisual experience by delimiting some of its possible boundaries: Each person interviewed offered spontaneous comparisons (without any suggestion on my part) of televisual experience vis-a-vis other forms of experience, and each person described a different mass medium as his/her primary reference point. This illustrates the importance of bracketing your own protocol topics used during the interview so that topics you had not anticipated can emerge. In my case, descriptions of televisual experience vis-a-vis other media experiences brings into relief the variety and degrees of involvement, its functions, and how it sensitizes the researcher to the nuances involved in seemingly innocuous word choices. One begins the process of understanding just how seeing is not watching and not looking, just as listening is not the same experience as hearing.

After establishing the thematic topics, I went back to the transcripts to extract specific references to other mediated experiences. I copied these onto notecards labelled "Film" "Music" "Radio" "Theater" and "Print" as initial thematic categories of the topic. After looking at and comparing all the references to film, I underlined what appeared to be key descriptions (e.g., "I don't get involved in film as I do TV;" "When you go see a movie, that's all you do"). Unable to reduce the key descriptions of film any further, I turned my attention to the thematic category of music, and repeated the description/reduction process. Upon comparing the key music descriptions with the key film descriptions, I noticed that music is depicted as being more like TV than film is. Like music (and unlike film), TV is a constant potential presence that provides the option and possibility for immediate involvement, an involvement that often requires distance and isolation. That last sentence represents a description of my interpretation of the reduction process.

Like transcription, the description phase involves another spiraling of description, reduction, and interpretation. The transcripts constitute the description. The researcher performs a reduction by choosing certain elements from the description and by submitting them to variation. In short, the rules which inform the act of description are: (a) attend to the phenomena as they are immediately present; (b) describe, don't explain; (c) horizontalize or equalize all immediate phenomena and do not assume an initial hierarchy of "realities" (Ihde, 1977, pp. 34–6). In this way, phenomenological description opens the field of experience in its fullness and its multiplicity in preparation for the phenomenological reduction.

THEMATIZING INTERVIEWS

The second step in the phenomenological method is the phenomenological reduction, or definition, wherein the direct experience as disclosed in the description becomes the object of our reflection. The researcher reflects on the first reflection in order to specify the structurings of lived-reality. In this step, elements of the description undergo variation. The reduction of the description constitutes a definition of the phenomenon. In phenomenological research, thematizing is a systematic way of developing and refining interpretations of the data. The coding process involves bringing together and analyzing all the data relevant to themes, concepts, and ideas generated from the data itself. During this stage of the procedure, vague ideas are refined, expanded, developed, or discarded. The reduction consists in abstracting words and phrases from the interviews that function as existential signifiers, or revelatory phrases (Colaizzi, 1973).

In analyzing interview transcripts, the goals of traditional research are altered. The aim is not to determine if there is consensus about experience, nor is it to find out why persons do what they do. Rather, phenomenology is concerned with the meaning structure of experience as a lived logic. By adhering to the experience as described, the reduction determines which aspects of the description are essential (truly part of consciousness) and which parts are merely assumed (methodological).

The basic rule which informs the reduction is: seek out structural or invariant features of the phenomenon (Ihde, 1977, p. 39). Through the technique of imaginative free variation, which contextualizes various features of the phenomenon within the whole, and which allows for comparison and contrast, a pattern of experience emerges. With it emerges the shape of the phenomenon as it is attended to in experience. Through imaginative free variation, that which is invariant and essential for the existence of the phenomenon to consciousness is described—its essence. Thus, the theme of the experience is articulated.

There are two phases to the reduction procedure which need to be further articulated. The first entails a focus on "the abstract and general properties of, ideas about, or forms of the phenomenon under investigation" (Lanigan, 1979, p. 38). The second entails restraint in the consideration of particular examples. That is, although the general themes are originally located in actual experience, the researcher should remain critically aware of the necessity to remain open and independent of the particularities of any actual experience so that the essential elements of the phenomenon may emerge in the fullness of their possibilities for experience. At this stage of the analysis, then, the original descriptions of particular experiences will have been transformed into more general, concise expressions. That is, specific references to a particular person, situation and so on will become references to the phenomenon in general.

In feminist terms, this means that the personal becomes political. In *Gyn/Ecology*, for instance, Daly carefully explicates the particularities of various procedures designed to control women's bodies/selves: Chinese foot-binding, Indian sutee, African clitoridectomy, European witchburnings, and American gynecology. She transforms what had previously been interpreted and reported as *cultural*-specific practices, into the more general, essential phenomenon of female oppression and genocide. Daly was able to bracket the particularities (female body parts, culture-specific ritual, etc.). by focusing on the general properties of particular descriptions (the female body).

The most important lesson of the reduction is the impossibility of a complete reduction (Merleau-Ponty, 1962, p. xiv). Finding the essences is a means for incarnating consciousness in personal and social human existence, that is, to ground essence (the political) in existence (the personal). As such, this maxim refutes constitutive or phenomenological idealism. The fact that our consciousness is always an "engaged consciousness" in the world becomes for Merleau-Ponty the fundamental principle in the understanding of our mutual involvement and participation in the world.

For Daly, it was only by explicating the "engaged consciouness" of female experience in patriarchal culture that she was able to articulate the fundamental principle of female oppression. The feminist researcher's task, then, is to take these critical discoveries and return them to the world in which we find ourselves and to describe as faithfully as possible what we find there.

The procedure(s) of reduction move reflexively from lived and unreflected-upon experiences (respondents' descriptions of lived experiences *and* the researcher's lived experiences of listening/reading) to reflection upon experiences and the mode of experiencing them (how respondents depict their experience and how the researcher engages in analysis), to the emergence of the previously repressed subject of experiences (general themes emerging from respondents' descriptions and the researcher's methodology). The subject becomes strictly thematic only reflectively. It is this movement to intentional analysis which separates reflection from ordinary introspection. The reflexive turn to the subject situates the reference of experience (the personal experiences of the respondent describing/the researcher analyzing) back into relation with the life of consciousness (the political/methodological). The final reflexive phase is that of the lived-body *(corps propre)*, the experiencing person.

PHENOMENOLOGICAL INTERPRETATION

The third phase of Merleau-Ponty's radical reflection attempts to understand the "meaning" which links the phenomenon under investigation with consciousness. The relationships established by the phenomenological reduction are now considered in relation to each other. The phenomenolgoical interpretation consists of two steps. In the first step, the list of revelatory phrases obtained from the reduction phase is critically examined and one or two selected as the meaning (signified) of the discourse. Second, a particular signified is used as the key part of the hermeneutic proposition, that is., a statement written by the researcher that gives the meaning implicit in the explicit discourse. A seemingly unimportant phrase/utterance can be (is) the preconscious, prereflective meaning used by the respondent. Confirmation of one's interpretation is often readily at hand with such respondent reactions as, "That's what I was trying to say," or "That's what I meant, but I didn't know I said it." In either case, both the informant and the re-searcher discover the sense in which the phrase is indeed revelatory of lived-meaning.

In the interpretation, I conduct what Merleau-Ponty (1968, p. 38) calls a hyper-reflection, that which takes itself and the changes it introduces into the phenomenon into account. Further, "it must use words not according to their pre-established signification, but in order to state this pre-logical bond." Mary Daly (1978, p. 315) describes a similar hyper-reflective maneuver with what she calls the "third passage": "this knowing/ acting/ Self-centering Process is itself the creating of a new, woman- identified environment. . . . It also involves dis-covering the sources of the Self's original movement, hearing the moving of this movement. It involves speaking forth the New Words which correspond to this deep listening, speaking the words of our lives." In the hyper-reflection, I must not only go *back* to the speech of the respondents, but I must also go *beyond* those already-speaking significations.

The goal of the interpretation is to dis-cover meanings which are not immediately apparent in the description and reduction (Spiegelberg, 1982, p. 695). That which is given in specific revelatory phrases serves as indicators to certain meanings which are not immediately apparent. The final movement of the interpretation synthesizes and synopsizes the previous movements into a "hermeneutic judgment or specification of existential meaning, i.e., the meaning of the phenomenon as the person lived it" (Lanigan, 1979, p. 40). The interpretation thus emphasizes the meaning of the phenomena as contingent upon their being ascribed value by embodied persons in concrete situations. In my research, a revelatory respondent phrase captured the lived meaning of the televisual: "eyes out of your head." This phrase suggests not simply the sometimes eye-popping rapidity of TV rhythm, but a movement out of and away from the reflective cognitive capacity of the "de-coder" to the prereflective affective activity of the person. Although eyes have their physical location in the human head, their powers of perception are distributed throughout the ensemble body. "Eyes out of your head" also suggests an embodied rationality—a differential ratio (ensemble) of prereflective choices and perceptual power. In addition, the phrase is revelatory of those moments in which persons grasp a sense of self in recognition that their vision differs from others. Thus, a person's eyes are commuted to those of living, embodied others, and becomes reflexive: my eyes are more in them than in me. In such cases, the person feels the Self to be a conspicuous and self-conscious "naked I/eye" abjectly displayed before the powerful Other.

"Eyes out of your head" also suggests the self-reflexiveness of televisual experience—the ability of the person to become an object for her/himself, to turn a critical eye on the seeing Self, to interrogate the I/eye who sees. My eyes come out of my head in order to turn reflexively toward my own expression of perception, in which case the TV provides a horizon against which my own consciousness (meaning) emerges in effect, the third step attempts to specify "meaning" that is essential in the phenomenon as described, and consciousness of the phenomenon as reduced. In what Lanigan (1979, p. 8) calls a "hermeneutic semiology," there is a specification of the value relationship that unites the phenomenological description and reduction. It may take the form of an implicit or explicit revelatory phrase by the person interviewed, which signifies the value (conscious experience) that functions as the relationship in the descriptions and the reductions. By attempting to determine the hermeneutic semiology inherent in experience, we are necessarily asking what value is to be found there, what meaning is generated from there.

The interpretation is an attempt to specify the preconscious and intentional meaning of the described and defined phenomenon. Since such a meaning can be located as "the original presence of that which never could be present in person ... conceivable only as the 'shadow' and the latency of our experience, that which is present to us only by remaining absent from us" (Madison, 1981, pp. 197–98), it is graspable only through interpretation.

CONCLUSION

The communication researcher needs to experiment with various methods, testing time and time again their serviceability. The question, "How should I approach my data?" is a question that needs to be asked at the level of the interview and at the level of the interpretation of data because of the ongoing and multidimensional character of the phenomenon of social reality and the situated perspective of the investigator. What is required is that the methodological principles that inform the doing of research not sever the phenomena from the method. The phenomena should be permitted to speak for themselves and thus guide the construction of methodological theory and procedure. The variety of methodologies in communication studies is not in itself a regrettable state of affairs. It would be a mistake to institutionalize any one methodological approach as the official prerequisite for understanding. However, the adequacy of each particular methodology needs to be determined in the context of its actual practice and performance, its ability to yield insights regarding women's communication patterns, their strategies for communicating in various contexts.

In devising some general guidelines for using phenomenology as a way to do feminist research into women's communication, I can only skim over a possible agenda. First, feminists have demonstrated the gendered and sexualized structures that characterize the methodologies and theories of communication research. Second, by explicating how our own discourse is structured, and how our research is conducted, we have begun to show how this area of inquiry is accessible to other feminist scholars. Third, so long as methods of interpreting interview data are seen as a set of social practices engaging persons who are specifically positioned within cultural categories—each person/researcher having a history, a world-view, and beliefs—this context affects what communication scholars believe need explaining, what questions they ask of others and themselves, what assumptions they make, and what they consider valid evidence to be.

The rereadings that the phenomenological method entails encourage the researcher to place herself at deliberately different angles in relation to the subject of interest: first in the interview situation and then in the three phases of interpretation, where each rereading necessarily includes and transforms insights gleaned from previous readings. Context—the terms of address and reception—is very important in determining the meaning of any given utterance or text. By placing oneself as close as possible to the person being interviewed (allowing her to speak), by remaining close to the utterances and to the text via careful transcription, and by systematic rereadings, the communication researcher greatly increases the chances for contextual fidelity. By varying one's positions—as listener, speaker, reader, and writer—within the discourse of a single subject and among various subjects, meaning is multiplied rather than arrested. By constantly referring to the materiality of the research situation, the researcher's perceived power and position can be constantly checked and varied. The intersubjective nature of the interpretive enterprise is, as Teresa de Lauretis (1984, p. 159) puts it, "an ongoing construction, not a fixed point of departure or arrival from which one then interacts with the world."

With this in mind, I offer semiotic phenomenology as one methodology appropriate for studying women's communication. The spiraling, interdependent three-step procedure of description, reduction, and interpretation is especially useful for the systematic explication of interviews.

REFERENCES

Bartky, S. L. (1977). Toward a phenomenology of feminist consciousness. In M. Vetterling-Braggin, F. A. Elliston, & J. English (Eds.), *Feminism and philosophy* (pp. 22–34). Totowa, NJ: Littlefield, Adams, & Co.

Bouchard, D. F. (Ed.) (1977). *Michel Foucault: Language, counter-memory, practice: Selected essays and interviews.* New York: Cornell University Press.

Cahill, C. (1984, November). *Women as audience: Feminism and the significance of gender for the study of interpersonal communication.* Paper presented to the Speech Communication Association, Chicago, IL.

Campbell, A. (1984). *The girls in the gang.* New York: Basil Blackwell.

Cixous, H. (1976). The laugh of the medusa (K. Cohen & P. Cohen, Trans.). In E. Marks & I. de Courtivron (Eds.), *New French feminisms* (pp. 245–64). New York: Schocken Books.

Colaizzi, P. F. (1973). *Reflection and research in psychology.* Dubuque, IA: Kendall/ Hunt.

Daly, M. (1978). *Gyn/Ecology: The metaethics of radical feminism.* Boston: Beacon.

Daly, M. (1984). *Pure lust: Elemental feminist philosophy.* Boston: Beacon.

de Lauretis, T. (1984). *Alice doesn't: Feminism, semiotics, cinema.* Bloomington: Indiana University Press.

Descombes, V. (1980). *Modern French philosophy* (L. Scott-Fox & J. M. Harding, Trans.). Cambridge: Cambridge University Press.

Eddings, B. M. (1980). Women in broadcasting. *Women's studies international quarterly, 3,* 1–13.

Gilligan, C. (1982). *In a different voice: Psychological theory and women's development.* Cambridge: Harvard University Press.

Ihde, D. (1977). *Experimental phenomenology: An introduction.* New York: Capricorn Books.

Irigaray, L. (1980). When our lips speak together (C. Burke, Trans.). *Signs, 6,* 69–79.

Kamler, H. (1983). *Communication: Sharing our stories of experience.* Seattle: Psychological Press.

Langellier, K. M., & Peterson, E. E. (1984, November). *Spinstorying: A communication analysis of women's storytelling.* Paper presented at the Speech Communication Association, Chicago, IL.

Lanigan, R. L. (1979). The phenomenology of human communication. *Philosophy Today, 23*(i), 3–15.

Lowe, D. M. (1982). *The history of bourgeois perception.* Chicago: University of Chicago Press.

Mackinnon, C. (1982). Feminism, Marxism, method, and the state: An agenda for theory. *Signs, 7,* 515–544.

Madison, G. B. (1981). *The phenomenology of Merleau-Ponty: A search for the limits of consciousness.* Athens: Ohio University Press.

Meese, E. A. (1986). *Crossing the double-cross: The practice of feminist criticism.* Chapel Hill & London: University of North Carolina Press.

Merleau-Ponty, M. (1962). *Phenomenology of perception* (C. Smith, Trans., F. Williams, Trans. rev.). London: Routledge & Kegan Paul. (Original work published 1948).

Merleau-Ponty, M. (1968). *The visible and the invisible* (C. Leford, Ed., A. Lingis, Trans.). Evanston: Northwestern University Press.

Merleau-Ponty, M. (1973). *The prose of the world* (C. Lefort, Ed.; J. O'Neill, Trans.). Evanston: Northwestern University Press. (Original work published 1969).

Modleski, T. (1986). Feminism and the power of interpretation: Some critical readings. In T. de Lauretis (Ed.), *Feminist studies/critical studies* (pp. 121–138). Bloomington: Indiana University Press.

Moraga, C. (1986). From a long line of vendidas: Chicanas and feminism. In T. de Lauretis (Ed.), *Feminist studies/critical studies* (pp. 173–190). Bloomington: Indiana University Press.

Nelson, J. L. (1986). The other side of signification: a semiotic phenomenology of televisual experience. Unpublished doctoral dissertation, Southern Illinois University, Carbondale IL.

Oakley, A. (1981). Interviewing women: A contradiction in terms. In H. Roberts (Ed.), *Doing feminist research* (pp. 30–61). London: Routledge & Kegan Paul.

O'Neale, S. (1986). Inhibiting midwives, usurping creators: The struggling emergence of black women in American fiction. In T. de Lauretis (Ed.), *Feminist studies/critical studies* (pp. 139–156). Bloomington: Indiana University Press.

Spender, D. (1985). *Man made language (2nd ed.)*. Boston: Routledge & Kegan Paul (Original work published 1980).

Spiegelberg, H. (1982). *The phenomenological movement (3rd ed.)*. The Hague: Martinus Nijhoff. (Original work published 1960).

Spivak, G. C. (1983). Displacement and the discourse of woman. In M. Krupnick (Ed.), *Displacement: Derrida and after* (pp. 169–195). Bloomington: Indiana University Press.

10

Triangulation in Gender Research: The Need for Converging Methodologies

CONSTANCE COURTNEY STALEY

PAMELA SHOCKLEY-ZALABAK
Dof Communication
University of Colorado at Colorado Springs

INTRODUCTION

Over the last 20 years, researchers have become increasingly interested in the communication differences of males and females. Although numerous studies detail sex differences, findings have often been buried in research designed to examine such major variables as self-disclosure, interpersonal interaction, and nonverbal behavior (Montgomery & Norton, 1981).

Within the last 10 years, the study of gender and communication has evolved as a specific research specialization among communication scholars. Now that researchers have compiled a sizeable body of literature on sex differences, gender and communication scholars have begun the process of critical review (Bates, 1984; Putnam, 1982; Solomon, 1984; Staley, 1986) and report that research results are fragmented, mixed, and controversial. Rarely in communication research has a unifying framework been used to examine male-female differences (Montgomery & Norton, 1981).

The gender and communication research picture is further confounded by two additional factors. First, researchers often operationalize variables differently from one study to the next; and second, contextual factors within research studies obviously influence outcomes. The research on communicative dominance, for example, investigates such variables as length of utterance (Swacker, 1975), number of topics generated by each speaker (Fishman, 1978), or number of interruptions made by each person (Zimmerman & West, 1975). While all of these operational definitions of conversational dominance may overlap conceptually, it is possible for one sex to be conversationally dominant in one study but not in another. While this problem is not unique to gender research, it nevertheless contributes to the perception among scholars that "gender role research is in a state of confusion" (Solomon, 1984, p. 98).

Findings may also conflict based on a variety of contextual variables, such as the size, makeup, and characteristics of the communicative group under observation, or the research context itself, such as laboratory versus organizational setting. For example, researchers such as Zimmerman and West (1975), Eakins and Eakins (1976) and Baird (1976) found that men interrupt others more frequently than do women. Camden and Kennedy (1982), however, found that female graduate students were more likely to interrupt in group settings than were male graduate students, concluding that interruptions in their study were an attempt to gain dominance, rather than a display of dominance. Likewise, many studies document perceived differences in male-female leadership style; however, researchers such as Osborn and Vicars (1976) and Brown (1979) conclude that differences may vary depending on the research context: "The widely held belief that women make inferior leaders seems to give way in actual work situations. . . . Practicing managers overwhelmingly feel that there is no difference between male and female leadership styles; whereas students generally hold the opposite to be true" (Brown, 1979, p. 607).

A further point to emerge from recent critiques of the literature on sex differences is the erroneous overlap between *self-reports* of male-female behaviors, *others'* reports of perceived behaviors, and *stereotyped projections* based on social conditioning (Staley, 1986). Often distinctions between these three distinct research categories become fuzzy, resulting in a single informal generalization which is then referred to as sex differences (Staley & Cohen, 1988). For example, the widely-held generalization that males are evaluated more favorably than females gives way upon close examination of the research perspectives employed in various studies.

In truth, investigating all three perspectives—self-reports, others' reports, and stereotyped projections—within their appropriate parameters contributes to our understanding of male and female communicative behavior. Many studies identify *expected* differences based on stereotypes of socially approved male and female roles. Kramer (1974), for example, found distinct differences between the stereotypes of male versus female speech. By comparison, few studies document *actual* differences between the speech of men and women, perhaps because actual behaviors are difficult to recognize given the influence of sex-role stereotyping. Comparisons of *self-perceptions* of male-female communication identify more similarities than differences (McDaris & Javidi, 1985; Montgomery & Norton, 1981; Staley & Cohen, 1988). To date, no single study we know of has investigated all three perspectives concurrently.

THE NEED FOR CONVERGING METHODOLOGIES

The purpose of this essay is twofold. First, we will provide a detailed example of the confusion in gender-communication research by surveying the mixed literature on evaluating male versus female organizational performance. We see this as a critical research area to investigate because of its relevance to the divergent career outcomes experienced by men and women.

Perhaps the single most important finding to emerge from the plethora of research comparing professional males and females is the lack of significant differences in both attitudes toward work and actual behaviors on the job (e.g., Bartol, 1977; Birdsall, 1980; Day & Stogdill, 1972; Donnell & Hall, 1980). On the other hand, the most important factor in determining the selection of potential managers and leaders may not be actual or even perceived behavior, but rather, how behavior is evaluated (Hollander & Julian, 1979). Nieva and Gutek (1980) suggest that a significant barrier for professional women is prejudicial evaluation of their qualifications and performance. Therefore, we have decided to review the conflicting research in this area by focusing on four levels of evaluation—self, peer, subordinate, and supervisor.

Second, we will propose an innovative research methodology which provides a holistic, integrated perspective critical to the study of women's communication—multilevel triangulation. Multiple methodologies, both quantitative and qualitative, and multilevel perspectives—self, peer, subordinate, and superior—have produced a collection of mixed results. And while mixed findings alone do not justify the call for methodological "revolution," we assert with Sypher and Sypher (1984) that "communication researchers ought to be generally concerned that the phenomena they study converge, at least to some extent, with independent indicators of the same phenomena" (p. 98). Triangulation, or the use of more than one method in the study of a single phenomenon (Denzin, 1970), can serve to enhance the confidence of gender researchers by capturing a "more complete, holistic, and contextual portrayal of the unit(s) under study" (Jick, 1979, in Tompkins & Cheney, 1983).

We believe that the study of women's communication is a viable research area, an area which has been overlooked until recently. For generations, research was conducted by male reseachers using male subjects and then generalized to all human beings (Gilligan, 1982). With the women's movement came the realization that women's experiences are diverse, complex, and divergent from the experiences of men, and thus was born a new research specialization. However, because the study of women has evolved as a "female" research area with a concentration of female researchers "impelled by the researcher's passion for the subject" (Foss &

Foss, 1986, p. 4), the opportunity exists for bias in the opposite direction. Although feminist research often acknowledges its bias (Spender, 1985), researchers must continue to search for innovative methodologies to best describe the experiences of women, not only through the use of innovative qualitative methodologies such as oral history, but through innovative methodologies that are objective *and* holistic.

ASSESSMENT OF THE LITERATURE

Evaluation: Self, Peers, Subordinates, Supervisors.

A detailed example of the confusion in gender-communication research may be seen in the mixed literature on evaluating male versus female performance in organizational settings. Some studies show no differences (e.g., Dipboye & Wiley, 1977; Frank & Drucker, 1977; Hall & Hall, 1976; Moses & Boehm, 1975); some studies show that males are evaluated more favorably than females (e.g., Deaux & Emswiller, 1974; Dipboye, Arvey, & Terpstra, 1977; Dipboye, Fromkin, & Wiback, 1975; Goldberg, 1968; Rosen & Jerdee, 1974; Schein, 1973); and some studies show that females are evaluated more favorably than males (e.g., Abramson, Goldberg, Greenberg, & Abramson, 1977; Hamner, Kim, Baird, & Bigoness, 1974; Jacobson & Effertz, 1974; Peters, O'Conner, Weekley, Pooyan, Frank, & Erenkrantz, 1983). Inconsistencies may be seen in the research on female professionals' self, peer, subordinate, and supervisor evaluation.

Nieva and Gutek (1980) suggest that a potential barrier to professional women is prejudicial evaluation of females' qualifications and performance. They note that while employee evaluation should be objectively based on merit, extensive documentation demonstrates deviation from these ideals. Glucklich and Povall (1979) studied 26 organizations and found that in 22 of the 26, one or more managers concerned with hiring, training, and promotions said they were "discriminating or intending to discriminate against men or women in the future" (p. 28). Women are more likely to be subjected to negative bias in evaluation when the required level of inference is high, when sex-role incongruence occurs, or when women are highly competent (Nieva & Gutek, 1980).

Inconsistencies in Self Evaluation

When female professionals evaluate their own performance in organizations, results are mixed. Snyder and Bruning (1979), for example, surveyed both supervisors and nonsupervisors and found that women reported themselves to be as competent as their male counterparts. These results stand in contrast to a study by Deaux (1979) in which women managers' self-ratings were lower than those of their male colleagues. Ezell, Odewahn, and Sherman (1980) asked 304 male managers and 271 female managers to complete questionnaires with scales measuring self-perceptions of ability, motivation, and environment, or the extent to which the individual receives feedback from and copes effectively with the work environment. In terms of overall results, female managers reported greater competence-motivation and competence-environment, but less competence-ability than male managers.

Inconsistencies in Peer Evaluation

When the performance of female professionals is evaluated by their peers, both male and female, the existence of sex-role conditioning in the work place becomes evident. Wood (1976) found that males reported anxiety about restructuring relationships with females who were once subordinates but have become peers. Haefner (1977), in surveying workers in two Illinois towns, found a clear preference for working with highly competent men over highly competent women. Donnell and Hall (1980) found that female managers are not as willing as male managers to share information with their colleagues—"confirming evidence of interpersonal noise at the peer level" (p. 7). In a more recent study, however, Tsui and Gutek (1984) found that female managers were given higher performance evaluations by peers than were their male counterparts.

When research on women professionals examines peer evaluations in terms of the sex-composition of the peer groups, female-female or female-male, findings are often negative. Matteson (1976), for example, found fewer positive attitudes toward women managers among male managers. Furthermore, attitudes toward women managers became less favorable for both males and females with increased work experience. Albrecht (1976) reported that female scientists are usually not sought out by their male colleagues, nor do these women seek out their male colleagues. Wood (1976) surveyed 100 male managers who identified two critical faults of female managers: Females were perceived to be overdemanding, particularly of other females, and they were perceived as unwilling to provide help to other females. While some research reports findings to the contrary (e.g., Jabes, 1980), Ezell, Odewahn, and Sherman (1980), in a survey of over 300 male and female managers, found that females believed other female managers were less competent than males in similar positions.

Inconsistencies in Subordinate Evaluation

Despite difficulties such as these in negotiating new roles for professional women in organizations, some researchers identify a growing body of empirical literature providing evidence that women are experiencing managerial success (White, Crino, & DeSanctis, 1981). Indeed, although management has traditionally been a male-dominated occupation, increasing evidence indicates that females can be as successful as males (Hennig & Jardim, 1977). On the other hand, research which is now several decades old indicated definite bias against female supervisors. Ellman (1963), for example, found that 81 percent of queried personnel executives agreed that men generally object to female supervisors; 51 percent of the sample believed that females object to female supervisors as well. More recently, however, Ezell, Odewahn, and Sherman, (1981) found that subordinates who have experienced working under female managers have more positive perceptions of female managers' motivation to perform effectively. Petty, Odewahn, Bruning, and Thomason (1977) found no differences among subordinates' job satisfaction levels due to the sex of the supervisor.

The job satisfaction of subordinates has been investigated frequently as an evaluation measure for male and female superiors (Osborn & Vicars, 1976; Petty et al., 1977); however, researchers have investigated other issues as well. Donnell and Hall (1980), for example, administered the *Management Relations Survey* (MRS) to 428 subordinates of 185 female managers and 504 subordinates of 185 male managers. In the first section of the MRS, subordinates assessed the communication practices of their managers. Subordinates reported no differences between the communication behaviors of male and female managers; however, subordinates of female managers reported that they generally solicited less feedback from their managers than did subordinates of male managers. Wexley and Pulakos (1983), in a sample of 286 manager–subordinate dyads, found that the more cognizant a subordinate is of his or her manager's work-related attitudes, the more favorably the subordinate appraises the manager's leadership performance. These results, however, occurred more reliably in same-sex, as opposed to mixed-sex, dyads.

Other researchers have investigated two basic dimensions of leadership behavior: "consideration," or warm, trusting, friendly behaviors, and "initiating structure," or behaviors which include overt attempts to organize group activities and achieve organizational goals (see, for example, Stogdill, 1974). Research shows generally that superiors are rated more highly when they score high in both dimensions (Stogdill, 1974); however, some studies suggest that both males and females prefer male superiors who exhibit more "initiating structure" behaviors and female superiors who exhibit more "consideration" behaviors (Bartol & Butterfield, 1976; Petty & Lee, 1975; Petty & Miles, 1976).

Results have sometimes indicated that successful female leadership performance is evaluated more highly than similar performance by males. Jacobson and Effertz (1974) found that group members rated female leadership more highly than they rated male leadership. They explain their findings by citing Samuel Johnson's remark on women preachers in the eighteenth century: "Sir, a woman preaching is like a dog's walking on his hind legs. It is not done well: but you are very surprised to find it done at all." (p. 393). Abramson, Goldberg, Greenberg, and Abramson (1977) have referred to similar findings as the "talking platypus phenomenon." Since we do not expect a dog to walk on its hind legs or a platypus to talk, we are pleasantly surprised. These researchers infer competent women produce a similar reaction. It should be pointed out, however, that these two studies were not carried out in organizational settings.

Inconsistencies in Supervisor Evaluations

Research has also asked how female professionals are evaluated as subordinates. Again, results are mixed. Evaluators are constrained by their judgments, values, and perceptions of role behaviors. If evaluators' perceptions of the female role are not compatible with their perceptions of the managerial role, conflicting sets of role expectations emerge and may affect evaluations of performance (White et al., 1981). Schein (1978) cautions that stereotyped thinking by superiors about a woman's capability to function effectively as a manager may limit her ability to perform well and to be promoted. If a superior perceives that a woman is less aggressive, competitive, or forceful than her male counterpart, her superior may not require of the woman tasks that utilize such skills. This, in turn, may limit the female professional, keep her from developing these abilities, promote within the organization an image that she cannot perform these tasks, and thereby restrict her promotional progress.

Along these lines, Kiesler (1975) identified a cognitive bias which occurs during the evaluation process: "actuarial prejudice," an expectation of inferior performance from subgroup members based on available information about the group. It may be the case that since there are fewer successful women than men in organizations, evaluators will expect all females to be less successful; therefore, these expectations will surface in performance evaluations. Patterson (1975), in a study of 192 male and female managers, found that females were consistently rated lower than males on evaluations of promotability and performance. Moses and Boehm (1975), on the other hand, found no sex differences in the potential ratings of 4,846 female managers and 8,885 male managers. Hall and Hall (1976) found no sex differences in ratings of job incumbents' ability, motivation, or overall task performance. Likewise, Deaux (1979) found no differences in the performance ratings given to female and male managers by superiors; however, Mobley (1982) found that females were rated higher than their male counterparts. Furthermore, Schwartz (cited in White et al., 1981) found that 95 percent of employers of women managers rated their performance on the job as excellent, very good, or good. Wood (1976), in polling nearly 100 male and female managers, discovered that most managers believe women are proving their competence and winning increased acceptance in organizations.

Of particular interest regarding evaluation of subordinates by superiors is the amount of mutual agreement between the two since superiors obviously influence, at least to some extent, training and development opportunities and the upward mobility of their subordinates. Research demonstrates that the perceptions of subordinates and superiors can differ significantly (e.g., Baird, 1977; Heneman, 1974; Thornton, 1968). However, Staley and Shockley-Zalabak (1986) investigated this issue for female professionals and their supervisors and reported little agreement between female professionals and their supervisors on their assessed communication competencies. In assessments of 15 areas of communication proficiency, a woman and her supervisor agreed only on the woman's proficiency in the areas of business writing, oral presentations, and communications technology—visible, overt skill sets. The authors suggest that the significance of their findings does not lie in the areas of agreement between female professionals and their supervisors. Rather, the lack of agreement in areas of critically complex competencies such as group, interpersonal relationships, motivating people, and delegating authority may be key to understanding the managerial development of female professionals and their subsequent promotional progress. Upward mobility in organizations is influenced by an array of communication skills, both visible and overt and complex and multifaceted.

METHODOLOGICAL PROPOSAL

Triangulation and Gender Research

The preceding overview of research on evaluation of male and female performance exemplifies the general perception among scholars that gender research is important yet is lacking in its ability to comprehensively explain gender experiences. Multiple methodologies, both quantitative and qualitative, and multilevel perspectives—self, peer, subordinate, and superior—have produced a collection of mixed results. In the remainder of this essay, we describe how the limitations of single-method studies can be resolved by the innovative use of triangulation. Although the examples of our triangulation approach are applied to professional women, the application of the methodology to the diverse contexts of female experiences holds promise. Our proposal is based on an assumption fundamental to a feminist perspective, namely, that "the study of gender and women, in particular, is a valuable endeavor" (Foss & Foss, 1986, p. 3). Moreover, the endeavor is essential if women's communication is to be understood and valued within varying social or professional contexts.

Triangulation can be described as the use of multiple and diverse data sources and collection techniques to study a single research question or understand complex phenomena. The underlying assumption for using triangulation is that multiple sources and diverse data contribute better than single sources and methods to our understanding of research questions and their contexts.

Triangulated designs permit both description and interpretation (Albrecht & Ropp, 1982) and can encompass assumptions from divergent paradigms (Faules, 1982). A research design is triangulated when researchers collect data to understand the phenomenon under study from a variety of similar and dissimilar sources, forms, and locations. Multilevel triangulation refers to a particular application of triangulation methodology when the researcher seeks data from multiple sources at structurally diverse organizational levels (supervisors, peers, subordinates) with whom the subject or subjects under study communicate. The methodology of triangulation (whether multilevel or not) brings a pluralism of approaches to bear on understanding experiences.

Olson (in Levinger & Raush, 1977) has argued that triangulation research can be understood in terms of both perspective and data collection methods. Perspective refers to insider (subject observer of self) versus outsider (observers of subject) and data collection refers to both subjective and objective methods. With diverse perspectives and data collection methods, triangulation encourages a more comprehensive examination of complex phenomena than the best of single method designs. Triangulated designs encourage the use of both qualitative and quantitative methods, thereby maximizing single method benefits while neutralizing single method drawbacks. Table 10–1 is a partial list of data sources and collection methods which are used in a variety of combinations for triangulated designs.

Single-method designs are appropriate when the experiences in question can be understood through examination of data collected from a single source or with a single method. Triangulation is appropriate either

Table 10-1. DATA SOURCES AND COLLECTION METHODS USED IN TRIANGULATED DESIGNS

Data Sources	Collection methods
The research subject	Interviews
Those with whom the subject interacts	Questionnaires
The researcher	Laboratory experiments
Demographic data	Observation
Socioeconomic data	Participant observation
Historical records	Content analysis
Personal records (diaries, letters, etc.)	Videotape, recordings

when single data sources cannot be expected to comprehensively explain the phenomena under study or when inconsistencies in single-method designs cannot be explained. Triangulated designs are used to collect data from multiple sources that are identified as relevant to the research question. Single-method designs are used to collect data from the single source identified as being the most relevant to the research question. For complex questions, multiple sources and forms enhance the possibility that researchers will discover important and often subtle interrelationships. Furthermore, triangulated designs do not require researchers to make often impossible judgments about what is the single "best" source or form of data for difficult and marginally understood problems.

Multiple methods of data collection guard against biases that are frequently introduced by single-method designs. Limitations in experimentation, for example, can be identified and better understood when experimentation is combined with observation and interviews. Experimentation is based on the development of preestablished categories for studying women's communication. In an experimentation design the extent of understanding is related to the accuracy and inclusiveness of the established categories. Observation and interviews, when combined with experimental categories, can provide support and credibility to the inclusiveness of the selected categories or can identify additional categories or variables of importance. Surveys may reflect stereotyped projections in phrasing of questions. A multiple-method design combining survey, self-reflection, and naturalistic observation could balance stereotyped projections in the survey with self-reflective comments of female participants and observation of "actual" behaviors. Self-reflection as a single data collection methodology also is subject to stereotypical responses. Female subjects can project responses they believe to be culturally acceptable, again introducing bias. This bias may be detected when actual behavior is compared to descriptions of behavior. Indeed the culturally acceptable self-reflection, when contrasted to actual behaviors, may be informative for understanding female experiences. This understanding, however, is more likely to emerge using data collected with multiple methods than with data collected with the best of single-method designs. Since both advantages and disadvantages are inherent in any research methodology, we advocate an approach which combines methodologies and, in multilevel triangulation, perspectives on the same communication phenomenon. Table 10–2 provides a list of the advantages and disadvantages of commonly used methodologies for studying women's communication.

Multiple methods of data collection permit examination of whether there is convergence of findings across methods. Convergence, similarity of results across diverse methods, enhances confidence in problem identification and explanation. On the other hand, divergent results also contribute to understanding and can raise important questions, define future re-

TABLE 10-2. ADVANTAGES AND DISADVANTAGES OF METHODOLOGIES FOR STUDYING WOMEN'S COMMUNICATION

Research Methodology	Advantages in the study of women's communication	Disadvantages in the study of women's communication
Self-reflection	Females know best the female experience	Responses may be projections of cultural stereotypes rather than "real" responses
Survey	Females know best the female experience	Researchers may inject bias and/or stereotyped projections into phrased questions
Naturalistic observation	"Actual" female behavior is observed	Cultural stereotypes or feminist bias may color interpretation of the data
Participant-Observation	Females subjects are also female researchers—subjective "accuracy"	Female researchers may inject their own biases and expectations into generation and interpretation of the data
(Quasi) Experimentation	Control of data generation may reduce researcher bias and, to some degree, cultural bias	Laboratory settings may preclude researchers from ascertaining the richness of women's experience
		Preconceived categories may be erroneously applied to the study of women's communication

search directions, and identify diversity and deviance. When researchers find contradictions in self-reflection and actual behavior, new and interesting questions emerge. What is it in the experience that produces the contradiction? Is it cultural expectation? Is it a limitation in self-awareness? Has the behavior been understood? Is this contradiction unique to females? Multiple collection methods yield both data convergence and divergence. As such, multiple collection methods are a strength of triangulation not available in more limited single-method approaches.

Triangulation as a methodology has been applied to the study of numerous groups. Triangulation has not, however, been extensively applied in gender research. The traditional methodology of triangulation is nontraditional when used to understand women's communication within varying contexts. Furthermore, triangulation in general, and multilevel triangulation, in particular, are suited to support a primary characteristic of a feminist perspective which suggests that feminist scholarship "utilizes women's experiences, which are manifest in their symbols, rituals, and regular practices, as a starting point through which to approach events or phenomena under investigation" (Foss & Foss, 1986, p. 3). Additionally, triangulated designs encourage the use of researcher's complex personal experiences and build on an assumption of the feminist perspective that the self is an important and valid source for intellectual discovery. We, therefore, propose triangulation as an important methodology for the study of women's communication.

Triangulation as a methodology for understanding female experiences holds promise because it encourages the convergence of traditional and less traditional data by admitting of multiple perspectives for the understanding of experience. Triangulation encourages a view of subjects as active participants who help to define research agendas, provide data, and verify data interpretation. Subjects are actively engaged in helping the researcher reflect their experiences rather than fit experiences into overly rigid research expectations or designs.

Active subject involvement can go hand in hand in a triangulated design with more traditional quantitative measures. Qualitative measures such as open-ended questionnaires, interviews, participant observation, content analysis, letters, diaries, and other written records can converge with demographic data, socioeconomic status measures, test results, and laboratory experiments to generate a more holistic picture of female experiences. Indeed, one has but to look at what critics consider lacking in the explanatory power of much current research to envision how triangulation might improve our understanding.

Few areas in communication research produce more confusing and seemingly contradictory findings and are more subject to criticism than those attempting to describe similarities and differences in the communication behaviors of males and females. Researchers have not been able to thoughtfully distinguish between male and female communicative experiences in similar contexts. For example, as we previously discussed, gender and communication research results are often mixed and controversial. It is also true that males and females exhibit similar behaviors, particularly in organizational contexts, yet do not experience similar career outcomes (Day & Stogdill, 1972; National Science Foundation, 1984; Devanna, in Fraker, 1984; U.S. Labor Department, 1985).

Research efforts comparing males and females in organizations have generally described an "event," for example, leadership behaviors, without being able to contextualize the event into the broader experience of promotional progress, compensation, credibility, job satisfaction, and so on. That is, an understanding of the event (leadership) does not provide an understanding of the overall experience. Triangulation offers an alternative methodology to encompass the event as part of the process which we call the experience. In other words, a triangulated design would not only study actual behaviors but would examine self and others' perceptions of behaviors as they contribute to outcomes such as performance effectiveness, promotional progress, compensation, and job satisfaction. Researchers using triangulated designs would hope to better understand, for example, why male and female professionals who have similar backgrounds, exhibit similar preferences for leadership, and leadership communication styles, experience differing vertical mobility rates in organizations. Specifically, we are proposing that a multilevel triangulation design could help us determine how preferences and behaviors converge with evaluation of behaviors to explain promotability and, therefore, help us to understand male and female organizational experiences. Furthermore, multilevel (self, supervisor, subordinate, peer) evaluation in a single design holds promise for better understanding many of the other seeming inconsistencies we have previously identified.

Earlier we described diversity in findings among several self, peer, and subordinate evaluation studies. Irrespective of the specific findings in the evaluation studies, single-method designs did not permit comprehensive examination of the underlying attitudes and experiences which contributed to evaluation. From these studies we come to understand the complexity and apparent inconsistencies of evaluation but are unable to contextualize evaluation into broader female/male experiences. Triangulated designs attempt to better reflect the complexity of the experience by relating, for example, evaluations to past experiences, attitudes, and expectations. The density of information obtained from qualitative data (interviews, records, stories, etc.) can be combined with the breadth of data from quantitative approaches (surveys, demographic data, mobility rates, etc.) to better understand the evaluation experience.

MULTILEVEL TRIANGULATION—A CASE STUDY FOR GENDER RESEARCH

To this point we have discussed recommended applications of triangulation methodology as a possibility for solving existing research problems, better understanding female experiences, and contributing to a holistic understanding of male/female similarities and differences. The benefits of triangulation are demonstrated in our research design to study male/female communication behavior during decision making. The purpose of the research was to compare male and female communication behaviors during decision making and to determine how behaviors were evaluated by business professionals in terms of effectiveness.

Two hundred male and female subjects participated in the research project which included a battery of self-report instruments, collection of demographic and career data, personal interviews about decision making and career progress, videotaped decision-making interactions with same sex and opposite sex others, content analysis by trained judges of interviews and videotapes, and evaluations of decision-making effectiveness from videotaped interactions by business professionals.

This multilevel triangulated design permitted the use of both qualitative and quantitative analyses to better understand communication behaviors and the evaluations of those behaviors. We were able to match subjects for videotaping on similarities in professional backgrounds and on similarities and differences of preference for dominance, leadership, communication apprehension, and conflict style preferences, thereby controlling for these important variables other than gender known to be influential in the decision-making process. Interview data were used to examine decision-making premises for participants. Content analysis of the tapes permitted examination of factors such as initiation of interaction, interruptions, control of time behaviors, and participation levels. Additionally, we were able to examine verbal factors such as social facilitative behaviors which showed agreement, released tension, or showed solidarity. Task facilitative behaviors were coded in information-seeking and -giving categories. Finally, a range of nonverbal behaviors such as head movements, postural shifts, and hand gestures was coded.

A scale representing a set of criteria for decision making was developed and used by volunteer business professionals to evaluate the effectiveness of taped interactions. Comparisons were possible between content analysis of behaviors and evaluations of effectiveness. Additionally, self-report instruments and demographic data were compared for males and females and with evaluations of effectiveness.

This design permitted us to examine important questions about communication not easily understood with any single data collection method. As researchers we were able to explore whether and how similarities and differences of preference for dominance, leadership, communication apprehension, and conflict style influenced initiation of interaction, interruptions, control of time behaviors, and participation levels. Additionally, we were able to examine whether or how gender interacted with these personal preferences. We explored similarities and differences in the use of task facilitative and social facilitative behaviors and determined how these behaviors were evaluated by others. We were able to compare actual behaviors (derived from content analysis) with the perceptions of decision-making effectiveness provided by volunteer business professionals. We were able to examine how preferences for communication influenced actual behaviors and how those behaviors were evaluated by others. We were able to examine whether males and females with similar preferences exhibited similar behaviors and how those behaviors were evaluated. We were able to examine how women interacted with other women (also men with men) and how those interactions were viewed. Finally, we were able to look at the promotional progress and compensation history of our participants as compared to their communication preferences and behaviors.

While this research design is not flawless, we do suggest, however, that data from the multilevel triangulated design gives us a more complete picture with which to approach our questions than any of the data taken in isolation. Additionally, the informal input from our participants facilitated the development of new questions and other ways of understanding and studying male and female communication. As such, triangulation methodology both seeks answers and raises questions, a valuable asset of any design.

SUMMARY

Triangulation methodology provides an alternative perspective for doing research on women's communication. Multilevel triangulation can encourage the use of qualitative and quantitative approaches with particular emphasis on the active participation of women and those with whom they most frequently interact (peers, supervisors, and subordinates for professional women). Triangulated designs are complicated and yield extensive amounts of data for analysis. However, the richness of the data potentially provides better pictures for understanding the experiences we need to study.

Triangulation as a methodology is appropriate for understanding the styles, forms, and strategies of/for communication exhibited by women. Triangulated designs contextualize communication behaviors into the diverse experiences of women and provide an essential link between communication behaviors and self-perceptions of experiences. Finally, triangulated designs encourage improved understanding of how others with whom women interact perceive communication exhibited by women.

REFERENCES

Abramson, P. R., Goldberg, P. A., Greenberg, J. H., & Abramson, L. M. (1977). The talking platypus phenomenon: Competency ratings as a function of sex and professional status. *Psychology of Women Quarterly, 2,* 114–124.

Albrecht, S. (1976). Informal interaction patterns of professional women. In M. Gerrard, J. S. Oliver, & M. Williams (Eds.), *Women in management.* Human Services Monograph Series, School of Social Work, University of Texas.

Albrecht, T. L., & Ropp, V. A. (1982). The study of network structuring in organizations through the use of method triangulation. *The Western Journal of Speech Communication, 46,* 162–178.

Baird, J. (1976). Sex differences in group communication: A review of relevant research. *The Quarterly Journal of Speech, 62,* 179–192.

Baird, L. S. (1977). Self and superior ratings of performance: As related to self-esteem and satisfaction with supervision. *Academy of Management Journal, 20* (2) 291–300.

Bartol, K. M. (1977). *Male versus female organizational leaders: A review of comparative literature.* Syracuse, NY: School of Management.

Bartol, K. M., & Butterfield, D. A. (1976). Sex effects in evaluating leaders. *Journal of Applied Psychology, 61* (4), 446–454.

Bates, B. (1984). Submerged concepts in gender/communication research. *Women's Studies in Communication, 7,* 101–104.

Birdsall, P. (1980). A comparative analysis of male and female managerial communication style in two organizations. *Journal of Vocational Behavior, 16,* 183–196.

Brown, S. M. (1979). Male versus female leaders: A comparison of empirical studies. *Sex Roles, 5* (5), 595–611.

Camden, C., & Kennedy, C. (1982, February). *Interruptions as an index of communication dominance.* Paper presented at the Western Speech Communication Association Convention, Denver, CO.

Day, D. R., & Stogdill, R. M. (1972). Leader behavior of male and female supervisors: A comparative study. *Personnel Psychology, 25,* 353–360.

Deaux, K. (1979). Self-evaluations of male and female managers. *Sex Roles, 5* (5), 571–580.

Deaux, K., & Emswiller, T. (1974). Explanations of successful performance on sex-linked tasks: What is skill for the male is luck for the female. *Journal of Personality and Social Psychology, 29,* 80–85.

Denzin, N. K. (1970). The methodologies of symbolic interaction: A critical review of research techniques. In G. P. Stone & H. A. Farberman (Eds.), *Social psychology through symbolic interaction* (pp. 447–465). Waltham, MA: Ginn-Blaisdell.

Dipboye, R. L., Arvey, R. D., & Terpstra, D. E. (1977). Sex and physical attractiveness of raters and applicants as determinants of resume evaluations. *Journal of Applied Psychology, 62*, 288–294.

Dipboye, R. L., Fromkin, H. L., & Wiback, K. (1975). Relative importance of applicant sex, attractiveness, and scholastic standing in evaluation of job applicant resumes. *Journal of Applied Psychology, 60* (1), 39–43.

Dipboye, R. L., & Wiley, J. W. (1977). Reactions of college recruiters to interviewee sex and self-presentation style. *Journal of Vocational Behavior, 10* (1), 1–12.

Donnell, S., & Hall, J. (1980). *Men and women as managers: A significant case of no significant differences.* The Woodlands, TX: Teleometrics International.

Eakins, B., & Eakins, G. (1976). Verbal turn-taking and exchanges in faculty dialogue. In B. L. Dubois & I. Crouch (Eds.), *Papers in Southwest English IV: Proceedings of the Conference on the Sociology of the Languages of American Women* (pp. 53–62). San Antonio, TX: Trinity University.

Ellman, E. S. (1963). *Managing women in business.* National Foremen's Institute, Bureau of Business Practice, National Sales Development Institute, Waterford, CT.

Ezell, H. F., Odewahn, C. A., & Sherman, J. D. (1980). Perceived competence of women managers in public human service organizations: A comparative view. *Journal of Management, 6* (2), 135–144.

Ezell, H. F., Odewahn, C. A., & Sherman, J. D. (1981). The effects of having been supervised by a woman on perceptions of female managerial competence. *Personnel Psychology, 34,* (2), 291–299.

Faules, D. (1982). The use of multi-methods in the organizational setting. *The Western Journal of Speech Communication, 46,* 150–161.

Fishman, P. M. (1978). Interaction: The work women do. *Social Problems, 25,* 397–406.

Foss, S. K., & Foss, K. A. (1986, April). *Challenge versus legitimacy: The dilemma of the feminist perspective.* Paper presented at the Gender and Communication Conference, Pennsylvania State University, State College, PA.

Fraker, S. (1984, April). Why women aren't getting to the top. *Fortune,* pp. 40–45.

Frank, F. D., & Drucker, J. (1977). The influence of evaluatee's sex on evaluations of a response on a managerial selection instrument. *Sex Roles, 3* (1), 59–64.

Gilligan, C. (1982). *In a different voice: Psychological theory and women's development.* Cambridge: Harvard University Press.

Goldberg, P. (1968). Are women prejudiced against women? *Trans-Action, 5* (5), 28–30.

Glucklich, P., & Povall, M. (1979). Equal opportunities: A case for action in default of the law. *Personnel Management, 11* (1), 28–31.

Haefner, J. E. (1977). Sources of discrimination among employees: A survey investigation. *Journal of Applied Psychology, 62* (3), 265–270.

Hall, F. S., & Hall, D. T. (1976). Effects of job incumbents' race and sex on evaluations of managerial performance. *Academy of Management Journal, 19* (3), 476–481.

Hamner, W. C., Kim, J. S., Baird, L., & Bigoness, W. (1974). Race and sex as determinants of ratings by potential employers in a simulated work-sampling task. *Journal of Applied Psychology, 59* (6), 705–711.

Heneman, H. G. (1974). Comparisons of self and superior ratings of managerial performance. *Journal of Applied Psychology, 59*(5), 638–642.

Hennig, M., & Jardim, A. (1977). *The managerial woman.* Garden City, NY: Anchor Press, Doubleday.

Hollander, E. P., & Julian, J. W. (1979). Contemporary trends in the analysis of the leadership process. *Psychological Bulletin, 71*(5), 387–397.

Jabes, J. (1980). Causal attributions and sex-role stereotypes in the perceptions of women managers. *Canadian Journal of Behavioral Science, 12*(1), 52–63.

Jacobson, M. B., & Effertz, J. (1974). Sex roles and leadership: Perceptions of the leaders and the led. *Organizational Behavior and Human Performance, 12*, 383–396.

Kiesler, S. B. (1975). Actuarial prejudice toward women and its implications. *Journal of Applied Social Psychology, 5* (3), 201–216.

Kramer, C. (1974). Women's speech: Separate but unequal? *Quarterly Journal of Speech, 60*, 14–24.

Levinger, G., & Raush, H. (1977). *Close relationships.* Amherst: University of Massachusetts Press.

Matteson, M. T. (1976). Attitudes toward women as managers: Sex or role differences? *Psychological Reports, 39*, 166.

McDaris, M. A., & Javidi, M. (1985, November). *Gender perceptions of communicator styles.* Paper presented at the Speech Communication Association Convention, Denver, CO.

Mobley, W. H. (1982). Supervisor and employee race and sex effects on performance appraisals: A field study of adverse impact and generalizability. *Academy of Management Journal, 25*(3), 598–606.

Montgomery, B. M., & Norton, R. W. (1981). Sex differences and similarities in communicator style. *Communication Monographs, 48*(2), 121–132.

Moses, J. L., & Boehm, V. R. (1975). Relationship of assessment-center performance to management progress of women. *Journal of Applied Psychology, 60*(4), 527–529.

National Science Foundation. (1984). Women and minorities in science and engineering. NSF: Washington, DC

Nieva, V., & Gutek, B. (1980). Sex effects on evaluation. *Academy of Management Review, 5*(2), 267–276.

Osborn, R. N., & Vicars, W. M. (1976). Sex stereotypes: An artifact in leader behavior and subordinate satisfaction analysis? *Academy of Management Journal, 19*, 439–449.

Patterson, R. A. (1975). Women in management: An experimental study of the effects of sex and marital status on job performance ratings, promotability ratings, and promotion decisions. *Dissertation Abstracts International, 36*, 3108B–3109B.

Peters, L. H., O'Connor, E. J., Weekley, J., Pooyan, A., Frank, B., & Erenkrantz, B. (1983). *Sex bias and managerial evolution: A replication and extension.*

Paper presented at the Academy of Management national meeting, Dallas, TX.

Petty, M. M., & Lee, G. K. (1975). Moderating effects of sex of supervisor and subordinate on relationships between supervisory behavior and subordinate satisfaction. *Journal of Applied Psychology, 60*(5), 624–628.

Petty, M. M., & Miles, R. H. (1976). Leader sex-role stereotyping in a female-dominated work culture. *Personnel Psychology, 29,* 393–404.

Petty, M. M., Odewahn, C. A., Bruning, N. S., & Thomason, T. L. (1977, August). An examination of the moderating effects of supervisor sex and subordinate sex upon the relationships between supervisory behavior and subordinate outcomes in mental health organizations. *Proceedings of the Academy of Management* (pp. 408–417). Orlando, FL: Academy of Management.

Putnam, L. L. (1982). In search of gender: A critique of communication and sex-roles research. *Women's Studies in Communication, 5,* 1–9.

Rosen, B., & Jerdee, T. H. (1974). Effects of applicant's sex and difficulty of job on evaluations of candidates for managerial positions. *Journal of Applied Psychology, 59*(4), 511–512.

Schein, V. E. (1973). The relationship between sex role stereotypes and requisite management characteristics. *Journal of Applied Psychology, 57*(2), 95–100.

Schein, V. E. (1978). Sex role stereotyping, ability and performance: Prior research and new directions. *Personnel Psychology, 31,* 259–268.

Snyder, R. A., & Bruning, N. S. (1979). Sex differences in perceived competence: An across organizations study. *Administration in Social Work, 3*(3), 349–355.

Solomon, M. (1984). A prolegomenon to research on gender role communication. *Women's Studies in Communication, 7,* 98–100.

Spender, D. (1985). *Man made language.* New York: Methuen.

Staley, C., & Shockley-Zalabak, P. (1986). Communication proficiency and future training needs of the female professional: Self-assessment versus supervisors' evaluations. *Human Relations, 39*(10), 891–902.

Staley, C. C. (1986). Gender and communication research: Deliberations, dilemmas, and directions. *Speech Communication Association of Pennsylvania Annual, 17,* 29–35.

Staley, C. C., & Cohen, J. L. (1988). Communicator style and social style: Similarities and differences between the sexes. *Communication Quarterly, 36*(3), 192–202.

Stogdill, R. M. (1974). *Handbook of leadership.* New York: Free Press.

Swacker, M. (1975). The sex of the speaker as a sociolinguistic variable. In B. Thorne & N. Henley (Eds.), *Language and sex: Difference and dominance* (pp. 78–83). Rowley, MA: Newbury House.

Sypher, B. D., & Sypher, H. E. (1984). Seeing ourselves as others see us: Convergence and divergence in assessments of communication behavior. *Communication Research, 11*(1), 97–115.

Thornton, G. C. (1968). The relationship between supervisory and self-appraisals of executive performance. *Personnel Psychology, 21*(4), 441–455.

Tompkins, P. K., & Cheney, G. (1983). Account analysis of organizations: Decision making and identification. In L. L. Putnam & M. E. Pacanowsky (Eds.), *Com-*

munication in organizations: An interpretive approach (pp. 123–146). Beverly Hills, CA: Sage.

Tsui, A. S., & Gutek, B. A. (1984). A role set analysis of gender differences in performance, affective relationships, and career success of industrial middle managers. *Academy of Management Journal, 27*(3), 619–635.

U.S. Department of Labor, Women's Bureau (1985). 20 Facts on Women Workers. Washington, DC: Government Printing Office.

Wexley, K. N., & Pulakos, E. D. (1983). The effects of perceptual congruence and sex on subordinates' performance appraisals of their managers. *Academy of Management Journal, 26*(4), 666–676.

White, M. C., Crino, M. D., & DeSanctis, G. L. (1981). A critical review of female performance, performance training and organizational initiatives designed to aid women in the work-role environment. *Personnel Psychology, 34*(2), 227–248.

Wood, M. M. (1976). Women in management: How is it working out? *Advanced Management Journal, 41*(1), 22–30.

Zimmerman, D. H., & West. C. (1975). Sex roles, interruptions and silences in conversation. In B. Thorne & N. Henley (Eds.), *Language and sex: Difference and dominance.* (pp. 105–129) Rowley, MA: Newbury House.

Author Index

A

Aarons, V., 76, *90*
Abramson, L.M., 245, 248, *257*
Abramson, P.R., 245, 248, *257*
Abzug, B., 137, *157*
Acker, J., 193, 196, 198, 200, 201, 216, *217*
Adams, K., 138, *157*
Addelson, K.D., 30, *36*
Albrecht, S., 246, *257*
Albrecht, T.L., 250, *257*
Althusser, L., 162, *189*
Anderson, J.A., 18, 22, *36*
Anderson, R., 198, *217*
Andrews, J.R., 137, 145, 147, 150, *157*
Andrews, P.H., 142, *157*
Archer, D., 129, *136*
Armitage, S.H., 193, 202, *217*
Arnett, R.C., 154, *157*, 198, *217, 218*
Arnkoff, D.B., 245, *258*
Arvey, R.D., 245, *258*

B

Baird, J.E., 138, 147, *157*, 245, 249, *257*
Baird, L.S., 243, *257*
Barnlund, D.C., 15, *36*
Barry, K., 193, 196, 198, 200, 201, 216, *217*
Barthes, R., 163, *189*
Bartky, S.L., 194, 198, *218, 227, 239*
Bartol, K.M., 244, 248, *257*
Barwick, L., 179, 187, *189*
Bate, B., 46, *62*
Bates, B., 242, *257*
Bateson, G., 95, 98, 101, 103, 106, 109, 110, *116*
de Beauvoir, S., 65, *89*
Beavin, J., 104, *117*
Belenky, M.F., 67, *89*, 95, 112, *116*
Benson, T., *36*
Berger, P.L., *89*
Bergstrom, J., 173, *189*
Berlo, D.K., 26, *36*

Berryman, C., 138, *157*
Berryman-Fink, C., 18, 22, 26, *39*
Bigoness, W., 245, *259*
Birdsall, P., 244, *257*
Birns, B., 44, *63*
Black, E., 147, *157*
Bleich, D., 140, 141, 142, *157*
Bleier, R., 18, 19, 20, 24, *36*
Blodgett, T.B., 56, *62*
Blum, A., 156, *157*
Bochner, A.P., 11, *36*, 69, *89*
Boehm, V.R., 245, 248, *259*
Bogdar, R., 59, *62*
Booth, W.C., 147, *157*
Borisoff, D., 138, *157*
Borker, R.A., 139, 140, *159*
Bormann, E.G., 26, *36*
Bormann, E.H., 147, *157*
Boscolo, L., 96, *116, 117*
Bouchard, D.F., 223, *239*
Bowers, J.W., 18, 23, *36*
Bowles, G., 194, *218*
Braden, W., 147, *160*
Bradley, B.E., 138, *157*
Bradley, P.H., 75, *89*, 146, *157*
Briere, J., 138, *158*
Briggs, C.L., 193, 202, *218*
Brockriede, W., 69, *89*, 145, 147, *158*
Brommel, B.J., 130, *134*
Brown, M.E., 179, *189*
Brown, S.M., 243, *257*
Brownmiller, S., 30, *36*
Brummett, B., 147, *158*
Bruning, N.S., 245, 247, *260*
Brunsdon, C., 181, 182, *189*
Buber, M., 154, *158*
Burgeon, M., 78, *90*

C

Cahill, C., 226, 227, 228, *239*
Camden, C., 243, *257*

Odewahn, C.A., 246, 247, *258*
O'Donnell, K., 156, *159*
Ohmann, R., 145, *159*
Olson, D.R., 119, 124, *135*
O'Neale, S., 229, *241*
Ong, W.J., 119, 124, 126, 127, 130, *135*, 178, 186, *190*
Osborn, R.N., 243, 247, *259*
Ostriker, A., 188, *190*
O'Sullivan, T., 162, *190*

P

Patterson, R.A., 248, *259*
Patterson, R.G., 150, *159*
Patton, M.Q., 202, 204, *219*
Pearce, W.B., 11, 15, 16, 24, 26, *38*, 69, 82, *90*
Pearson, J.C., 19, *38*, 54, *63*, 130, *135*, 138, 139, 146, *159*
Peters, L.H., 245, *259*
Peterson, E.E., 119, 120, *135*, 197, 200, 204, 216, *219*, 228, *240*
Petty, M.M., 247, 248, *260*
Phillips, G.M., 22, *38*, 46, 61, *64*
Pingree, S., 168, *189*
Polkinghorne, D., 193, 194, 198, 201, 205, *219*
Povall, M., 245, *258*
Prata, G., 96, *117*
Pulakos, E.D., 247, *261*
Putnam, L.L., 72, 79, *90*, 242, *260*
Pylyshyn, Z.W., 123, *135*

R

Radway, J., *190*
Ragan, S.L., 76, *90*
Railsback, C.C., 147, *159*
Rakow, L.F., 12, 19, *38*, 49, *63*, 72, 77, *90*, 197, *219*
Randall, P., 80, *90*
Raush, H., 250, *259*
Rawlins, W.K., 47, 51, *63*
Raymond, R., 74, *90*
Reinharz, S., 34, 35, *38*, 53, 57, *63*, 194, 200, *219*
Ricoeur, P., 118, *136*
Riessmann, C.K., 203, *219*
Roberts, J.L., 68, *90*
Roberts, M., 58, *63*
Robinson, J.A., 203, 210, *219*, *136*

Roche, M., 198, 201, *220*
Rogers, P.L., 129, *136*
Ropp, V.A., 250, *257*
Rorty, R., 69, *90*
Rose, H., 51, 52, 55, *63*
Rosen, B., 245, *260*
Rosenfield, L., 31, *38*
Rosenthal, R., 112, *117*, 129, *136*
Rosnow, R.L., 112, *117*
Rothenberg, P.S., 198, *219*
Rubin, G., 185, *190*

S

Sacks, H., 133, *136*
Safran, C., 56, *63*
Saunders, D., 162, *190*
Schachtel, E., 52, *63*
Schaef, A.W., 67, *90*
Schein, V.E., 245, 248, *260*
Schlueter, D.W., 47, *64*
Schrag, C.D., 198, *220*
Scollon, R., 123, *136*
Scollon, S.B.K., 123, *136*
Scott, R.L., 76, 77, *90*
Secord, P., 69, *89*
Selltiz, C., 47, 54, 57, 58, 60, *64*
Selvini-Palazzoli, M., 96, 97, 99, *117*
Sereno, K.K., *39*
Shedletsky, L.J., 68, *91*
Sherman, J.D., 246, *258*
Shockley-Zalabak, P., 249, *260*
Showalter, E., 148, 149, *159*, 186, *190*
Simons, H.W., 145, *159*
Smith, P., 195, *219*
Smith-Rosenberg, C., 186, *190*
Smythe, M., 47, *64*
Snyder, R.A., 245, *260*
Solomon, M., 47, *64*, 78, *91*, 242, 243, *260*
Spender, D., 29, 31, 32, *39*, 49, *64*, 66, 68, 74, *91*, 99, 108, 110, 111, *117*, 119, 120, *136*, 138, 139, 151, *159*, 195, 199, *220*, 225, *241*, 245, *260*
Sperber, D., 123, *136*
Spiegelberg, H., 225, 227, 237, *241*
Spitzack, C., 12, 19, 21, 28, *39*, 127, *136*, 140, 145, 147, 149, *159*
Spitzberg, B., 22, *39*
Spivak, G.C., 225, *241*
Sprague, J., 46, 47, *64*
Spretnak, C., 69, *91*

Subject Index

D

Discourse
academic, 164–165
feminine, 162–163, 171–175
oral-literate, 124–126, 178, 186
gender differences in, 126–130
patriarchal, 162
Dualisms
culture-nature, 19–22, 52–53
feminist critiques of, 19–22
knower and known, 34–36, 43, 50–51,
164–165, 201

F

Family therapy
Milan Model of, 99–105
assumptions shared with feminism, 96,
108–113
origins of, 99–105
Feminist consciousness, 198–199
Feminist literary theory, 148–150
Feminist research
accommodations made to dominant research
paradigm, 75–81
critiques of, 29–32
definition of, 66–68, 148, 195–196, 200–201
in communication scholarship, 74
in rhetorical theory and criticism, 148–151
implications of, 112–114
practices in, 33–36, 51–54, 108–112, 203,
215–216, 227–228
resistance to, 1–2, 30–33, 48–49, 73

G

Gender
differences in language and perception,
138–142
in public speaking, 145–146
stereotyped perceptions of, 143

differences in moral decision making,
128–129
differences in organizational performance,
245–249
feminist view of, 67
identity, 42–43
Gossip
as data, 187–188
definition of, 174–176
functions of, 177

H

Harassment, sexual, 56
Hegemony, 161–162

I

Ideology
in research process, 26–27
Intersubjectivity, 35, 227

M

Methodology
in communication research, 13–14
deception of participants, 35
group interviews, 204, 209–213
interviewing, 101–104, 165, 202
feminist approaches to, 206–208, 213–
215
transcriptions of, 228–231
participant observation, 57–59
personal documents, 60–61
phenomenology, 196–201, 224–227,
231–238
assumptions shared with feminism,
194–195, 225–228
triangulation, 250–254
unstructured interviews, 59–60, 129

269